Walter Thornbury

Two Centuries of Song

Or, Lyrics, madrigals, sonnets, and other occasional verses of the English poets of

the last two hundred years

Walter Thornbury

Two Centuries of Song
Or, Lyrics, madrigals, sonnets, and other occasional verses of the English poets of the last two hundred years

ISBN/EAN: 9783744774802

Printed in Europe, USA, Canada, Australia, Japan

Cover: Foto ©Thomas Meinert / pixelio.de

More available books at **www.hansebooks.com**

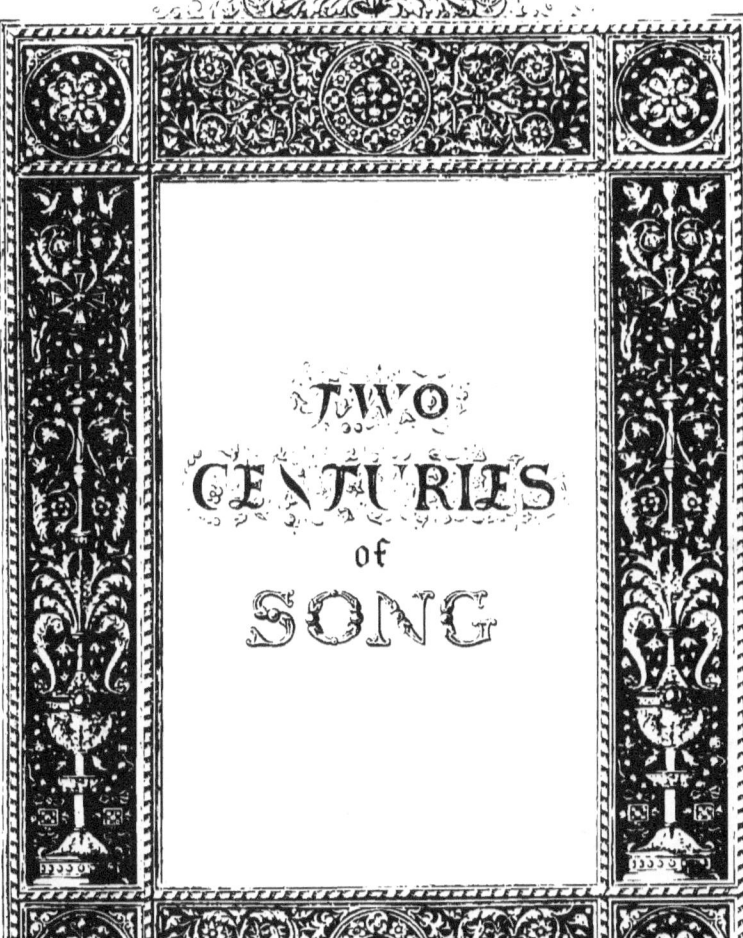
TWO CENTURIES of SONG

TWO CENTURIES OF SONG;

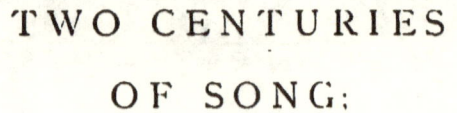

OR,

LYRICS, MADRIGALS, SONNETS,
AND OTHER OCCASIONAL VERSES OF THE ENGLISH POETS
OF THE LAST TWO HUNDRED YEARS.

WITH CRITICAL AND BIOGRAPHICAL NOTES
BY
WALTER THORNBURY.

Author of "Haunted London," "Greatheart," "Tales for the Marines," &c.

ILLUSTRATED BY ORIGINAL PICTURES OF EMINENT ARTISTS,
DRAWN AND ENGRAVED ESPECIALLY FOR THIS WORK.
WITH COLOURED BORDERS, DESIGNED BY HENRY SHAW, F.S.A., ETC. ETC.

LONDON:
SAMPSON LOW, SON, AND MARSTON,
MILTON HOUSE, LUDGATE HILL.
1867.

Preface.

Our first intention was to have made this volume a sort of Wardian glass-case, wherein the butterflies of Parnassus might have freely disported themselves. Waller, Prior, and Praed were to have been the Argus, Peacock, and Emperor of the collection. But this plan we soon found would be too limited. Even Shelley and Tennyson would have had no real claims to places among those gay-coloured flutterers. We therefore enlarged our scheme, to include such poems as the Laureate's "Invitation," Goldsmith's "Haunch of Venison," Cowley's "Chronicle," and Lord Macaulay's "Valentine." It is difficult precisely to define what *Vers de Société* really are; we have presumed them to be poems written for refined circles of educated people, and composed for friends, on special, often on personal, occasions. It is the best of such poems that we have sought to select.

If the vertebrated is in any way better than the invertebrated book; if a carefully-culled and pleasantly-contrasted nosegay is any better than a bundle of entangled and bruised flowers, our book will surely be deemed no worse for its historical order and chronological arrangement. In this wise we are partially enabled to trace the origin, development, and decay of certain styles and fashions in verse. From such changes we may learn to grow more tolerant and more catholic in our tastes. What we despise, our forefathers often loved; what we delight in, our children will perhaps refuse to read.

It would have indeed been a hopeless task in alchemy to have endeavoured to compress even the essence of the minor poems of two centuries into a volume of under four hundred pages. We had, after all, but a small *flaçon*, however daintily cut, and there was much to put into it. The limitation of room must be our apology for many omissions of which we are only too conscious. We have, on all accounts, to regret the immutability of the great scientific fact, that a pint measure will only hold a pint. With more flower-beds, we could to our advantage have had more flowers.

We have commenced our Collection with three Poems of GEORGE WITHER. The date of the death of that amiable poet takes us back to within a very few years of the Restoration. We have no "exquisite reason," as Sir Andrew Aguecheek choicely expresses it, for this limitation; but still we think we have "reason enough." Nor was a frontier line drawn across the year 1660 at a mere venture; for our *Vers de Société* were mainly derived from the French, and introduced into England by those exiles who returned with Charles from Breda. With so much less genius than the Elizabethan writers, the gentlemen poets, *circa* 1660—1670, wrote symmetrical lines, and

PREFACE.

studied harmony and euphony even if they neglected strength. Waller and his successors did not plant oaks nor pile pyramids; but it cannot be denied that they had taste and elegance. The Elizabethan dramatists spent their time in toiling at the forges of thought; courtiers like Waller amused themselves with the mere coloured subtleties of fancy's *marqueterie*. Cowley and his *confrères* did not write verses more courtly, airy, or elegant than those of Suckling or Lovelace. The poets of the Restoration stand foremost in our selection, merely because they mark a literary era and a special style.

When our readers discover, under the head of *Dryden*, that we have inserted but two rather trivial songs, and under that of *Scott*, only some rather unimportant verses, they must be kind enough to bear in mind the plan of our volume. It was not intended to include epics and elegiacs, stories in verse, dramatic extracts, satires, translations, epigrams, or even poems of the highest order, merely because they were *chefs-d'œuvres*. Our object was rather to select occasional verses and poems written to friends, short bright pieces that might specially show the personality of the poet, and display as much as possible his individuality—album verses, in fact, but album verses of high quality, and written by our best poets, living or dead. We wished our book to be as full of good and savoury things as that cauldron at the marriage-feast, into which Sancho dipped so much to his heart's content.

In conclusion, we have to express gratitude to many living authors for kind and generous permission to quote their

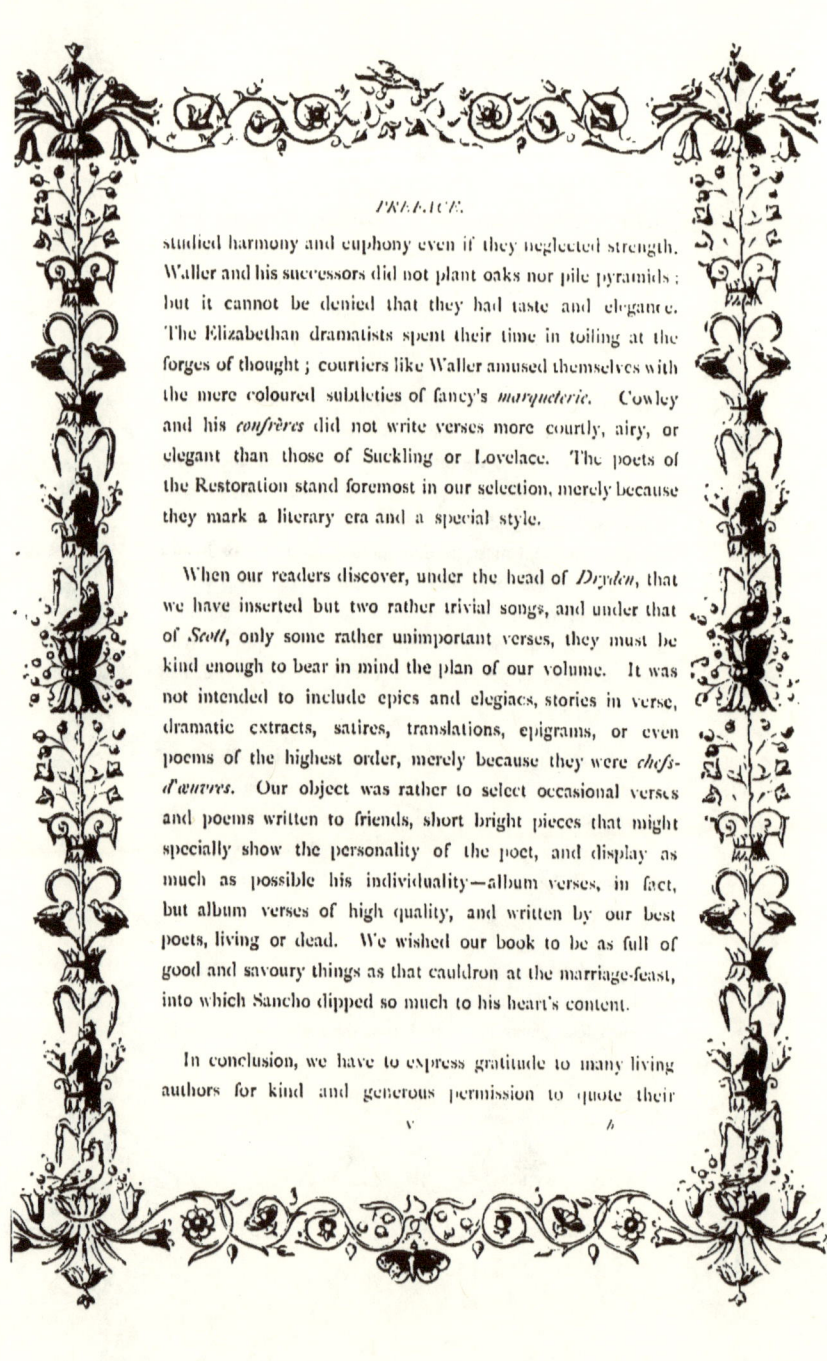

PREFACE.

poems, and to the publishers of London, for their liberal-minded alacrity in swelling our stores; we have also to thank Mr. Jonathan Bouchier for his untiring aid; and Mr. Cundall, for his zealous and judicious superintendence of the art department of this work.

We cannot but deeply regret the omission of many eminent names; but when a dining-room table will only hold a dozen agreeable and clever people, it is surely not wise to ask twenty-four.

Dorking, Oct. 1866.

Table of Contents.

	Page
GEORGE WITHER.—The Shepherd's Resolution	1
Madrigal	2
Sonnet upon a Stolen Kiss	3
ABRAHAM COWLEY.—Anacreontic: Drinking	4
The Chronicle	4
ROBERT HERRICK.—The Bag of the Bee	7
The Country Life	7
The Night Piece.—To Julia	9
To the Virgins, to make much of their Time	10
To Daffodils	11
To Blossoms	11
To Primroses filled with Morning Dew	12
To Corinna, to go a-Maying	13
JOHN MILTON.—To Cyriac Skinner	15
To Mr. Lawrence	16
On his being arrived to the Age of Twenty-three	16
Song on May Morning	17
ANDREW MARVELL.—The Garden	18
The Nymph complaining for the Death of her Fawn	20
THE EARL OF ROCHESTER.—	
Song: My dear Mistress has a Heart	24
Love and Life	25
IZAAK WALTON.—The Angler's Wish	26
EDMUND WALLER.—The Bud	28
Go, Lovely Rose	29
On a Girdle	29
To a Lady singing a Song of his composing	30
To Phyllis	30
CHARLES COTTON.—Invitation to Izaak Walton	31
GEORGE VILLIERS, DUKE OF BUCKINGHAM.—	
Song: Come, let us now resolve at last	33
JOHN DRYDEN.—Song to Britannia, in "King Arthur"	34
The Fair Stranger	35
SIR CHARLES SEDLEY.—Song: Not, Celia, that I juster am	36
Song: Love still has something of the Sea	37
Song: Hears not my Phyllis how the birds	38
Song: Phyllis is my only joy	39
To a very Young Lady	39
CHARLES SACKVILLE, EARL OF DORSET.—	
Song: Written at Sea, in the first Dutch War, 1665, the night before an Engagement	41

CONTENTS.

	Page
DR. WALTER POPE.—The Old Man's Wish	44
MATTHEW PRIOR.—Ode: The Merchant, to secure his Treasure.	48
An Answer to Chloe jealous	49
To Chloe	50
Chloe Hunting	50
To Chloe Weeping	51
Cupid Mistaken	51
The Lady's Looking-Glass	52
On Beauty: a Riddle	53
Song: If Wine and Music have the Power	54
The Female Phaeton	55
The Garland	56
JOHN GAY.—To a Lady, on her passion for Old China	58
GEORGE GRANVILLE, LORD LANSDOWNE.—	
Song: Love is by Fancy led about	61
HENRY CAREY.—Sally in our Alley	62
ALEXANDER POPE.—Epistle to Mrs. Blount, on her leaving the Town after the Coronation	64
Ode on Solitude	66
Imitation of Swift: The Happy Life of a Country Parson	66
AMBROSE PHILIPS.—	
To Miss Charlotte Pulteney, in her Mother's arms	68
COLLEY CIBBER.—The Blind Boy	69
WILLIAM OLDYS.—Song, made extempore by a Gentleman, occasioned by a Fly drinking out of his Cup of Ale	70
JOHN BYROM.—A Pastoral	71
WILLIAM SHENSTONE.—Hope	74
ROBERT DODSLEY.—The Parting Kiss	76
JOHN GILBERT COOPER—Away! let nought to Love displeasing	77
THOMAS GRAY.—On the Death of a Favourite Cat, drowned in a tub of Gold Fishes	79
TOBIAS GEORGE SMOLLETT.—Ode to Leven Water	81
PAUL WHITEHEAD.—Hunting Song	82
OLIVER GOLDSMITH.—Stanzas on Woman	83
The Haunch of Venison	83
SIR GILBERT ELLIOT.—Amynta	87
DR. JOHN LANGHORNE.—To a Redbreast	88
DR. SAMUEL JOHNSON.—	
To Mrs. Thrale, on her completing her Thirty-fifth Year	89
To Miss Hickman, playing on the Spinnet	90
JOHN LOGAN.—To the Cuckoo	91
THOMAS WARTON.—	
Written on a Blank Leaf of Dugdale's "Monasticon"	93
On Revisiting the River Loddon	93
THOMAS BLACKLOCK.—Ode to Aurora on Melissa's Birth-day	94
SAMUEL BISHOP.—To Mrs. Bishop, on the Anniversary of her Wedding-day, which was also her Birth-day, with a Ring	96
ROBERT BURNS.—Of a' the airts the Wind can blaw	97
A Rosebud by my early walk	98

	Page
BEAU BRUMMELL.—The Butterfly's Funeral	159
THEODORE E. HOOK.—Lines from the Heart	161
ALLAN CUNNINGHAM.—The Poet's Bridal-day Song	163
DOCTOR MAGINN.—My Soldier-Boy	165
ROBERT SOUTHEY.—The Holly Tree	166
THOMAS CAMPBELL.—Field Flowers	168
THOMAS HOOD.—It was not in the Winter	170
LAMAN BLANCHARD.—The Poet's Heart	172
REV. RICHARD HARRIS BARHAM.—	
Song: There sits a Bird on yonder Tree	174
Reflections in Westminster Abbey	175
As I laye a-thynkynge	176
ANNE BRONTË.—Home	178
CHARLOTTE BRONTË.—The Letter	179
WILLIAM WORDSWORTH.—Louisa	182
She dwelt among the untrodden Ways	183
Poor Susan	183
She was a Phantom of Delight	184
Yarrow unvisited	185
I wandered lonely	187
WILLIAM LISLE BOWLES.—Water-Party on Beaulieu River	188
THOMAS MOORE.—Take back the Virgin Page	190
The Origin of the Harp	191
There's a Bower of Roses by Bendemeer's Stream	192
SAMUEL ROGERS.—To ——	193
A Wish	193
On —— asleep	194
An Italian Song	194
LEIGH HUNT.—Rondeau	196
To J. H. Four Years Old	196
An Angel in the House	199
LORD MACAULAY.—Song: O stay, Madonna! stay	200
Valentine to the Hon. Mary C. Stanhope	201
ROBERT B. BROUGH.—A Story from Boccaccio	203
STEWART LOCKYER.—The Toast	209
ELIZABETH BARRETT BROWNING.—Wine of Cyprus	211
WILLIAM MAKEPEACE THACKERAY.—The Ballad of Bouillabaisse	218
The Age of Wisdom	220
The Mahogany Tree	221
The Cane-bottomed Chair	222
ALARIC ALEXANDER WATTS.—Ten Years Ago	224
ADELAIDE ANNE PROCTER.—My Picture Gallery	227
WALTER SAVAGE LANDOR.—On receiving a Monthly Rose	230
To John Foster	231
Sixteen	232
FRANCIS MAHONY (FATHER PROUT).—	
Paraphrase of Horace, Book I. Ode 9	233
The Shandon Bells	234
The Town of Passage	235

LIVING AUTHORS.

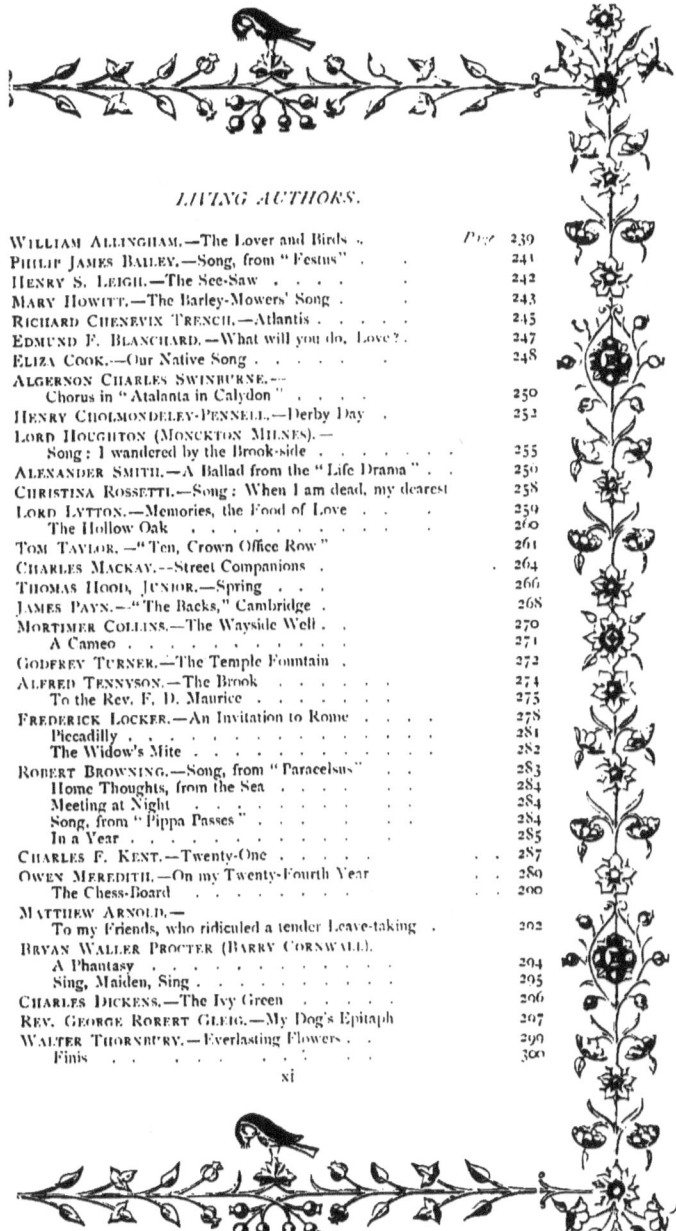

	Page
WILLIAM ALLINGHAM.—The Lover and Birds	239
PHILIP JAMES BAILEY.—Song, from "Festus"	241
HENRY S. LEIGH.—The See-Saw	242
MARY HOWITT.—The Barley-Mowers' Song	243
RICHARD CHENEVIX TRENCH.—Atlantis	245
EDMUND F. BLANCHARD.—What will you do, Love?	247
ELIZA COOK.—Our Native Song	248
ALGERNON CHARLES SWINBURNE.—	
Chorus in "Atalanta in Calydon"	250
HENRY CHOLMONDELEY-PENNELL.—Derby Day	252
LORD HOUGHTON (MONCKTON MILNES).—	
Song: I wandered by the Brook-side	255
ALEXANDER SMITH.—A Ballad from the "Life Drama"	256
CHRISTINA ROSSETTI.—Song: When I am dead, my dearest	258
LORD LYTTON.—Memories, the Food of Love	259
The Hollow Oak	260
TOM TAYLOR.—"Ten, Crown Office Row"	261
CHARLES MACKAY.—Street Companions	264
THOMAS HOOD, JUNIOR.—Spring	266
JAMES PAYN.—"The Backs," Cambridge	268
MORTIMER COLLINS.—The Wayside Well	270
A Cameo	271
GODFREY TURNER.—The Temple Fountain	272
ALFRED TENNYSON.—The Brook	274
To the Rev. F. D. Maurice	275
FREDERICK LOCKER.—An Invitation to Rome	278
Piccadilly	281
The Widow's Mite	282
ROBERT BROWNING.—Song, from "Paracelsus"	283
Home Thoughts, from the Sea	284
Meeting at Night	284
Song, from "Pippa Passes"	284
In a Year	285
CHARLES F. KENT.—Twenty-One	287
OWEN MEREDITH.—On my Twenty-Fourth Year	289
The Chess-Board	290
MATTHEW ARNOLD,—	
To my Friends, who ridiculed a tender Leave-taking	292
BRYAN WALLER PROCTER (BARRY CORNWALL).	
A Phantasy	294
Sing, Maiden, Sing	295
CHARLES DICKENS.—The Ivy Green	296
REV. GEORGE ROBERT GLEIG.—My Dog's Epitaph	297
WALTER THORNBURY.—Everlasting Flowers	299
Finis	300

List of Illustrations.

	DRAWN BY	ENGRAVED BY	PAGE
THE STOLEN KISS	*I. Lamont*	*Orrin Smith*	3
PAVING LABOURERS	*H. S. Marks*	*Orrin Smith*	8
MILTON'S HOME	*E. K. Johnson*	*H. Harral*	15
CHAMBER MUSIC	*T. Morten*	*H. Harral*	28
PHYLLIS	*G. Leslie*	*W. J. Linton*	38
SUNSET BY THE SEA	*W. P. Burton*	*H. Harral*	48
THE LITTLE GOSSIP	*G. H. Thomas*	*W. Thomas*	68
COLIN AND PHEBE	*W. Small*	*H. Harral*	71
THE WHIPPER-IN	*G. B. Goddard*	*W. Thomas*	82
THE SPINNET	*E. K. Johnson*	*H. Harral*	90
THE FIRST PRIMROSES	*E. Wimperis*	*W. J. Linton*	102
WHEN THE KYE COMES HAME	*F. B. Barwell*	*W. J. Linton*	138
INDIAN LANDSCAPE	*J. Wolf*	*H. Harral*	192
HOME, SWEET HOME	*E. Wimperis*	*W. J. Palmer*	248
EARLY SPRING	*Edmund Warren*	*W. Thomas*	266
THE WAYSIDE WELL	*E. Wimperis*	*W. J. Palmer*	270
PHILIP'S FARM	*W. P. Burton*	*H. Harral*	274
BAFFLED	*J. Wolf*	*H. Harral*	283
THE IMPENDING CHECK-MATE	*T. Morten*	*W. Thomas*	290

The Ornamental Title Page and Borders designed by HENRY SHAW, F.S.A. *and engraved by* R. B. UTTING.

GEORGE WITHER.

1588—1667.

PLAYFUL fancy, pure taste, and artless delicacy of sentiment, (says Mr. Ellis) distinguish the poetry of George Wither.—Is it not difficult to imagine the leader of a troop of Parliamentary horse anticipating Wordsworth in his exquisite appreciation of the smallest of Nature's beauties? In the Marshalsea Wither wrote some of his tenderest verses; and whether stern Major-general for Cromwell in Surrey, or in the Gate House pining for liberty, he seems to have maintained the same undeviating fervour and a high changeless love of all that was beautiful and good.

THE SHEPHERD'S RESOLUTION.

Shall I, wasting in despair,
Die because a woman's fair?
Or my cheeks make pale with care
'Cause another's rosy are?
Be she fairer than the day,
Or the flowery meads in May—
    If she be not so to me,
    What care I how fair she be?

Shall my foolish heart be pined
'Cause I see a woman kind;
Or a well-disposèd nature
Joinèd with a lovely feature?

Be she meeker, kinder, than
Turtle-dove or pelican,
    If she be not so to me,
    What care I how kind she be?

Shall a woman's virtues move
Me to perish for her love?
Or her merit's value known
Make me quite forget mine own?
Be she with that goodness blest
Which may gain her name of Best,
    If she seem not such to me,
    What care I how good she be?

'Cause her fortune seems too high,
Shall I play the fool and die?
Those that bear a noble mind
Where they want of riches find,
Think what with them they would do,
Who without them dare to woo;
    And unless that mind I see,
    What care I though great she be?

Great or good, or kind or fair,
I will ne'er the more despair;
If she love me, this believe,
I will die ere she shall grieve;
If she slight me when I woo,
I can scorn and let her go;
    For if she be not for me,
    What care I for whom she be?

MADRIGAL.

Amaryllis I did woo,
And I courted Phyllis too;
Daphne for her love I chose,
Chloris, for that damask rose
In her cheek, I held so dear,
Yea, a thousand liked well near;

THE STOLEN KISS.

And, in love with all together,
Fearèd the enjoying either:
'Cause to be of one possessed
Barred the hope of all the rest.

SONNET UPON A STOLEN KISS.

Now gentle sleep hath closèd up those eyes,
Which, waking, kept my boldest thoughts in awe;
And free access unto that sweet lip lies,
From whence I long the rosy breath to draw.
Methinks no wrong it were, if I should steal
From those two melting rubies one poor kiss;
None sees the theft that would the theft reveal,
Nor rob I her of ought what she can miss:
Nay, should I twenty kisses take away,
There would be little sign I would do so;
Why then should I this robbery delay?
Oh! she may wake, and therewith angry grow!
Well, if she do, I'll back restore that one,
And twenty hundred thousand more for loan.

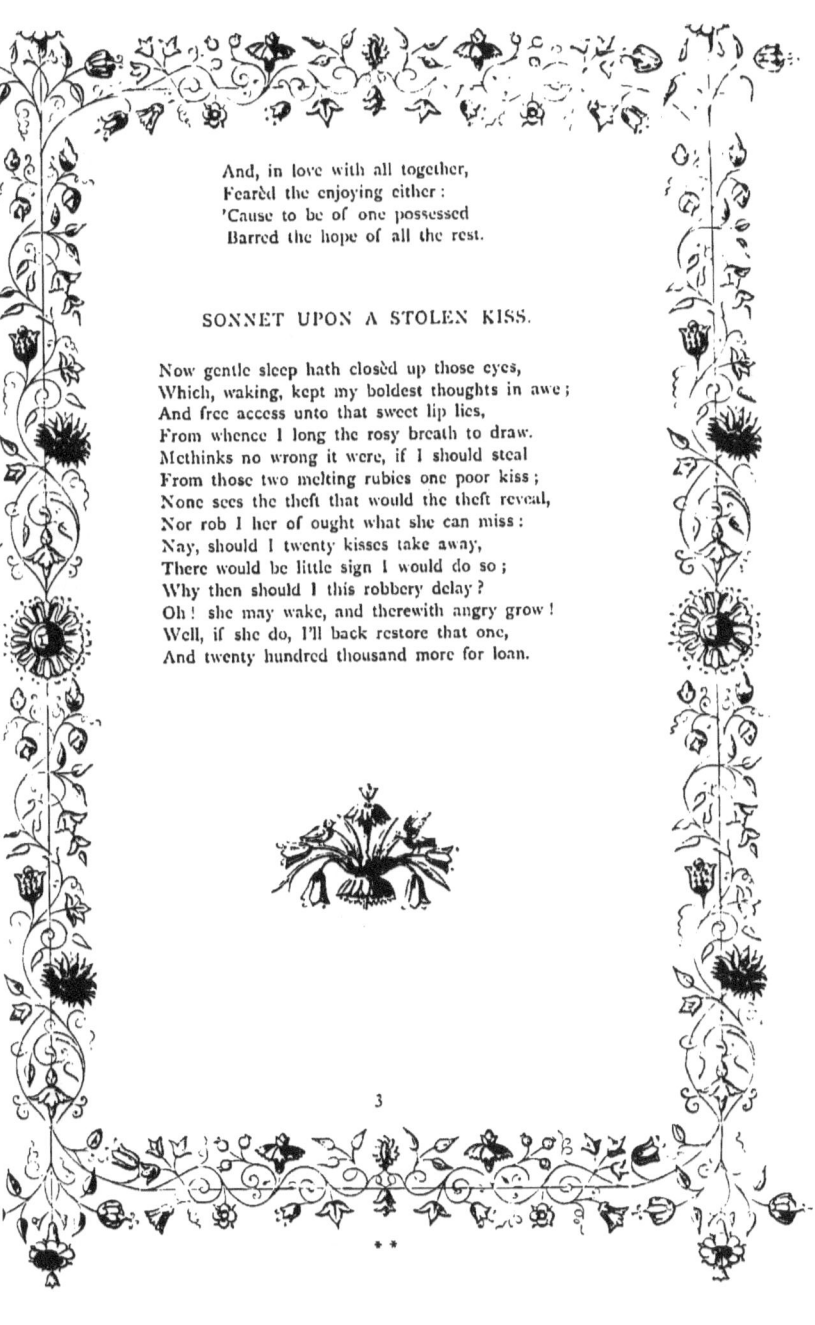

ABRAHAM COWLEY.
1618—1667.

THIS amiable and witty poet left no verse behind him so airy graceful, and gay, as the specimens we append. Amidst a chaotic drift of cumbrous religious poems, and fantastic efforts to versify the labours of the Royal Society, the diver may discover some pearls like these to repay his labours.

ANACREONTIC: DRINKING.

The thirsty earth soaks up the rain,
And drinks, and gapes for drink again.
The plants suck in the earth, and are
With constant drinking fresh and fair.
The sea itself, which one would think
Should have but little need of drink,
Drinks ten thousand rivers up,
So filled that they o'erflow the cup.
The busy sun—and one would guess
By's drunken fiery face no less—
Drinks up the sea, and when he has done,
The moon and stars drink up the sun.
They drink and dance by their own light:
They drink and revel all the night.
Nothing in Nature's sober found,
But an eternal health goes round.
Fill up the bowl then, fill it high,
Fill all the glasses there, for why
Should every creature drink but I,
Why, men of morals, tell me why?

THE CHRONICLE.

Margarita first possest,
    If I remember well, my breast.
    Margarita first of all;
But when a while the wanton maid
With my restless heart had played
    Martha took the flying ball.

Martha soon did it resign
    To the beauteous Catherine.
Beauteous Catherine gave place
Though loath and angry she to part
With the possession of my heart -
    To Eliza's conquering face.

Eliza till this hour might reign,
    Had she not evil counsels ta'en ;
Fundamental laws she broke,
And still new favourites she chose,
Till up in arms my passions rose
    And cast away her yoke.

Mary then and gentle Anne
    Both to reign at once began
Alternately they swayed ;
And sometimes Mary was the fair,
And sometimes Anne the crown did wear,
    Sometimes I both obeyed.

Another Mary then arose,
    And did vigorous laws impose ;
A mighty tyrant she !
Long, alas ! should I have been
Under that iron-sceptered queen,
    Had not Rebecca set me free.

When fair Rebecca set me free,
    'Twas then a golden time with me.
But soon those pleasures fled ;
For the gracious princess died
In her youth and beauty's pride,
    And Judith reigned in her stead.

One month, three days, and half an hour,
    Judith held the sovereign power.
Wondrous beautiful her face ;
But so weak and small her wit
That she to govern was unfit,—
    And so Susanna took her place.

But when Isabella came,
    Armed with a resistless flame
And the artillery of her eye,

    Whilst she proudly marched about,
Greater conquests to find out,
    She beat out Susan, by the bye.

But in her place I then obeyed
    Black-eyed Bess, her viceroy maid,
    To whom ensued a vacancy.
Thousand worse passions then possest
The interregnum of my breast:
    Bless me from such an anarchy!

Gentle Henrietta then,
    And a third Mary next began;
    Then Joan, and Jane, and Audria,
And then a pretty Thomasine,
And then another Catherine,
    And then a long 'et cetera.'

But should I now to you relate
    The strength and riches of their state,
    The powder, patches, and the pins,
The ribbons, jewels, and the rings,
The lace, the paint, and warlike things
    That make up all their magazines:

If I should tell the politic arts
    To take and keep men's hearts;
    The letters, embassies, and spies,
The frowns, and smiles, and flatteries,
The quarrels, tears, and perjuries,
    Numberless, nameless mysteries;

And all the little lime-twigs laid
    By Machiavel, the waiting-maid;
    I more voluminous should grow—
Chiefly if I like them should tell
All change of weathers that befell—
    Than Holinshed or Stow.

But I will briefer with them be,
    Since few of them were long with me.
    A higher and a nobler strain
My present emperess does claim,
Heleonora, first o' th' name,
    Whom God grant long to reign!

ROBERT HERRICK.

1591—1674.

THE vicar of a Devonshire village, Herrick, was no quiet saintly preacher of the Gospel like George Herbert of Bemerton. He loved to press the grape clusters with Ben Jonson, in the "Sun, the Dog and Triple Tun," and to listen to the revelling poets in the Apollo Chamber, hard by Temple Bar. In calmer moments, in the dewy evening, in the tranquil meadows of Dean Prior, however, this graceful poet found time to watch the primroses glowing in the dusk; time also to record their beauty and their transitoriness, and to weave into verse a thousand pleasant thoughts on the charms of a country life.

THE BAG OF THE BEE.

About the sweet bag of a bee,
  Two Cupids fell at odds;
And whose the pretty prize should be,
  They vowed to ask the gods.

Which Venus hearing thither came,
  And for their boldness stript them;
And, taking thence from each his flame,
  With rods of myrtle whipt them.

Which done, to still their wanton cries,
  When quiet grown she'd seen them,
She kissed and wiped their dove-like eyes,
  And gave the bag between them.

THE COUNTRY LIFE.

Sweet country life, to such unknown,
Whose lives are others, not their own!
But, serving courts and cities, be
Less happy, less enjoying thee.

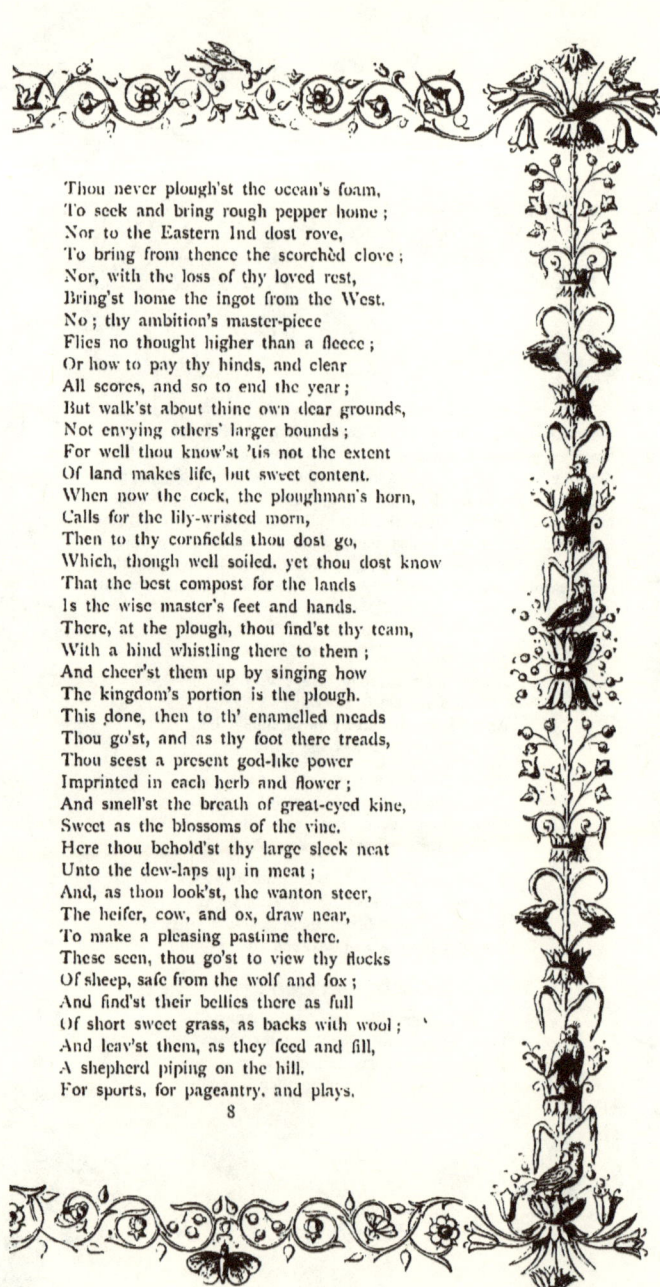

Thou never plough'st the ocean's foam,
To seek and bring rough pepper home;
Nor to the Eastern Ind dost rove,
To bring from thence the scorchèd clove;
Nor, with the loss of thy loved rest,
Bring'st home the ingot from the West.
No; thy ambition's master-piece
Flies no thought higher than a fleece;
Or how to pay thy hinds, and clear
All scores, and so to end the year;
But walk'st about thine own dear grounds,
Not envying others' larger bounds;
For well thou know'st 'tis not the extent
Of land makes life, but sweet content.
When now the cock, the ploughman's horn,
Calls for the lily-wristed morn,
Then to thy cornfields thou dost go,
Which, though well soiled, yet thou dost know
That the best compost for the lands
Is the wise master's feet and hands.
There, at the plough, thou find'st thy team,
With a hind whistling there to them;
And cheer'st them up by singing how
The kingdom's portion is the plough.
This done, then to th' enamelled meads
Thou go'st, and as thy foot there treads,
Thou seest a present god-like power
Imprinted in each herb and flower;
And smell'st the breath of great-eyed kine,
Sweet as the blossoms of the vine.
Here thou behold'st thy large sleek neat
Unto the dew-laps up in meat;
And, as thou look'st, the wanton steer,
The heifer, cow, and ox, draw near,
To make a pleasing pastime there.
These seen, thou go'st to view thy flocks
Of sheep, safe from the wolf and fox;
And find'st their bellies there as full
Of short sweet grass, as backs with wool;
And leav'st them, as they feed and fill,
A shepherd piping on the hill.
For sports, for pageantry, and plays.

Thou hast thy eyes and holy-days,
On which the young men and maids meet
To exercise their dancing feet;
Tripping the comely country-round,
With daffodils and daisies crowned.
Thy wakes, thy quintels, here thou hast,
Thy May-poles, too, with garlands graced;
Thy morris-dance, thy Whitsun-ale,
Thy shearing feast, which never fail:
Thy harvest-home, thy wassail-bowl,
That's tost up after fox i' th' hole;
Thy mummeries, thy Twelfth-night kings
And queens, thy Christmas revellings;
Thy nut-brown mirth, thy russet wit,
And no man pays too dear for it.
To these thou hast thy time to go,
And trace the hare in the treacherous snow:
Thy witty wiles to draw, and get
The lark into the trammel net;
Thou hast thy cock-rood, and thy glade,
To take the precious pheasant made;
Thy lime-twigs, snares, and pitfalls, then,
To catch the pilfering birds, not men.
O happy life, if that their good
The husbandmen but understood!
Who all the day themselves do please.
And younglings, with such sports as these;
And, lying down, have nought t' affright
Sweet sleep, that makes more short the night.

THE NIGHT-PIECE.—TO JULIA.

Her eyes the glow-worm lend thee,
The shooting stars attend thee;
   And the elves also,
   Whose little eyes glow
Like the sparks of fire, befriend thee.

No will-o'-th'-wisp mislight thee,
Nor snake or slow-worm bite thee;
   But on, on thy way,
   Not making a stay,
Since ghost there's none to affright thee.

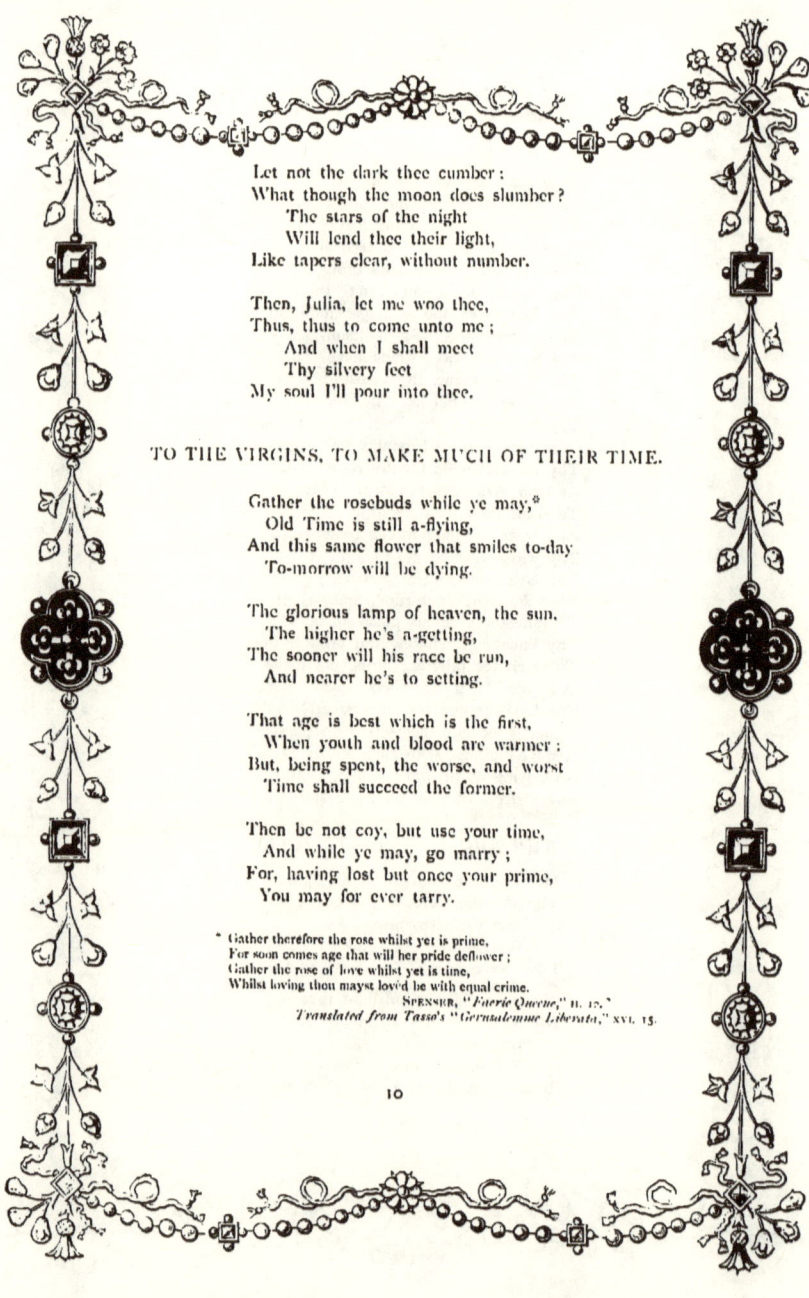

Let not the dark thee cumber:
What though the moon does slumber?
 The stars of the night
 Will lend thee their light,
Like tapers clear, without number.

Then, Julia, let me woo thee,
Thus, thus to come unto me;
 And when I shall meet
 Thy silvery feet
My soul I'll pour into thee.

TO THE VIRGINS, TO MAKE MUCH OF THEIR TIME.

Gather the rosebuds while ye may,*
 Old Time is still a-flying,
And this same flower that smiles to-day
 To-morrow will be dying.

The glorious lamp of heaven, the sun,
 The higher he's a-getting,
The sooner will his race be run,
 And nearer he's to setting.

That age is best which is the first,
 When youth and blood are warmer:
But, being spent, the worse, and worst
 Time shall succeed the former.

Then be not coy, but use your time,
 And while ye may, go marry;
For, having lost but once your prime,
 You may for ever tarry.

<small>* Gather therefore the rose whilst yet is prime,
For soon comes age that will her pride deflower;
Gather the rose of love whilst yet is time,
Whilst loving thou mayst loved be with equal crime.
    SPENSER, "*Faerie Queene*," II. 12.
 Translated from Tasso's "*Gerusalemme Liberata*," XVI. 15.</small>

TO DAFFODILS.

Fair Daffodils, we weep to see
    You haste away so soon ;
As yet the early-rising sun
    Has not attained his noon.
      Stay, stay,
    Until the hasting day
      Has run
    But to the even-song ;
And, having prayed together, we
    Will go with you along.

We have short time to stay, as you,
    We have as short a spring ;
As quick a growth to meet decay
    As you, or any thing.
      We die,
    As your hours do, and dry
      Away
Like to the summer's rain ;
Or as the pearls of morning's dew
    Ne'er to be found again.

TO BLOSSOMS.

Fair pledges of a fruitful tree,
    Why do ye fall so fast?
    Your date is not so past
But you may stay yet here awhile
    To blush and gently smile,
      And go at last.

What, were ye born to be
    An hour or half's delight,
    And so to bid good-night?
'Twas pity Nature brought ye forth
    Merely to shew your worth,
      And lose you quite.

But you are lovely leaves, where we
May read how soon things have
Their end, though ne'er so brave:
And after they have shown their pride
Like you, awhile, they glide
Into the grave.

TO PRIMROSES FILLED WITH MORNING DEW.

Why do ye weep, sweet babes? Can tears
Speak grief in you,
Who were but born
Just as the modest morn
Teemed her refreshing dew?
Alas! you have not known that shower
That mars a flower,
Nor felt the unkind
Breath of a blasting wind;
Nor are ye worn with years,
Or warped as we,
Who think it strange to see
Such pretty flowers, like to orphans young,
Speaking by tears before ye have a tongue.

Speak, whimpering younglings, and make known
The reason why
Ye droop and weep;
Is it for want of sleep,
Or childish lullaby?
Or that ye have not seen as yet
The violet?
Or brought a kiss
From that sweet heart to this?
No, no; this sorrow shewn
By your tears shed,
Would have this lecture read—
'That things of greatest, so of meanest worth,
Conceiv'd with grief are, and with tears brought forth.'

TO CORINNA, TO GO A MAYING

Get up, get up, for shame, the blooming morn
Upon her wings presents the god unshorn.
    See how Aurora throws her fair
    Fresh-quilted colours through the air;
    Get up, sweet slug-a-bed, and see
    The dew bespangling herb and tree.
Each flower has wept, and bowed toward the east,
Above an hour since, yet you are not drest,
    Nay, not so much as out of bed ;
    When all the birds have matins said,
    And sung their thankful hymns : 'tis sin,
    Nay, profanation, to keep in,
When as a thousand virgins on this day
Spring sooner than the lark to fetch in May.

Rise, and put on your foliage, and be seen
To come forth, like the spring-time, fresh and green.
    And sweet as Flora. Take no care
    For jewels for your gown or hair ;
    Fear not, the leaves will strew
    Gems in abundance upon you ;
Besides, the childhood of the day has kept,
Against you come, some orient pearls unwept.
    Come, and receive them while the light
    Hangs on the dew-locks of the night :
    And Titan on the Eastern hill
    Retires himself, or else stands still
Till you come forth. Wash, dress, be brief in praying :
Few beads are best when once we go a Maying.

Come, my Corinna, come ; and, coming, mark
How each field turns a street, each street a park
    Made green, and trimmed with trees ; see how
    Devotion gives each house a bough,
    Or branch ; each porch, each door, ere this,
    An ark, a tabernacle, is,
Made up of white-thorn neatly interwove :
As if here were those cooler shades of love.

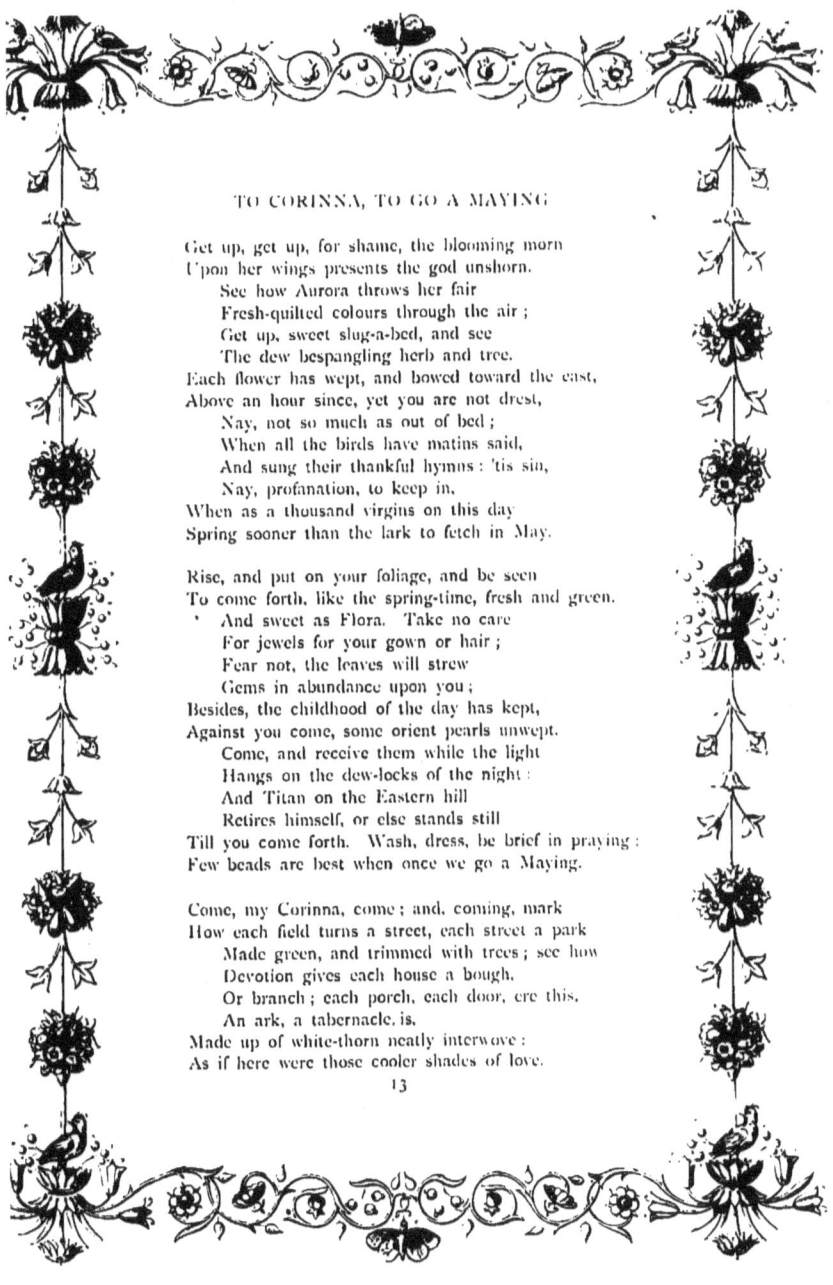

Can such delight be in the street
And open fields, and we not see't?
Come, we'll abroad, and let's obey
The proclamation made for May:
And sin no more, as we have done, by staying,
But, my Corinna, come, let's go a Maying.

There's not a budding boy or girl, this day,
But is got up, and gone to bring in May.
    A deal of youth, ere this, is come*
    Back, and with white-thorn laden home.
    Some have despatched their cakes and cream
    Before that we have left to dream;
And some have wept, and wooed, and plighted troth,
And chose their priest, ere we can cast off sloth:
    ✧   ✧   ✧   ✧   ✧
Come, let us go, while we are in our prime,
And take the harmless folly of the time.
    We shall grow old apace, and die
    Before we know our liberty.
    Our life is short, and our days run
    As fast away as does the sun;
And as a vapour, or a drop of rain
Once lost, can ne'er be found again;
    So when or you or I are made
    A fable, song, or fleeting shade;
    All love, all liking, all delight
    Lies drowned with us in endless night.
Then, while time serves, and we are but decaying,
Come, my Corinna, come, let's go a Maying.

    * Young folk now flocken in everywhere
    To gather May-buskets and smelling brere;
    And home they hasten the posts to dight,
    And all the Kirk-pillars ere daylight,
    With hawthorn buds and sweet eglantine.
        SPENSER, "*Shepherd's Calendar*," *May.*

MILTON'S HOME

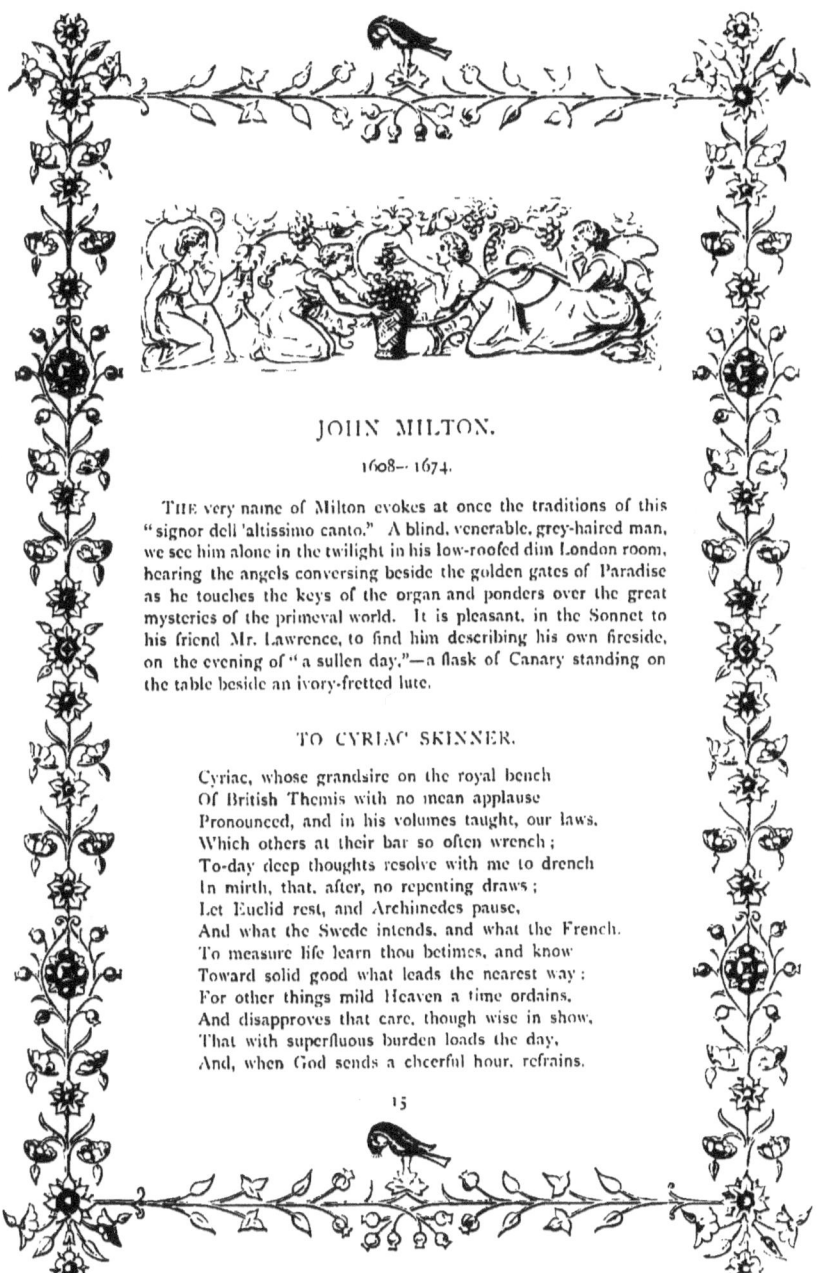

JOHN MILTON.

1608–1674.

THE very name of Milton evokes at once the traditions of this "signor dell 'altissimo canto." A blind, venerable, grey-haired man, we see him alone in the twilight in his low-roofed dim London room, hearing the angels conversing beside the golden gates of Paradise as he touches the keys of the organ and ponders over the great mysteries of the primeval world. It is pleasant, in the Sonnet to his friend Mr. Lawrence, to find him describing his own fireside, on the evening of "a sullen day,"—a flask of Canary standing on the table beside an ivory-fretted lute.

TO CYRIAC SKINNER.

Cyriac, whose grandsire on the royal bench
Of British Themis with no mean applause
Pronounced, and in his volumes taught, our laws,
Which others at their bar so often wrench;
To-day deep thoughts resolve with me to drench
In mirth, that, after, no repenting draws;
Let Euclid rest, and Archimedes pause,
And what the Swede intends, and what the French.
To measure life learn thou betimes, and know
Toward solid good what leads the nearest way;
For other things mild Heaven a time ordains,
And disapproves that care, though wise in show,
That with superfluous burden loads the day,
And, when God sends a cheerful hour, refrains.

TO MR. LAWRENCE.

Lawrence, of virtuous father virtuous son,
Now that the fields are dank and ways are mire,
Where shall we sometimes meet, and by the fire
Help waste a sullen day, what may be won
From the hard season gaining? Time will run
On smoother, till Favonius reinspire
The frozen earth, and clothe in fresh attire
The lily and rose, that neither sowed nor spun.
What neat repast shall feast us, light and choice,
Of Attic taste, with wine, whence we may rise
To hear the lute well touched, or artful voice
Warble immortal notes and Tuscan air?*
He who of those delights can judge, and spare
To interpose them oft, is not unwise.

ON HIS BEING ARRIVED TO THE AGE OF TWENTY-THREE.

How soon hath Time, the subtle thief of youth,
Stolen on his wing my three-and-twentieth year!
My hasting days fly on with full career,
But my late spring no bud or blossom shew'th.
Perhaps my semblance might deceive the truth
That I to manhood am arrived so near;
And inward ripeness doth much less appear,
That some more timely-happy spirits endu'th.
Yet be it less or more, or soon or slow,
It shall be still in strictest measure even
To that same lot, however mean or high,
Toward which Time leads me, and the will of Heaven;
All is, if I have grace to use it so,
As ever in my great Task-Master's eye.

---

* In this truly Miltonic line we seem to have a foretaste of the incomparable harmonies the "Paradise Lost"

SONG ON MAY MORNING.

Now the bright morning-star, day's harbinger,
Comes dancing from the east, and leads with her
The flowery May, who from her green lap throws
The yellow cowslip and the pale primrose.
    Hail, bounteous May, that dost inspire
    Mirth, and youth, and warm desire!
    Woods and groves are of thy dressing;
    Hill and dale doth boast thy blessing.
Thus we salute thee with our early song,
And welcome thee, and wish thee long.

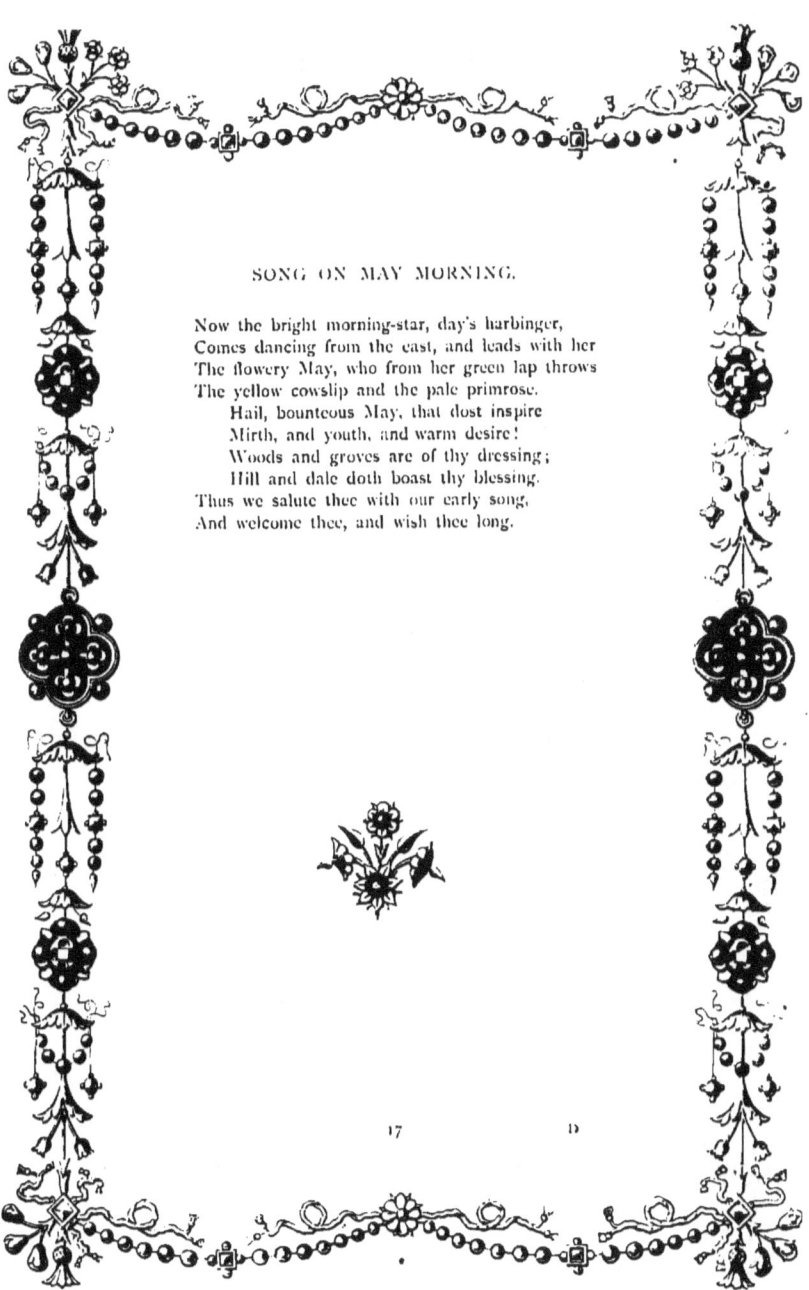

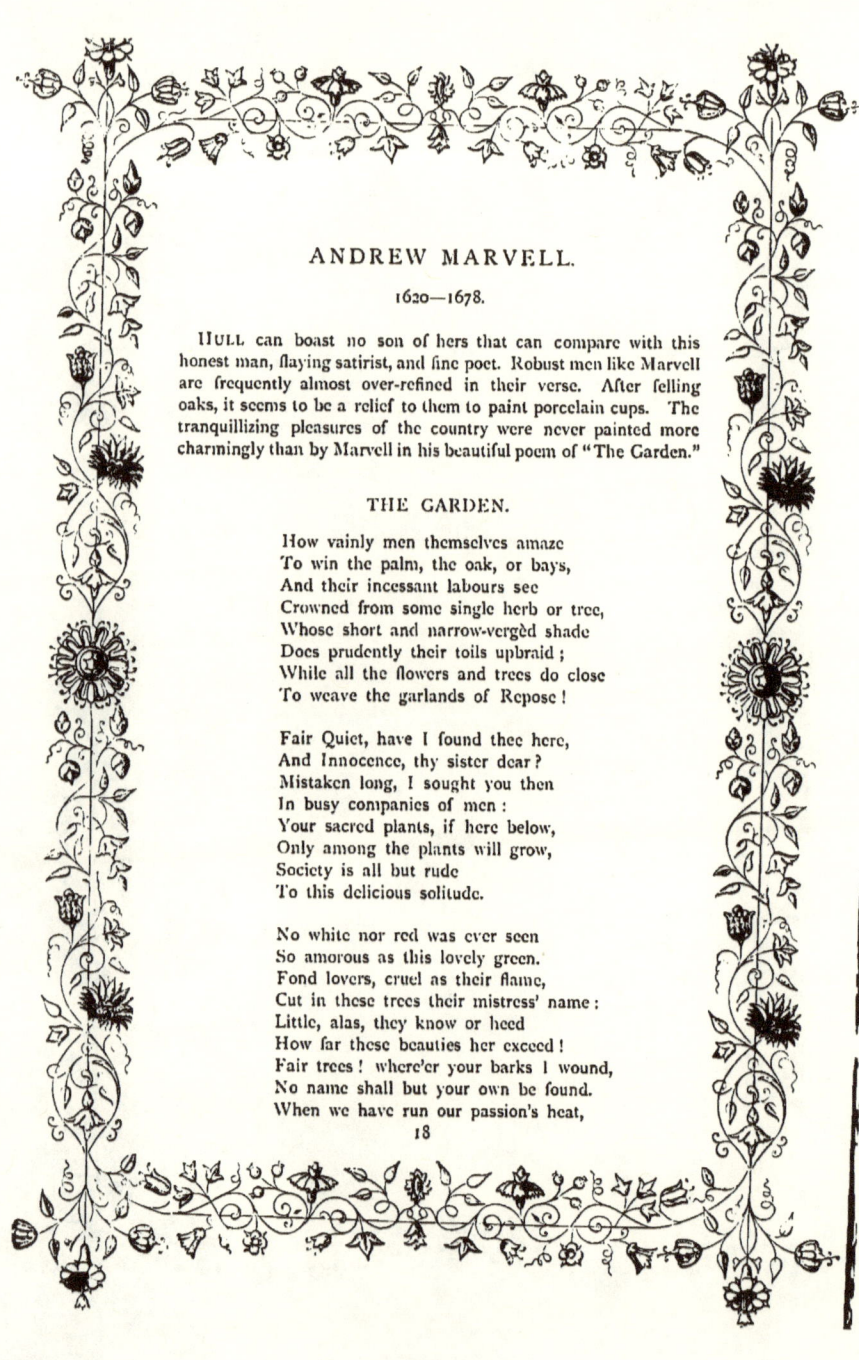

ANDREW MARVELL.

1620—1678.

HULL can boast no son of hers that can compare with this honest man, flaying satirist, and fine poet. Robust men like Marvell are frequently almost over-refined in their verse. After felling oaks, it seems to be a relief to them to paint porcelain cups. The tranquillizing pleasures of the country were never painted more charmingly than by Marvell in his beautiful poem of "The Garden."

THE GARDEN.

How vainly men themselves amaze
To win the palm, the oak, or bays,
And their incessant labours see
Crowned from some single herb or tree,
Whose short and narrow-vergèd shade
Does prudently their toils upbraid;
While all the flowers and trees do close
To weave the garlands of Repose!

Fair Quiet, have I found thee here,
And Innocence, thy sister dear?
Mistaken long, I sought you then
In busy companies of men:
Your sacred plants, if here below,
Only among the plants will grow,
Society is all but rude
To this delicious solitude.

No white nor red was ever seen
So amorous as this lovely green.
Fond lovers, cruel as their flame,
Cut in these trees their mistress' name:
Little, alas, they know or heed
How far these beauties her exceed!
Fair trees! where'er your barks I wound,
No name shall but your own be found.
When we have run our passion's heat,

Love hither makes his best retreat :
The gods, who mortal beauty chase,
Still in a tree did end their race :
Apollo hunted Daphne so
Only that she might laurel grow :
And Pan did after Syrinx speed
Not as a nymph, but for a reed.

What wondrous life is this I lead !
Ripe apples drop about my head ;
The luscious clusters of the vine
Upon my mouth do crush their wine ;
The nectarine and curious peach
Into my hands themselves do reach ;
Stumbling on melons, as I pass,
Ensnared with flowers, I fall on grass.

Meanwhile the mind from pleasure less
Withdraws into its happiness ;
The mind, that ocean where each kind
Does straight its own resemblance find ;
Yet it creates, transcending these,
Far other worlds, and other seas ;
Annihilating all that's made
To a green thought in a green shade.

Here at the fountain's sliding foot,
Or at some fruit-tree's mossy root,
Casting the body's vest aside,
My soul into the boughs does glide ;
There, like a bird, it sits and sings,
Then whets and claps its silver wings,
And, till prepared for longer flight,
Waves in its plumes the various light.*
Such was that happy Garden-state †

---

* "Waves in the eye of heaven her many-coloured wings."
                                    GRAY, *Bard.*
† Campbell seems to have been of a different opinion ; he says,
      "The world was sad, the Garden was a wild,
      And man, the hermit, sighed till woman smiled."
                                    Pleasures of Hope.

While man there walked without a mate:
After a place so pure and sweet,
What other help could yet be meet!
But 'twas beyond a mortal's share
To wander solitary there:
Two paradises are in one
To live in Paradise alone.

How well the skilful gardener drew
Of flowers and herbs this dial new!
Where, from above, the milder sun
Does through a fragrant zodiac run;
And, as it works, the industrious bee
Computes its time as well as we.
How could such sweet and wholesome hours
Be reckoned, but with herbs and flowers!

THE NYMPH COMPLAINING FOR THE DEATH OF HER FAWN.

The wanton troopers riding by
Have shot my fawn, and it will die.
Ungentle men! they cannot thrive
Who killed thee. Thou ne'er didst, alive,
Them any harm, alas! nor could
Thy death yet do them any good.
I'm sure I never wish'd them ill,
Nor do I for all this, nor will:
But, if my simple prayers may yet
Prevail with Heaven to forget
Thy murder, I will join my tears
Rather than fail. But, O my fears!
It cannot die so. Heaven's King
Keeps register of everything,
And nothing may we use in vain;
Even beasts must be with justice slain
Else men are made their deodands.
Though they should wash their guilty hands
In this warm life-blood which doth part
From thine and wound me to the heart,

Yet could they not be clean, their stain
Is dyed in such a purple grain.
There is not such another in
The world to offer for their sin.

Inconstant Sylvio, when yet
I had not found him counterfeit,
One morning, I remember well,
Tied in this silver chain and bell,
Gave it to me: nay, and I know
What he said then, I'm sure I do:
Said he, "Look how your huntsman here
Hath taught a fawn to hunt his deer."
But Sylvio soon had me beguiled;
This waxèd tame, while he grew wild,
And quite regardless of my smart
Left me his fawn, but took his heart.

Thenceforth I set myself to play
My solitary time away
With this; and very well content
Could so mine idle life have spent;
For it was full of sport, and light
Of foot and heart, and did invite
Me to its game: it seemed to bless
Itself in me; how could I less
Than love it? O, I cannot be
Unkind to a beast that loveth me!

Had it lived long, I do not know
Whether it too might have done so
As Sylvio did; his gifts might be
Perhaps as false, or more, than he;
But I am sure, for aught that I
Could in so short a time espy,
Thy love was far more better than
The love of false and cruel man.

With sweetest milk and sugar first
I it at my own fingers nursed;
And as it grew, so every day
It waxed more white and sweet than they.

It had so sweet a breath! And oft
I blush'd to see its foot more soft
And white, shall I say than my hand?
Nay, any lady's of the land.

It is a wondrous thing how fleet
'Twas on those little silver feet;
With what a pretty skipping grace
It oft would challenge me the race;
And, when it had left me far away,
'Twould stay, and run again, and stay;
For it was nimbler much than hinds,
And trod as if on the four winds.

I have a garden of my own,
But so with roses overgrown,
And lilies, that you would it guess
To be a little wilderness;
And all the spring-time of the year
It only lovèd to be there.
Among the beds of lilies I
Have sought it oft, where it should lie,
Yet could not, till itself would rise,
Find it, although before mine eyes;
For in the flaxen lilies' shade
It like a bank of lilies laid.
Upon the roses it would feed
Until its lips e'en seemed to bleed,
And then to me 'twould boldly trip,
And print those roses on my lip.
But all its chief delight was still
On roses thus itself to fill,
And its pure virgin limbs to fold
In whitest sheets of lilies cold:
Had it lived long it would have been
Lilies without, roses within.

O help! O help! I see it faint
And die as calmly as a saint!
See how it weeps! the tears do come
Sad, slowly, dropping like a gum.
So weeps the wounded balsam; so

The holy frankincense doth flow ;
The brotherless Heliades
Melt in such amber tears as these.

I in a golden vial will
Keep these two crystal tears, and fill
It till it doth o'erflow with mine,
Then place it in Diana's shrine.

Now my sweet fawn is vanished to
Whither the swans and turtles go ;
In fair Elysium to endure
With milk-white lambs and ermines pure.
O do not run too fast : for I
Will but bespeak thy grave, and die.

First, my unhappy statue shall
Be cut in marble ; and withal,
Let it be weeping too ; but there
The engraver sure his art may spare :
For I so truly thee bemoan,
That I shall weep though I be stone,
Until my tears, still dropping, wear
My breast, themselves engraving there ;
Then at my feet shalt thou be laid,
Of purest alabaster made ;
For I would have thine image be
White as I can, though not as thee.

THE EARL OF ROCHESTER.

1647—1680.

THE verse of John Wilmot, Earl of Rochester, is more artificial than that of Sedley. It does not come from the heart, but the head.

SONG.

My dear mistress has a heart
Soft as those kind looks she gave me,
  When with love's resistless art
And her eyes she did enslave me.
  But her constancy's so weak,
She's so wild and apt to wander,
  That my jealous heart would break
Should we live one day asunder.

  Melting joys about her move,
Killing pleasures, wounding blisses;
  She can dress her eyes in love,
And her lips can warm with kisses.
  Angels listen when she speaks;
She's my delight, all mankind's wonder;
  But my jealous heart would break
Should we live one day asunder.

LOVE AND LIFE.

All my past life is mine no more,
  The flying hours are gone;
Like transitory dreams given o'er,
Whose images are kept in store
  By memory alone.

The time that is to come is not;
  How can it then be mine?
The present moment's all my lot,
And that, as fast as it is got,
  Phyllis, is only thine.

Then talk not of inconstancy,
  False hearts, and broken vows;
If I by miracle can be
This live-long minute true to thee,
  'Tis all that heaven allows.

IZAAK WALTON.

1593—1683.

IN troublous times, and amidst the fret and anxieties of business Izaak Walton kept his heart pure and stainless as that of a child. Under shady sycamore trees on the Lea bank, and in the cool shadow of honeysuckle hedges, on the road to Tottenham, the brave old citizen meditated and angled, now catching a fish, now fishing for a metaphor. A simple tradesman, and yet a friend of grave divines and witty courtiers, Walton sounded both the bass and the upper strings of fortune, and must have spent ninety as calm-flowing and happy years as any son of Adam that ever drew breath. To use his own words, 'when the lawyer was swallowed up with business, and the statesman contriving plots, he sat on cowslip-banks hearing the birds sing, and possessed himself in as much quietness as the silent silver stream which rippled softly beside him.'

THE ANGLER'S WISH.

I in these flowery meads would be:
These crystal streams should solace me:
To whose harmonious bubbling noise
I with my angle would rejoice,
    Sit here and see the turtle-dove
    Court his chaste mate to acts of love:

Or on that bank feel the west wind
Breathe health and plenty: please my mind,
To see sweet dewdrops kiss these flowers,
And then washed off by April showers;
    Here, hear my Kenna sing a song;
    There, see a blackbird feed her young,

Or a laverock build her nest:
Here, give my weary spirits rest,
And raise my low-pitched thoughts above
Earth, or what poor mortals love:
    Thus, free from lawsuits and the noise
    Of princes' courts, I would rejoice ;

Or with my Bryan and a book
Loiter long days near Shawford brook ;
There sit by him and eat my meat ;
There see the sun both rise and set ;
There bid good morning to next day ;
There meditate my time away ;
    And angle on, and beg to have
    A quiet passage to a welcome grave.

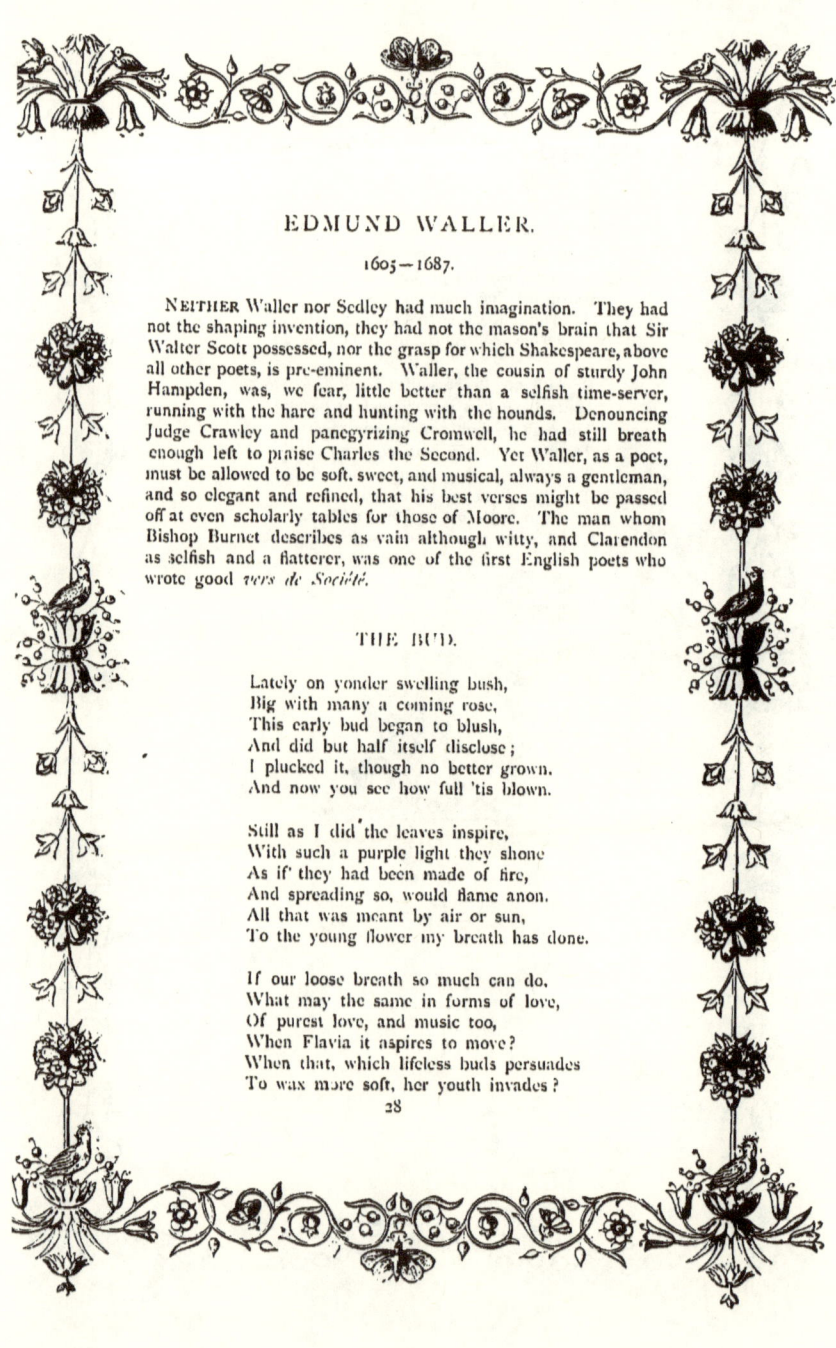

EDMUND WALLER.

1605—1687.

NEITHER Waller nor Sedley had much imagination. They had not the shaping invention, they had not the mason's brain that Sir Walter Scott possessed, nor the grasp for which Shakespeare, above all other poets, is pre-eminent. Waller, the cousin of sturdy John Hampden, was, we fear, little better than a selfish time-server, running with the hare and hunting with the hounds. Denouncing Judge Crawley and panegyrizing Cromwell, he had still breath enough left to praise Charles the Second. Yet Waller, as a poet, must be allowed to be soft, sweet, and musical, always a gentleman, and so elegant and refined, that his best verses might be passed off at even scholarly tables for those of Moore. The man whom Bishop Burnet describes as vain although witty, and Clarendon as selfish and a flatterer, was one of the first English poets who wrote good *vers de Société*.

THE BUD.

Lately on yonder swelling bush,
Big with many a coming rose,
This early bud began to blush,
And did but half itself disclose;
I plucked it, though no better grown,
And now you see how full 'tis blown.

Still as I did the leaves inspire,
With such a purple light they shone
As if they had been made of fire,
And spreading so, would flame anon.
All that was meant by air or sun,
To the young flower my breath has done.

If our loose breath so much can do,
What may the same in forms of love,
Of purest love, and music too,
When Flavia it aspires to move?
When that, which lifeless buds persuades
To wax more soft, her youth invades?

GO, LOVELY ROSE.

Go, lovely Rose!
  Tell her that wastes her time and me,
That now she knows,
  When I resemble her to thee,
  How sweet and fair she seems to be.

Tell her that's young,
  And shuns to have her graces spied,
That hadst thou sprung
  In deserts where no men abide
  Thou must have uncommended died.

Small is the worth
  Of beauty from the light retired;
Bid her come forth,
  Suffer herself to be desired,
  And not blush so to be admired.

Then die! that she
  The common fate of all things rare
May read in thee;
  How small a part of time they share
  That are so wondrous sweet and fair!

ON A GIRDLE.

That which her slender waist confined
Shall now my joyful temples bind;
No monarch but would give his crown
His arms might do what this has done.

It was my heaven's extremest sphere,
The pale which held that lovely deer.
My joy, my grief, my hope, my love,
Did all within this circle move!

A narrow compass! and yet there
Dwelt all that's good, and all that's fair.
Give me but what this ribbon bound,
Take all the rest the sun goes round.

TO A LADY SINGING A SONG OF HIS COMPOSING.

Chloris! yourself you so excel
    When you vouchsafe to breathe my thought,
That, like a spirit, with this spell
    Of my own teaching I am caught.

That eagle's fate and mine are one,
    Which on the shaft that made him die
Espied a feather of his own
    Wherewith he wont to soar so high.

Had Echo with so sweet a grace
    Narcissus' loud complaints returned,
Not for reflection of his face,
    But of his voice, the boy had burned.

TO PHYLLIS.

Phyllis! why should we delay
Pleasures shorter than the day?
Could we (which we never can!)
Stretch our lives beyond their span,
Beauty like a shadow flies,
And our youth before us dies.
Or would youth and beauty stay,
Love hath wings and will away.
Love hath swifter wings than Time,
Change in love to heaven does climb.
Gods that never change their state
Vary oft their love and hate.

Phyllis! to this truth we owe
All the love betwixt us two.
Let not you and I enquire
What has been our past desire;
On what shepherds you have smiled,
Or what nymphs I have beguiled;
Leave it to the planets too,
What we shall hereafter do;
For the joys we now may prove,
Take advice of present love.

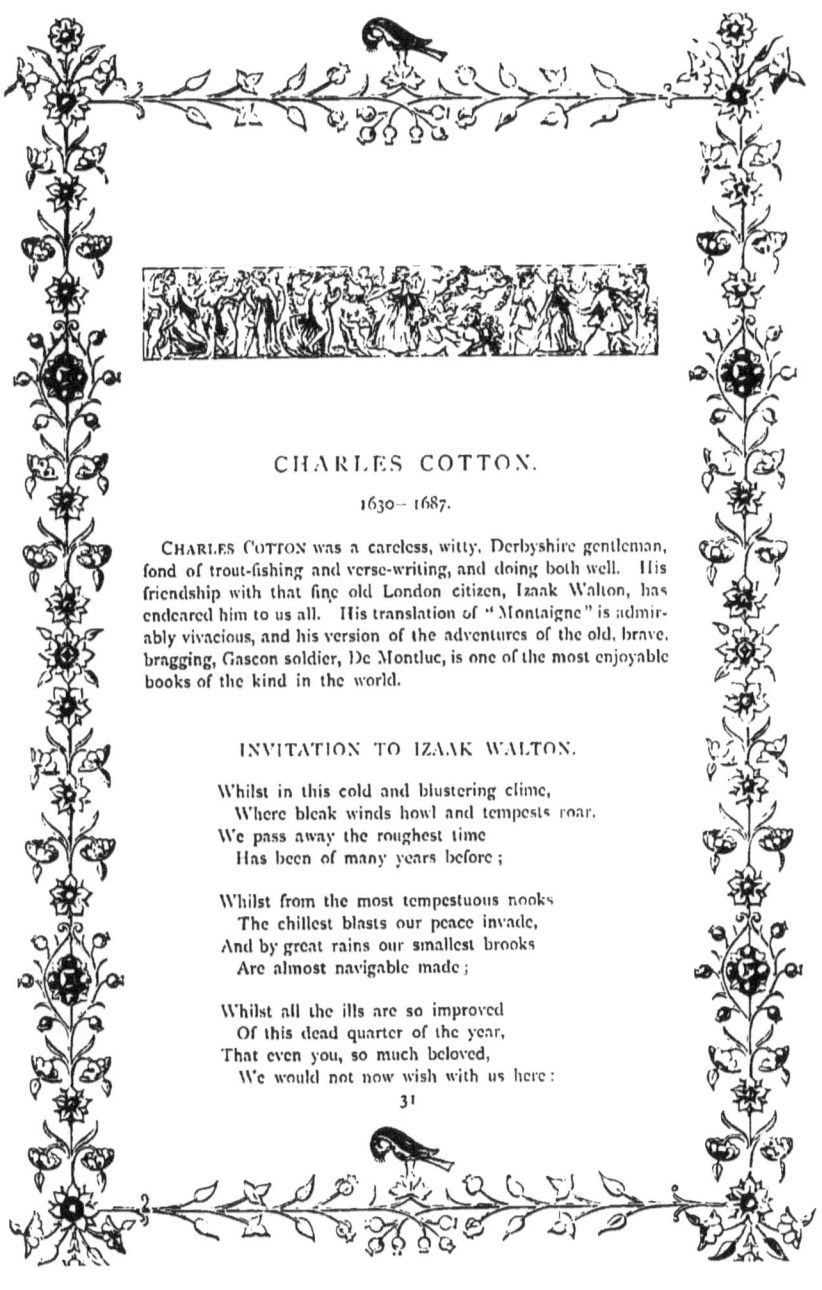

CHARLES COTTON.

1630—1687.

CHARLES COTTON was a careless, witty, Derbyshire gentleman, fond of trout-fishing and verse-writing, and doing both well. His friendship with that fine old London citizen, Izaak Walton, has endeared him to us all. His translation of "Montaigne" is admirably vivacious, and his version of the adventures of the old, brave, bragging, Gascon soldier, De Montluc, is one of the most enjoyable books of the kind in the world.

INVITATION TO IZAAK WALTON.

Whilst in this cold and blustering clime,
    Where bleak winds howl and tempests roar,
We pass away the roughest time
    Has been of many years before;

Whilst from the most tempestuous nooks
    The chillest blasts our peace invade,
And by great rains our smallest brooks
    Are almost navigable made;

Whilst all the ills are so improved
    Of this dead quarter of the year,
That even you, so much beloved,
    We would not now wish with us here:

In this estate, I say, it is
  Some comfort to us to suppose
That in a better clime than this
  You, our dear friend, have more repose;

And some delight to me the while,
  Though Nature now does weep in vain,
To think that I have seen her smile,
  And haply may I do again.

If the all-ruling Power please
  We live to see another May,
We'll recompense an age of these
  Foul days in one fine fishing-day.

We then shall have a day or two,
  Perhaps a week, wherein to try
What the best master's hand can do
  With the most deadly killing fly.

A day with not too bright a beam;
  A warm, but not a scorching sun;
A southern gale to curl the stream;
  And, master, half our work is done.

Then, whilst behind some bush we wait
  The scaly people to betray,
We'll prove it just with treacherous bait
  To make the preying trout our prey;

And think ourselves in such an hour
  Happier than those, though not so high,
Who, like leviathans, devour
  Of meaner men the smaller fry.

This, my best friend, at my poor home
  Shall be our pastime and our theme;
But then—should you not deign to come
  You make all this a flattering dream.

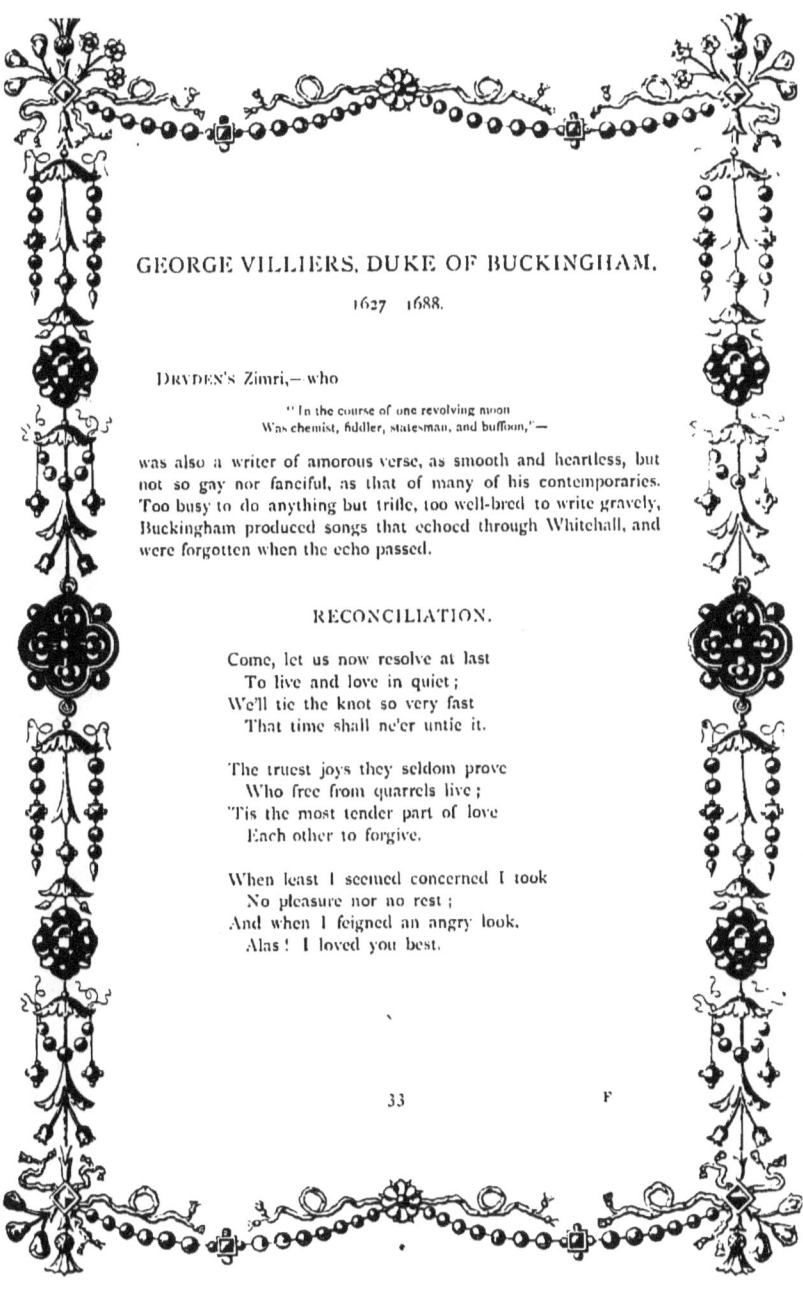

GEORGE VILLIERS, DUKE OF BUCKINGHAM.

1627—1688.

DRYDEN'S Zimri,—who

"In the course of one revolving moon
Was chemist, fiddler, statesman, and buffoon,"—

was also a writer of amorous verse, as smooth and heartless, but not so gay nor fanciful, as that of many of his contemporaries. Too busy to do anything but trifle, too well-bred to write gravely, Buckingham produced songs that echoed through Whitehall, and were forgotten when the echo passed.

RECONCILIATION.

Come, let us now resolve at last
　To live and love in quiet;
We'll tie the knot so very fast
　That time shall ne'er untie it.

The truest joys they seldom prove
　Who free from quarrels live;
'Tis the most tender part of love
　Each other to forgive.

When least I seemed concerned I took
　No pleasure nor no rest;
And when I feigned an angry look,
　Alas! I loved you best.

JOHN DRYDEN.

1631—1700.

DRYDEN was the eldest son of a Northamptonshire gentleman; he began by eulogizing Cromwell; went on to praise Charles the Second; wrote licentious plays for money, though himself a quiet, respectable man; and ended by turning Roman Catholic. Such a character can scarcely be pleasant to contemplate, and we must deplore that the great poet lived in so unhappy and vicious an age. There is a long and elastic swing in his satirical verse that makes its lashes cut as deep almost as Juvenal's; but Dryden wanted grace, taste, purity, and above all—heart.

SONG TO BRITANNIA, IN "KING ARTHUR."

Fairest isle, all isles excelling,
    Seat of pleasures and of loves:
Venus here will choose her dwelling,
    And forsake her Cyprian groves.

Cupid from his favourite nation
    Care and envy will remove;
Jealousy, that poisons passion,
    And despair, that dies for love.

Gentle murmurs, sweet complaining,
    Sighs, that blow the fire of love;
Soft repulses, kind disdaining,
    Shall be all the pains you prove.

Every swain shall pay his duty,
    Grateful every nymph shall prove;
And as these excel in beauty,
    Those shall be renowned for love.

THE FAIR STRANGER.

Happy and free, securely blest,
No beauty could disturb my rest;
My amorous heart was in despair
To find a new victorious fair.

Till you descending on our plains
With foreign force renew my chains;
Where now you rule without control,
The mighty sovereign of my soul.

Your smiles have more of conquering charms
Than all your native country's arms:
Their troops we can expel with ease,
Who vanquish only when we please.

But in your eyes, oh! there's the spell;
Who can see them, and not rebel?
You make us captives by your stay,
Yet kill us if you go away.

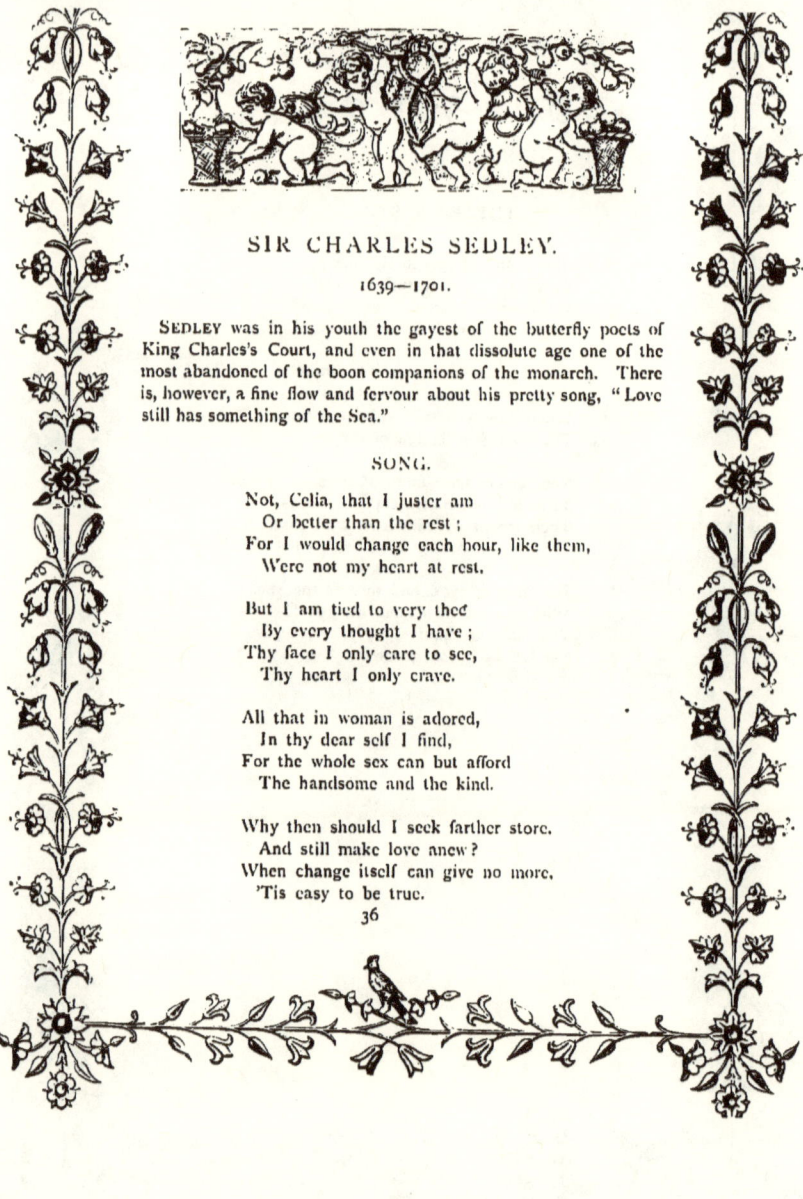

SIR CHARLES SEDLEY.

1639—1701.

SEDLEY was in his youth the gayest of the butterfly poets of King Charles's Court, and even in that dissolute age one of the most abandoned of the boon companions of the monarch. There is, however, a fine flow and fervour about his pretty song, "Love still has something of the Sea."

SONG.

Not, Celia, that I juster am
    Or better than the rest;
For I would change each hour, like them,
    Were not my heart at rest.

But I am tied to very thee
    By every thought I have;
Thy face I only care to see,
    Thy heart I only crave.

All that in woman is adored,
    In thy dear self I find,
For the whole sex can but afford
    The handsome and the kind.

Why then should I seek farther store,
    And still make love anew?
When change itself can give no more,
    'Tis easy to be true.

SONG.

Love still has something of the sea
    From whence his mother rose;
No time his slaves from doubt can free,
    Nor give their thoughts repose.

They are becalmed in clearest days,
    And in rough weather tossed;
They wither under cold delays,
    Or are in tempests lost.

One while they seem to touch the port,
    Then straight into the main
Some angry wind, in cruel sport,
    The vessel drives again.

At first disdain and pride they fear,
    Which if they chance to 'scape,
Rivals and falsehood soon appear
    In a more dreadful shape.

'Tis cruel to prolong a pain;
    And to defer a joy,
Believe me, gentle Celemene,
    Offends the wingèd boy.

An hundred thousand oaths your fears
    Perhaps would not remove;
And if I gazed a thousand years,
    I could no deeper love.

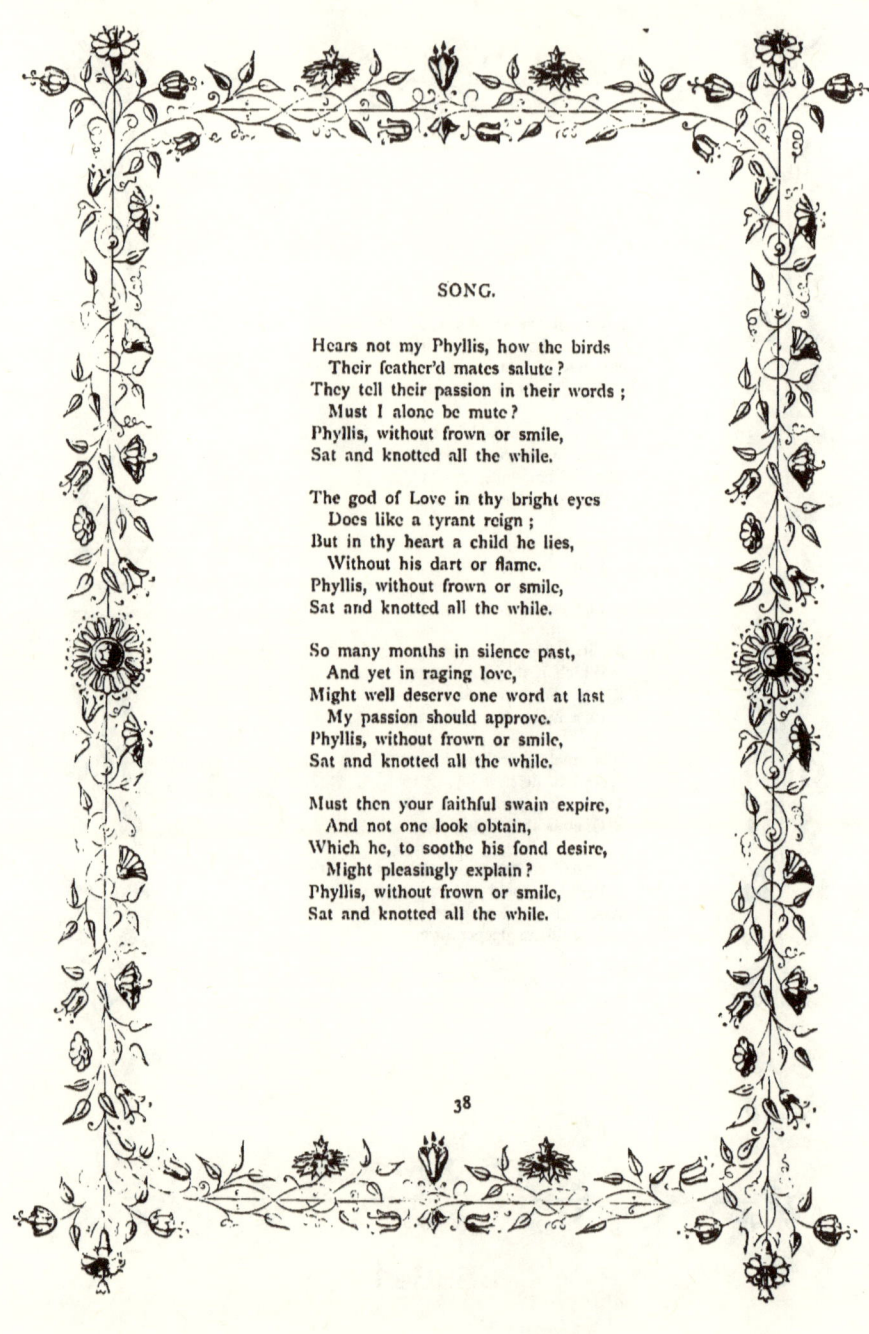

SONG.

Hears not my Phyllis, how the birds
   Their feather'd mates salute?
They tell their passion in their words;
   Must I alone be mute?
Phyllis, without frown or smile,
Sat and knotted all the while.

The god of Love in thy bright eyes
   Does like a tyrant reign;
But in thy heart a child he lies,
   Without his dart or flame.
Phyllis, without frown or smile,
Sat and knotted all the while.

So many months in silence past,
   And yet in raging love,
Might well deserve one word at last
   My passion should approve.
Phyllis, without frown or smile,
Sat and knotted all the while.

Must then your faithful swain expire,
   And not one look obtain,
Which he, to soothe his fond desire,
   Might pleasingly explain?
Phyllis, without frown or smile,
Sat and knotted all the while.

PHYLLIS.

SONG.

Phyllis is my only joy,
  Faithless as the winds or seas;
Sometimes coming, sometimes coy,
  Yet she never fails to please;
    If with a frown
    I am cast down,
    Phyllis smiling,
    And beguiling,
Makes me happier than before.

Tho', alas! too late I find
  Nothing can her fancy fix,
Yet the moment she is kind
  I forgive her all her tricks;
    Which, tho' I see,
    I can't get free;
    She deceiving,
    I believing;
What need lovers wish for more?

TO A VERY YOUNG LADY.

Ah, Chloris! could I now but sit
  As unconcerned as when
Your infant beauty could beget
  No happiness or pain!

When I the dawn used to admire,
  And praised the coming day,
I little thought the rising fire
  Would take my rest away.

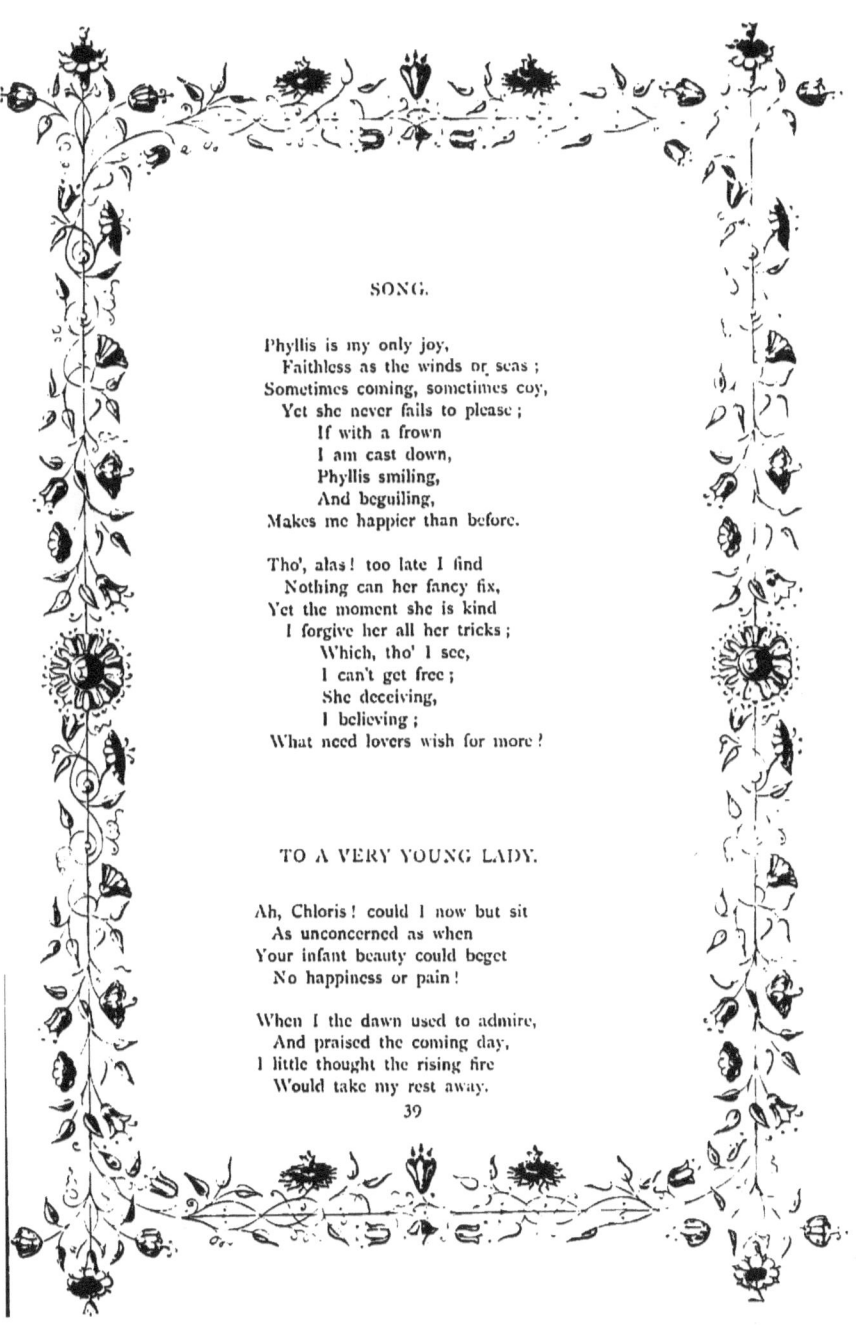

Your charms in harmless childhood lay
   Like metals in a mine;
Age from no face takes more away
   Than youth concealed in thine.
But as your charms insensibly
   To their perfection prest,
So love as unperceived did fly,
   And centered in my breast.

My passion with your beauty grew,
   While Cupid at my heart
Still as his mother favoured you
   Threw a new flaming dart:
Each gloried in their wanton part;
   To make a lover, he
Employed the utmost of his art—
   To make a beauty, she.

Though now I slowly bend to love,
   Uncertain of my fate,
If your fair self my chains approve
   I shall my freedom hate.
Lovers, like dying men, may well
   At first disordered be,
Since none alive can truly tell
   What fortune they must see.

From Sedley's play, "The Mulberry Garden." These verses have often been attributed to Duncan Forbes of Culloden.

CHARLES SACKVILLE, EARL OF DORSET.

1637—1705-6.

PRIOR (and who was a better judge of light verse?) thought the gay Earl's song one of the prettiest ever made; and it is certainly as airy and gallant as such a song could be. We seem to rock up and down as we read it. There is the sunny case, the playful elegance of a lighthearted courtier about it. The excitement of the coming battle (one of the most tremendous fought in that reign) had no doubt risen like Champagne into the man's witty, careless brain.

SONG

WRITTEN AT SEA IN THE FIRST DUTCH WAR, 1665, THE NIGHT BEFORE AN ENGAGEMENT.

To all you ladies now at land
  We men at sea indite;
But first would have you understand
  How hard it is to write;
The muses now, and Neptune too,
We must implore to write to you.
        With a fa la, la, la, la.

For though the muses should prove kind,
  And fill our empty brain;
Yet if rough Neptune rouse the wind
  To wave the azure main,
Our paper, pen, and ink, and we,
Roll up and down our ships at sea.
        With a fa la, &c.

Then if we write not by each post
  Think not we are unkind,
Nor yet conclude our ships are lost
  By Dutchmen or by wind:

Our tears we'll send a speedier way;
The tide shall bring them twice a day.
　　　With a fa la, &c.

The King with wonder and surprise
　Will swear the seas grow bold,
Because the tides will higher rise
　Than e'er they used of old:
But let him know it is our tears
Bring floods of grief to Whitehall-stairs.
　　　With a fa la, &c.

Should foggy Opdam chance to know
　Our sad and dismal story,
The Dutch would scorn so weak a foe,
　And quit their fort at Goree;
For what resistance can they find
From men who've left their hearts behind?
　　　With a fa la, &c.

Let wind and weather do its worst,
　Be you to us but kind;
Let Dutchmen vapour, Spaniards curse,
　No sorrow we shall find:
'Tis then no matter how things go,
Or who's our friend, or who's our foe.
　　　With a fa la, &c.

To pass our tedious hours away
　We throw a merry main;
Or else at serious ombre play;
　But why should we in vain
Each other's ruin thus pursue?
We were undone when we left you.
　　　With a fa la, &c.

But now our fears tempestuous grow,
　And cast our hopes away;
Whilst you, regardless of our woe,
　Sit careless at a play:
Perhaps permit some happier man
To kiss your hand, or flirt your fan.
　　　With a fa la, &c.

When any mournful tune you hear
  That dies in every note,
As if it sighed with each man's care
  For being so remote,
Think then how often love we've made
To you when all those tunes were played.
        With a fa la, &c.

In justice you can not refuse
  To think of our distress,
When we for hopes of honour lose
  Our certain happiness ;
All those designs are but to prove
Ourselves more worthy of your love.
        With a fa la, &c.

And now we've told you all our loves,
  And likewise all our fears,
In hopes this declaration moves
  Some pity for our tears ;
Let's hear of no inconstancy,
We have too much of that at sea.
        With a fa la, la, la, la.

DR. WALTER POPE.

1640—1714.

THERE is not much known of this pleasant old Epicurean Dean of Wadham, except that he quarrelled with irascible Anthony Wood, and kept up firm friendships with Bishop Wilkins, and Dr. Seth Ward, Bishop of Salisbury. Vincent Bourne turned the 'Old Man's Wish,' into charming Latin, with an Horatian feeling worthy of all praise.

THE OLD MAN'S WISH.

If I live to be old, for I find I go down,
Let this be my fate, in a country town
May I have a warm house, with a stone at the gate,
And a cleanly young girl to rub my bald pate.

CHORUS.

May I govern my passion with an absolute sway,
And grow wiser and better as my strength wears away;
Without gout or pang, by a gentle decay.

May my little house stand on the side of a hill,
With an easy descent to a mead and a mill,
That when I've a mind I may hear my boy read,
In the mill, if it rains; if it's dry, in the mead.
  May I govern, &c.

Near a shady grove, and a murmuring brook,
With the ocean at distance, whereon I may look,
With a spacious plain, without hedge or stile,
And an easy pad-nag to ride out a mile ;
    May I govern, &c.

With Horace and Petrarch, and two or three more
Of the best wits that reigned in the ages before ;
With roast mutton, rather than venison or teal,
And clean tho' coarse linen at every meal ;
    May I govern, &c.

With a pudding on Sundays, with stout humming liquor,
And remnants of Latin to welcome the Vicar ;
With Monte-Fiascone, or Burgundy wine,
To drink the king's health as oft as I dine ;
    May I govern, &c.

May my wine be vermilion, may my malt-drink be pale,
In neither extreme, or too mild or too stale :
In lieu of desserts, unwholesome and dear,
Let Lodi or Parmesan bring up the rear.
    May I govern, &c.

Nor Tory or Whig, observator or trimmer,
May I be, nor against the law's torrent a swimmer.
May I mind what I speak, what I write, and hear read,
And with matters of State ne'er trouble my head.*
    May I govern, &c.

Let the gods, who dispose of every king's crown,
Whomsoever they please set up and pull down ;
I'll pay the whole shilling imposed on my head,
Though I go without claret that night to my bed.
    May I govern, &c.

* " Leave princes' affairs undescanted on,
And tend to such doings as stands thee upon."
    Pusser.

I'll bleed without grumbling, though fresh taxes appear
As oft as new moons, or weeks in a year.
For why should I let a seditious word fall,
Since my lands in Utopia pay nothing at all?
    May I govern, &c.

Though I care not for riches, may I not be so poor
That the rich without shame cannot enter my door;
May they court my converse, may they take much delight
My old stories to hear in a winter's long night.
    May I govern, &c.

My small stock of wit may I not misapply
To flatter ill men, be they never so high;
Nor misspend the few moments I steal from the grave
In fawning and cringing like a dog or a slave.
    May I govern, &c,

May none whom I love to so great riches rise
As to slight their acquaintance and their old friends despise;
So low or so high may none of them be
As to move either pity or envy in me.
    May I govern, &c.

A friendship I wish for—(but, alas! 'tis in vain),
So firm, that no change of times, envy, or gain,
Or flattery, or woman, should have power to untie:
Jove's storehouse is empty, and can't it supply.
    May I govern, &c.

I hope I shall have no occasion to send
For priests or physicians till I'm so near mine end
That I have ate all my bread and drank my last glass;
Let them come then and set their seals to my pass.
    May I govern, &c.

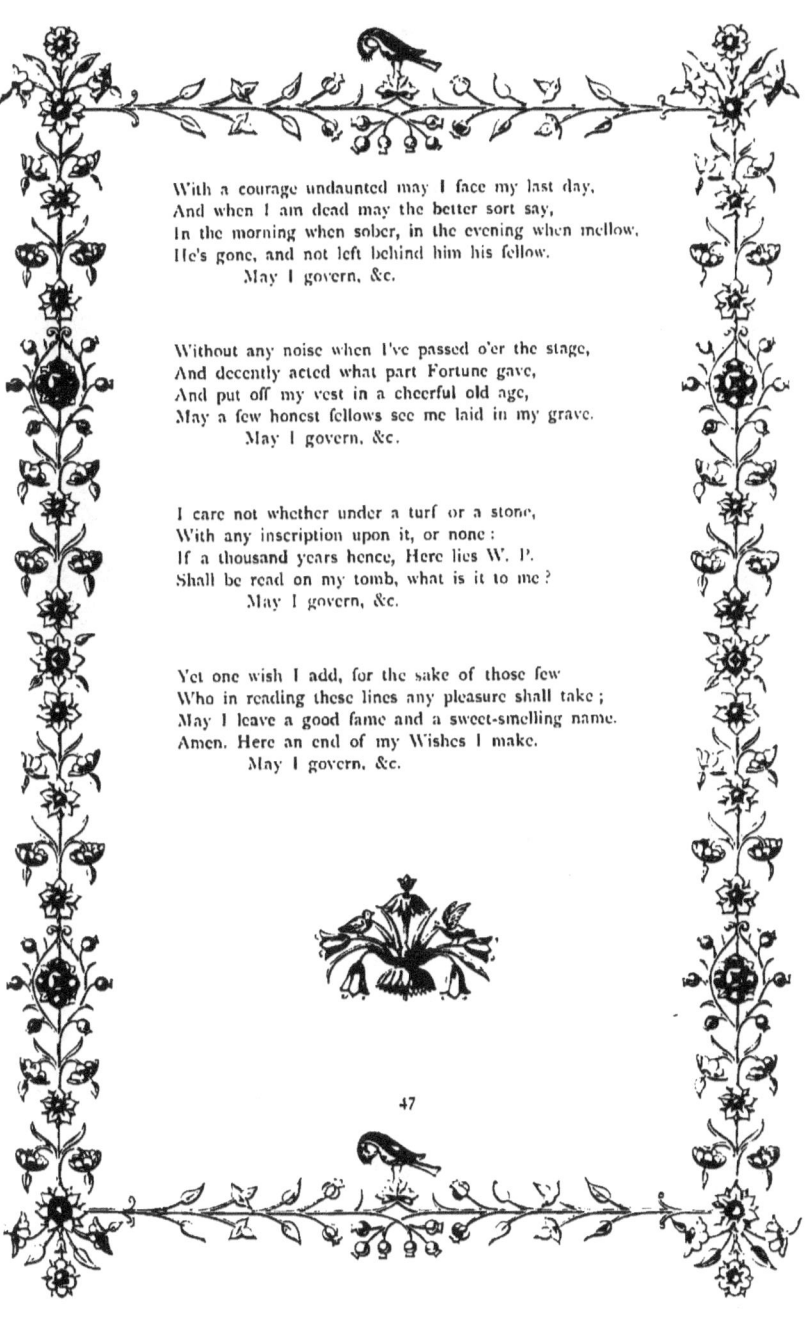

With a courage undaunted may I face my last day,
And when I am dead may the better sort say,
In the morning when sober, in the evening when mellow,
He's gone, and not left behind him his fellow.
    May I govern, &c.

Without any noise when I've passed o'er the stage,
And decently acted what part Fortune gave,
And put off my vest in a cheerful old age,
May a few honest fellows see me laid in my grave.
    May I govern, &c.

I care not whether under a turf or a stone,
With any inscription upon it, or none:
If a thousand years hence, Here lies W. P.
Shall be read on my tomb, what is it to me?
    May I govern, &c.

Yet one wish I add, for the sake of those few
Who in reading these lines any pleasure shall take;
May I leave a good fame and a sweet-smelling name.
Amen. Here an end of my Wishes I make.
    May I govern, &c.

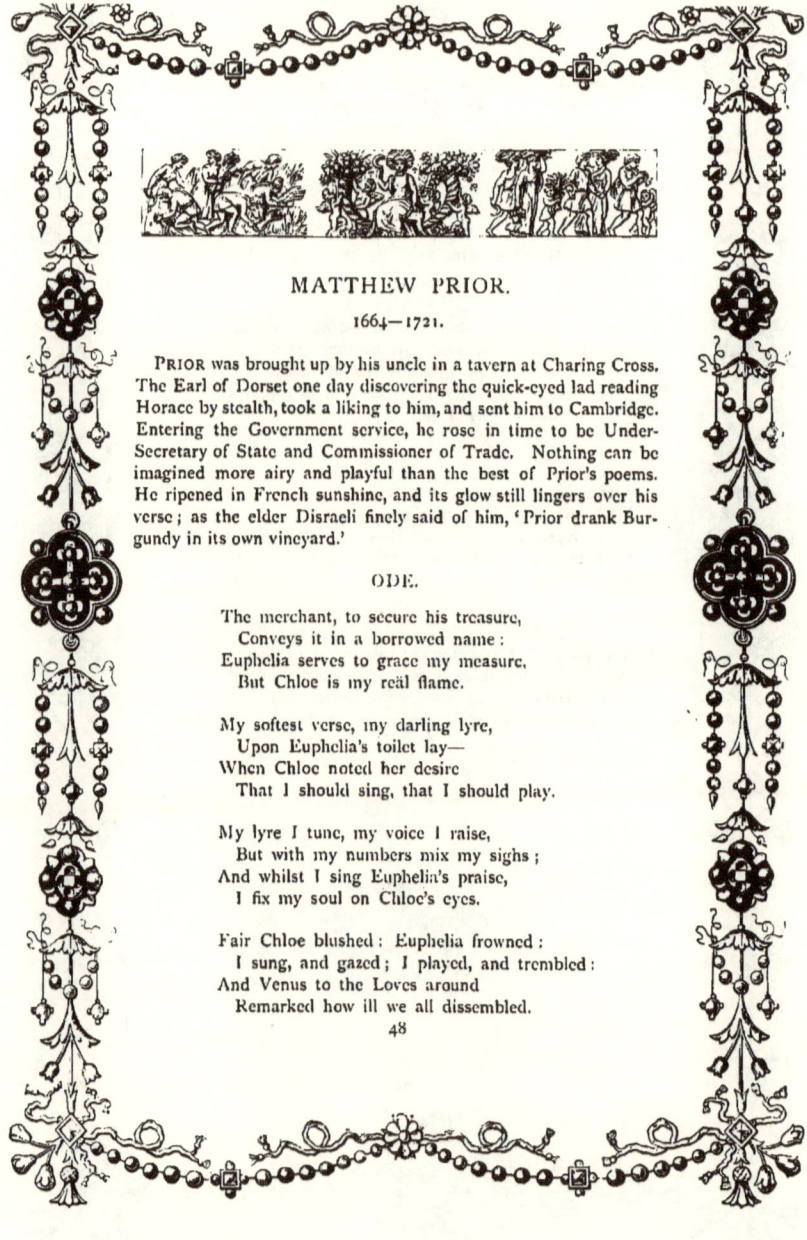

MATTHEW PRIOR.
1664—1721.

PRIOR was brought up by his uncle in a tavern at Charing Cross. The Earl of Dorset one day discovering the quick-eyed lad reading Horace by stealth, took a liking to him, and sent him to Cambridge. Entering the Government service, he rose in time to be Under-Secretary of State and Commissioner of Trade. Nothing can be imagined more airy and playful than the best of Prior's poems. He ripened in French sunshine, and its glow still lingers over his verse; as the elder Disraeli finely said of him, 'Prior drank Burgundy in its own vineyard.'

ODE.

The merchant, to secure his treasure,
   Conveys it in a borrowed name:
Euphelia serves to grace my measure,
   But Chloe is my reäl flame.

My softest verse, my darling lyre,
   Upon Euphelia's toilet lay—
When Chloe noted her desire
   That I should sing, that I should play.

My lyre I tune, my voice I raise,
   But with my numbers mix my sighs;
And whilst I sing Euphelia's praise,
   I fix my soul on Chloe's eyes.

Fair Chloe blushed: Euphelia frowned:
   I sung, and gazed; I played, and trembled:
And Venus to the Loves around
   Remarked how ill we all dissembled.

SUNSET BY THE SEA.

AN ANSWER TO CHLOE JEALOUS.

Dear Chloe, how blubbered is that pretty face![*]
    Thy cheek all on fire, and thy hair all uncurled:
Prithee, quit this caprice, and, as old Falstaff says,
    Let us e'en talk a little like folks of this world.

How canst thou presume thou hast leave to destroy
    The beauties which Venus but lent to thy keeping?
Those looks were designed to inspire love and joy:
    More ordinary eyes may serve people for weeping.

To be vexed at a trifle or two that I writ,
    Your judgment at once and my passion you wrong;
You take that for fact which will scarce be found wit:
    Odd's-life! must one swear to the truth of a song?

What I speak, my fair Chloe, and what I write, shows
    The difference there is betwixt nature and art:
I court others in verse; but I love thee in prose:
    And they have my whimsies, but thou hast my heart.

The god of us verse-men (you know, child) the sun,
    How after his journeys he sets up his rest:
If at morning o'er earth 'tis his fancy to run,
    At night he reclines on his Thetis's breast.

So when I am wearied with wandering all day,
    To thee, my delight, in the evening I come;
No matter what beauties I saw in my way,
    They were but my visits, but thou art my home.

Then finish, dear Chloe, this pastoral war,
    And let us like Horace and Lydia agree;
For thou art a girl as much brighter than her,
    As he was a poet sublimer than me.

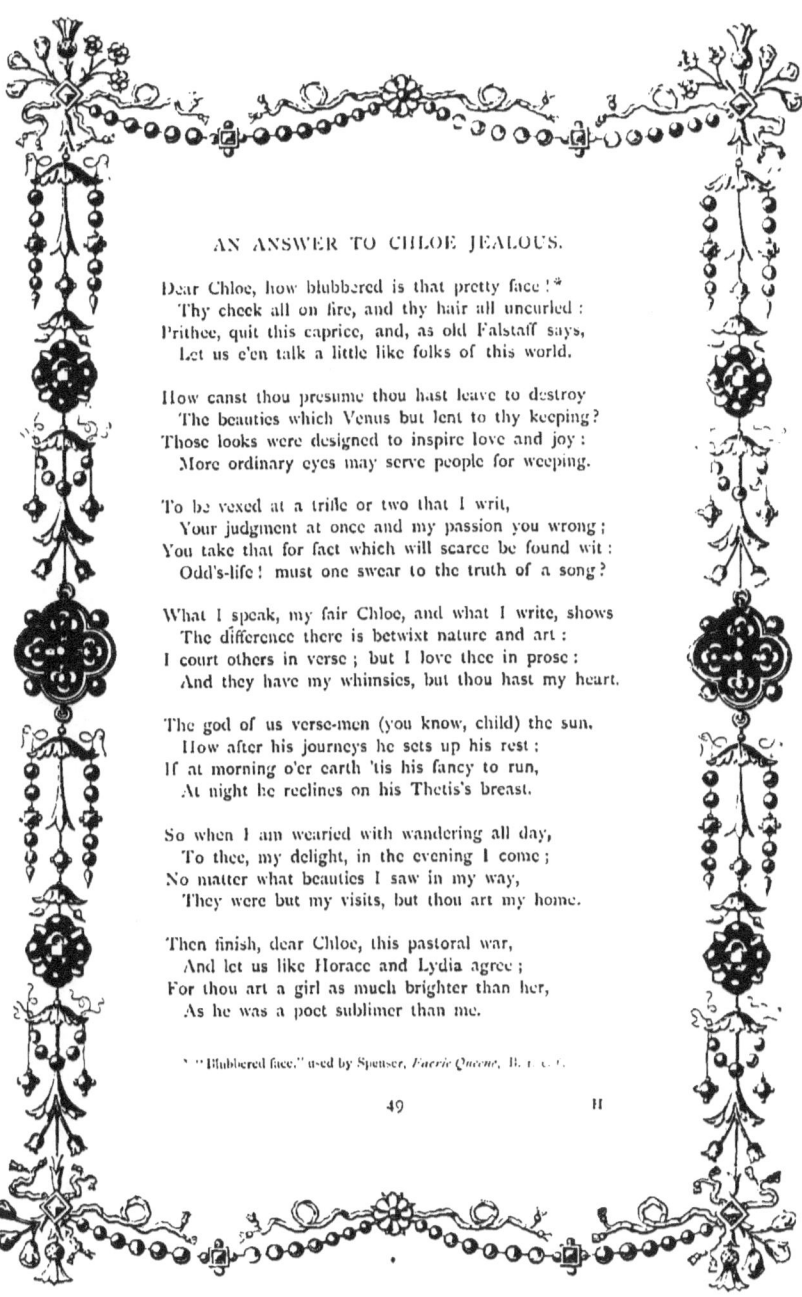

[*] "Blubbered face," used by Spenser, *Faerie Queene*, B. 1. c. 1.

TO CHLOE.

Whilst I am scorched with hot desire
  In vain cold friendship you return:
Your drops of pity on my fire,
  Alas! but make it fiercer burn.

Ah! would you have the flame suppresst
  That kills the heart it heats too fast,
Take half my passion to your breast:
  The rest in mine shall ever last.

CHLOE HUNTING.

Behind her neck her comely tresses tied,
Her ivory quiver graceful by her side,
A-hunting Chloe went: she lost her way,
And through the woods uncertain chanced to stray.
Apollo passing by beheld the maid,
And, "Sister dear, bright Cynthia, turn," he said:
"The hunted hind lies close in yonder brake."
Loud Cupid laughed to see the god's mistake;
And, laughing, cried, "Learn better, great divine,
To know thy kindred and to honour mine.
Rightly advised far hence thy sister seek,
Or on Meander's bank or Latmus' peak.
But in this nymph my friend, my sister know:
She draws my arrows, and she bends my bow;
Fair Thames she haunts, and every neighbouring grove
Sacred to soft recess and gentle love.
Go, with thy Cynthia hurl the pointed spear
At the rough boar, or chase the flying deer:
I and my Chloe take a nobler aim;
At human hearts we fling, nor ever miss the game.

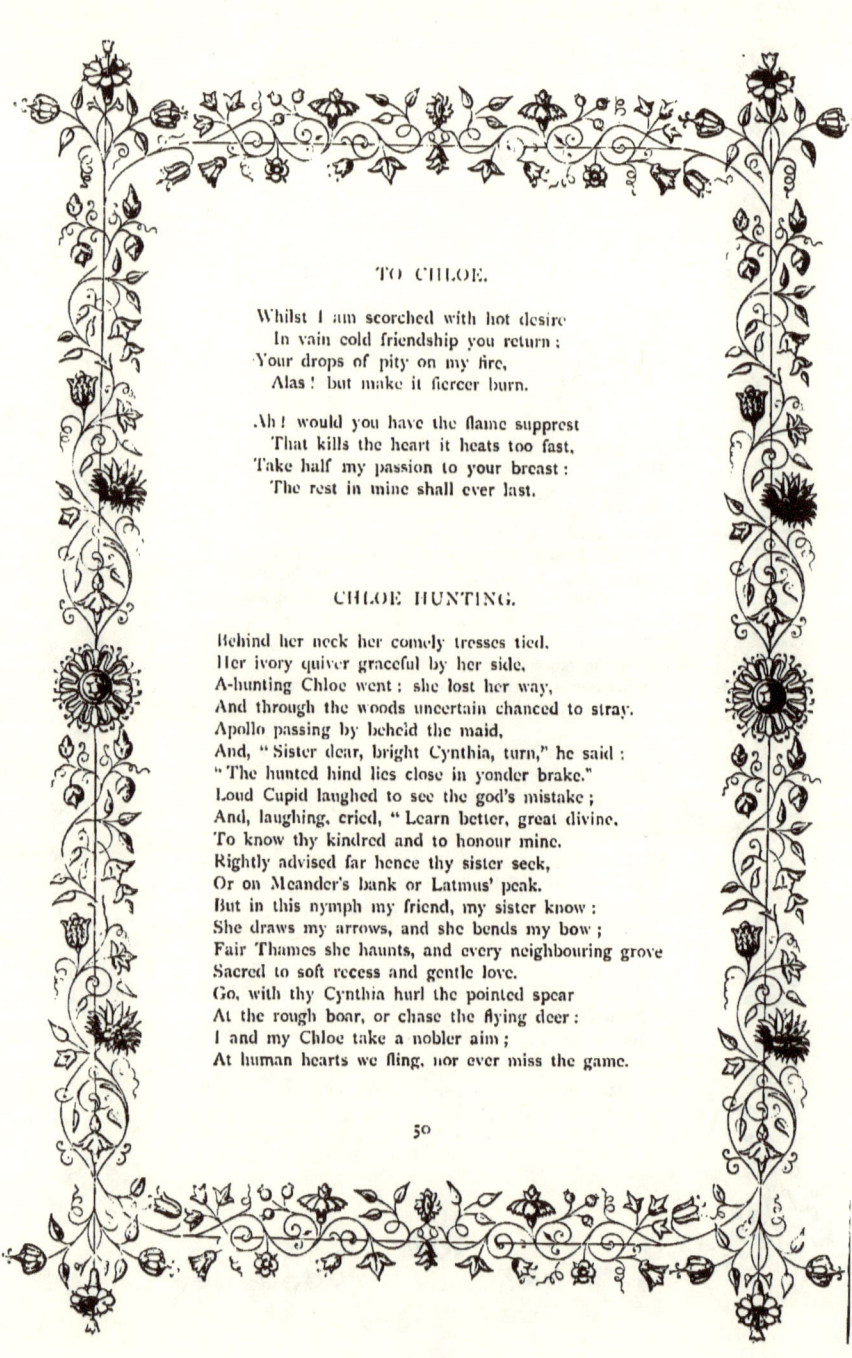

TO CHLOE WEEPING.

See, whilst thou weep'st, fair Chloe, see
The world in sympathy with thee.
The cheerful birds no longer sing,
Each droops his head and hangs his wing.
The clouds have bent their bosom lower,
And shed their sorrows in a shower:
The brooks beyond their limits flow,
And louder murmurs speak their woe:
The nymphs and swains adopt thy cares,
They heave thy sighs and weep thy tears.
Fantastic nymph! that grief should move
Thy heart obdurate against love.
Strange tears! whose power can soften all
But that dear breast on which they fall.

CUPID MISTAKEN.

As after noon, one summer's day,
  Venus stood bathing in a river,
Cupid a-shooting went that way,
  New strung his bow, new filled his quiver.

With skill he chose his sharpest dart,
  With all his might his bow he drew;
Swift to his beauteous parent's heart
  The too well guided arrow flew.

"I faint! I die!" the goddess cried:
"O cruel! couldst thou find none other
To wreak thy spleen on? parricide!
  Like Nero, thou hast slain thy mother."

Poor Cupid, sobbing, scarce could speak—
"Indeed, Mamma, I did not know ye:
Alas! how easy my mistake;
  I took you for your likeness, Chloe."

THE LADY'S LOOKING-GLASS.

IMITATION OF A GREEK IDYLLIUM.

Celia and I, the other day,
Walked o'er the sand-hills to the sea:
The setting sun adorned the coast,
His beams entire, his fierceness lost:
And on the surface of the deep
The winds lay only not asleep:
The nymph did, like the scene, appear
Serenely pleasant, calmly fair:
Soft fell her words as flew the air.
With secret joy I heard her say
That she would never miss one day
A walk so fine, a sight so gay.
But, oh the change! The winds grow high,
Impending tempests charge the sky,
The lightning flies, the thunder roars,
And big waves lash the frightened shores.
Struck with the horror of the sight
She turns her head and wings her flight;
And, trembling, vows she'll ne'er again
Approach the shore or view the main.

"Once more at least look back," said I,
"Thyself in that large glass descry:
When thou art in good humour drest,
When gentle reason rules thy breast,
The sun upon the calmest sea
Appears not half so bright as thee:
'Tis then that with delight I rove
Upon the boundless depth of love:
I bless my chain, I hand my oar,
Nor think on all I left on shore.

"But when vain doubt and groundless fear
Do that dear foolish bosom tear;
When the big lip and watery eye
Tell me the rising storm is nigh;

'Tis then thou art yon angry main
Deformed by winds and dashed by rain;
And the poor sailor that must try
Its fury labours less than I.
Shipwrecked, in vain to land I make,
While love and fate still drive me back:
Forced to doat on thee thy own way,
I chide thee first, and then obey:
Wretched when from thee, vexed when nigh,
I with thee, or without thee, die."

ON BEAUTY: A RIDDLE.

Resolve me, Chloe, what is this,
Or forfeit me one precious kiss?
'Tis the first offspring of the Graces,
Bears different forms in different places,
Acknowledged fine where'er beheld,
Yet fancied finer when concealed.
'Twas Flora's wealth, and Circe's charm,
Pandora's box of good and harm:
'Twas Mars' wish, Endymion's dream,
Apelles' draught, and Ovid's theme.
This guided Theseus through the maze,
And sent him home with life and praise:
But this undid the Phrygian boy,
And blew the flames that ruined Troy.
This shewed great kindness to old Greece,
And helped rich Jason to the fleece.
This through the East just vengeance hurled,
And lost poor Antony the world.
Injured, though Lucrece found her doom,
This banished tyranny from Rome;
For this Alcides learned to spin,
His club laid down and lion's skin:
For this Apollo deigned to keep
With servile care a mortal's sheep.
For this the father of the gods,
Content to leave his high abodes,

In borrowed figures loosely ran,
Europa's bull, and Leda's swan:
For this he reassumes the nod
While Semele commands the god;
Launches the bolt and shakes the poles,
Though Momus laughs and Juno scolds.

Here listening Chloe smiled and said,
"Your riddle is not hard to read:
I guess it."—Fair one, if you do,
Need I, alas! the theme pursue?
For this, thou seest, for this I leave
Whate'er this world thinks wise or grave,
Ambition, business, friendship, news,
My useful books and serious Muse.
For this I willingly decline
The mirth of feasts and joys of wine;
And choose to sit and talk with thee,
As thy great orders may decree.

IF WINE AND MUSIC HAVE THE POWER.

If wine and music have the power
  To ease the sickness of the soul,
Let Phœbus every string explore,
  And Bacchus fill the sprightly bowl.
Let them their friendly aid employ
  To make my Chloe's absence light,
And seek for pleasure, to destroy
  The sorrows of this live-long night.

But she to-morrow will return:
  Venus, be thou to-morrow great;
Thy myrtles strow, thy odours burn,
  And meet thy favourite nymph in state.
Kind goddess, to no other powers
  Let us to-morrow's blessings own;
Thy darling Loves shall guide the hours,
  And all the day be thine alone.

THE FEMALE PHAETON.

Thus Kitty,* beautiful and young,
   And, wild as colt untamed,
Bespoke the fair from whence she sprung,
   With little rage inflamed:

Inflamed with rage at sad restraint
   Which wise Mamma ordained;
And sorely vexed to play the saint
   Whilst wit and beauty reigned.

" Shall I thumb holy books, confined
   With Abigails, forsaken?
Kitty's for other things designed,
   Or I am much mistaken.

" Must lady Jenny frisk about
   And visit with her cousins?
At balls must *she* make all the rout,
   And bring home hearts by dozens?

" What has she better, pray, than I,
   What hidden charms to boast,
That all mankind for her should die,
   Whilst I am scarce a toast?

" Dearest Mamma! for once let me
   Unchained my fortune try;
I'll have my Earl as well as she,
   Or know the reason why.

" I'll soon with Jenny's pride quit score,
   Make all her lovers fall:
They'll grieve I was not loosed before,
   She, I was loosed at all."

* Afterwards Duchess of Queensbury, and a friend of that good-natured poet Gay

THE GARLAND.

The pride of every grove I chose,
　The violet sweet and lily fair,
The dappled pink and blushing rose,
　To deck my charming Chloe's hair.

At morn the nymph vouchsafed to place
　Upon her brow the various wreath;
The flowers less blooming than her face,
　The scent less fragrant than her breath.

The flowers she wore along the day,
　And every nymph and shepherd said
That in her hair they looked more gay
　Than glowing in their native bed.

Undressed at evening, when she found
　Their odours lost, their colours past,
She changed her look, and on the ground
　Her garland and her eyes she cast.

That eye dropped sense distinct and clear
　As any Muse's tongue could speak,
When from its lid a pearly tear
　Ran trickling down her beauteous cheek.

Dissembling what I knew too well,
　"My love, my life," said I, "explain
This change of humour; prithee, tell—
　That falling tear—what does it mean?"

She sighed, she smiled; and to the flowers
　Pointing, the lovely moralist said,
"See, friend, in some few fleeting hours,
　See yonder, what a change is made.

"Ah me! the blooming pride of May
And that of Beauty are but one;
At morn both flourish bright and gay,
Both fade at evening, pale, and gone.

"At dawn poor Stella danced and sung;
The amorous youth around her bowed;
At night her fatal knell was rung;
I saw and kissed her in her shroud.

"Such as she is who died to-day,
Such I, alas! may be to-morrow:
Go, Damon, bid thy Muse display
The justice of thy Chloe's sorrow."

JOHN GAY.

1688 – 1732.

GAY was a fat, careless, loveable man, before whose drollery even Swift relented; nor did Pope discharge one poisoned arrow at him.

TO A LADY, ON HER PASSION FOR OLD CHINA.

What ecstasies her bosom fire!
How her eyes languish with desire!
How blest, how happy, should I be
Were that fond glance bestowed on me!
New doubts and fears within me war:
What rival's near?—a china jar!

China's the passion of her soul:
A cup, a plate, a dish, a bowl,
Can kindle wishes in her breast,
Inflame with joy, or break her rest.

Some gems collect, some medals prize,
And view the rust with lovers' eyes;
Some court the stars at midnight hours;
Some doat on Nature's charms in flowers:
But every beauty I can trace
In Laura's mind, in Laura's face;
My stars are in this brightest sphere.
My lily and my rose is here.

Philosophers, more grave than wise,
Hunt science down in butterflies;
Or, fondly poring on a spider,
Stretch human contemplation wider.
Fossils give joy to Galen's soul;
He digs for knowledge like a mole;
In shells so learn'd, that all agree
No fish that swims knows more than he!
In such pursuits if wisdom lies,
Who, Laura, shall thy taste despise?

Where I some antique jar behold,
Or white, or blue, or speck'd with gold,
Vessels so pure and so refined
Appear the types of womankind:
Are they not valued for their beauty,
Too fair, too fine for household duty?
With flowers, and gold, and azure dyed,
Of every house the grace and pride?
How white, how polish'd is their skin,
And valued most when only seen!
She, who before was highest prized,
Is for a crack or flaw despised.
I grant they're frail; yet they're so rare,
The treasure cannot cost too dear!
But man is made of coarser stuff,
And serves convenience well enough.
He's a strong earthen vessel, made
For drudging, labour, toil, and trade;
And, when wives lose their other self,
With ease they bear the loss of pelf.

Husbands, more covetous than sage,
Condemn this china-buying rage;
They count that woman's prudence little,
Who sets her heart on things so brittle.
But are those wise men's inclinations
Fix'd on more strong, more sure foundations?
If all that's frail we must despise,
No human view or scheme is wise.
Are not Ambition's hopes as weak?
They swell like bubbles, shine, and break.

A courtier's promise is so slight,
'Tis made at noon, and broke at night.
The man who loves a country life
Breaks all the comforts of his wife;
And if he quit his farm and plough,
His wife in town may break her vow.
Love, Laura, love, while youth is warm,
For each new winter breaks a charm;
And woman's not like china sold,
But cheaper grows in growing old;
Then quickly choose the prudent part,
Or else you break a faithful heart.

GEORGE GRANVILLE, LORD LANSDOWNE.

1667   1734-5.

A FRIEND and patron of Pope, commended by Waller, and a Treasurer in Queen's Anne's household, Lord Lansdowne wrote like a gentleman; praising and petting the poets, he was praised by them. Although shut up in the Tower as an adherent of the Pretender, Lord Lansdowne escaped the block, and returned to the world to appear again in Parliament and to edit his poems.

LOVE IS BY FANCY LED ABOUT.

Love is by fancy led about
From hope to fear, from joy to doubt;
   Whom we now an angel call,
Divinely graced in every feature,
Straight's a deformed, a perjured creature;
   Love and hate are fancy all.

'Tis but as fancy shall present
Objects of grief, or of content,
   That the lover's blest, or dies;
Visions of mighty pain or pleasure,
Imagined want, imagined treasure.
   All in powerful fancy lies.

HENRY CAREY.

1700—1743.

THIS is one of the prettiest and most natural of English love songs. Carey had been watching an apprentice and his betrothed in Vauxhall, enjoying their cakes and ale—he came home and wrote this song. After a wild career, this mad genius destroyed himself at his house in Cold Bath Fields.

SALLY IN OUR ALLEY.

Of all the girls that are so smart,
   There's none like pretty Sally;
She is the darling of my heart,
   And she lives in our alley.
There is no lady in the land
   Is half so sweet as Sally;
She is the darling of my heart,
   And she lives in our alley.

Her father he makes cabbage-nets
   And through the streets does cry 'em;
Her mother she sells laces long
   To such as please to buy 'em:
But sure such folks could ne'er beget
   So sweet a girl as Sally!
She is the darling of my heart,
   And she lives in our alley.

When she is by, I leave my work,
   I love her so sincerely;
My master comes like any Turk,
   And bangs me most severely,—
But let him bang his bellyful,
   I'll bear it all for Sally;
She is the darling of my heart,
   And she lives in our alley.

Of all the days that's in the week
  I dearly love but one day—
And that's the day that comes betwixt
  A Saturday and Monday:
For then I'm drest all in my best
  To walk abroad with Sally;
She is the darling of my heart,
  And she lives in our alley.

My master carries me to church,
  And often am I blamed
Because I leave him in the lurch
  As soon as text is named;
I leave the church in sermon-time
  And slink away to Sally;
She is the darling of my heart,
  And she lives in our alley.

When Christmas comes about again,
  O then I shall have money;
I'll hoard it up, and box it all,
  I'll give it to my honey:
I would it were ten thousand pound,
  I'd give it all to Sally;
She is the darling of my heart,
  And she lives in our alley.

My master and the neighbours all
  Make game of me and Sally,
And, but for her, I'd better be
  A slave, and row a galley;
But when my seven long years are out
  O then I'll marry Sally,—
O then we'll wed, and then we'll bed,
  But not in our alley!

ALEXANDER POPE.

1688—1744.

Pope was too fond of money to waste much time on occasional verse. The epistle to Mrs. Blount is, however, a pretty Dutch picture of country life in Queen Anne's time.

EPISTLE TO MRS. BLOUNT,
ON HER LEAVING THE TOWN AFTER THE CORONATION.

As some fond virgin, whom her mother's care
Drags from the town to wholesome country air,
Just when she learns to roll a melting eye,
And hear a spark, yet think no danger nigh;
From the dear man unwilling she must sever,
Yet takes one kiss before she parts for ever:
Thus from the world fair Zephalinda flew,
Saw others happy, and with sighs withdrew;
Not that their pleasures caused her discontent,
She sighed not that they stayed, but that she went.

She went, to plain-work, and to purling brooks,
Old-fashioned halls, dull aunts, and croaking rooks:
She went from opera, park, assembly, play,
To morning walks, and prayers three hours a day;
To part her time 'twixt reading and bohea,
To muse, and spill her solitary tea,
Or o'er cold coffee trifle with the spoon,
Count the slow clock, and dine exact at noon:
Divert her eyes with pictures in the fire,
Hum half a tune, tell stories to the squire;
Up to her godly garret after seven,
There starve and pray, for that's the way to heaven.

Some squire, perhaps, you take delight to rack,
Whose game is whist, whose treat a toast in sack !
Who visits with a gun, presents you birds,
Then gives a smacking buss, and cries,—No words !
Or with his hound comes hallooing from the stable ;
Makes love with nods, and knees beneath a table ;
Whose laughs are hearty, though his jests are coarse,
And loves you best of all things—but his horse.*

In some fair evening, on your elbow laid,
You dream of triumphs in the rural shade ;
In pensive thought recall the fancied scene,
See coronations rise on every green ;
Before you pass the imaginary sights
Of lords, and earls, and dukes, and gartered knights,
While the spread fan o'ershades your closing eyes ;
Then give one flirt and all the vision flies.
Thus vanish sceptres, coronets, and balls,
And leave you in lone woods, or empty walls !

So when your slave, at some dear idle time
(Not plagued with head-aches, or the want of rhyme)
Stands in the streets, abstracted from the crew,
And while he seems to study, thinks of you ;
Just when his fancy paints your sprightly eyes,
Or sees the blush of soft Parthenia rise,
GAY pats my shoulder, and you vanish quite,
Streets, chairs, and coxcombs rush upon my sight ;
Vexed to be still in town, I knit my brow,
Look sour, and hum a tune, as you may now.

* " He will hold thee, when his passion shall have spent its novel force,
Something better than his dog, a little dearer than his horse."
TENNYSON: *Locksley Hall*

ODE ON SOLITUDE.

Happy the man, whose wish and care
   A few paternal acres bound,
Content to breathe his native air
      In his own ground.

Whose herds with milk, whose fields with bread
   Whose flocks supply him with attire,
Whose trees in summer yield him shade,
      In winter fire.

Blest, who can unconcern'dly find
   Hours, days, and years, slide soft away
In health of body, peace of mind,
      Quiet by day,

Sound sleep by night; study and ease
   Together mixed; sweet recreation,
And innocence, which most does please
      With meditation.

Thus let me live, unseen, unknown;
   Thus unlamented let me die;
Steal from the world, and not a stone
      Tell where I lie.

IMITATION OF SWIFT.

THE HAPPY LIFE OF A COUNTRY PARSON.

Parson, these things in thy possessing
Are better than the bishop's blessing.
A wife that makes conserves; a steed
That carries double when there's need;
October store, and best Virginia,
Tithe-pig, and mortuary guinea;

Gazettes sent gratis down, and franked,
For which thy patron's weekly thanked;
A large Concordance, bound long since;
Sermons to Charles the First, when Prince;
A Chronicle of ancient standing;
A Chrysostom to smooth thy band in;
The Polyglott—three parts,—my text,
Howbeit,—likewise—now to my next:
Lo here the Septuagint,—and Paul,
To sum the whole,—the close of all.
He that has these may pass his life,
Drink with the 'squire, and kiss his wife;
On Sundays preach, and eat his fill;
And fast on Fridays—if he will;
Toast Church and Queen, explain the news,
Talk with church-wardens about pews,
Pray heartily for some new gift,
And shake his head at Doctor Swift.

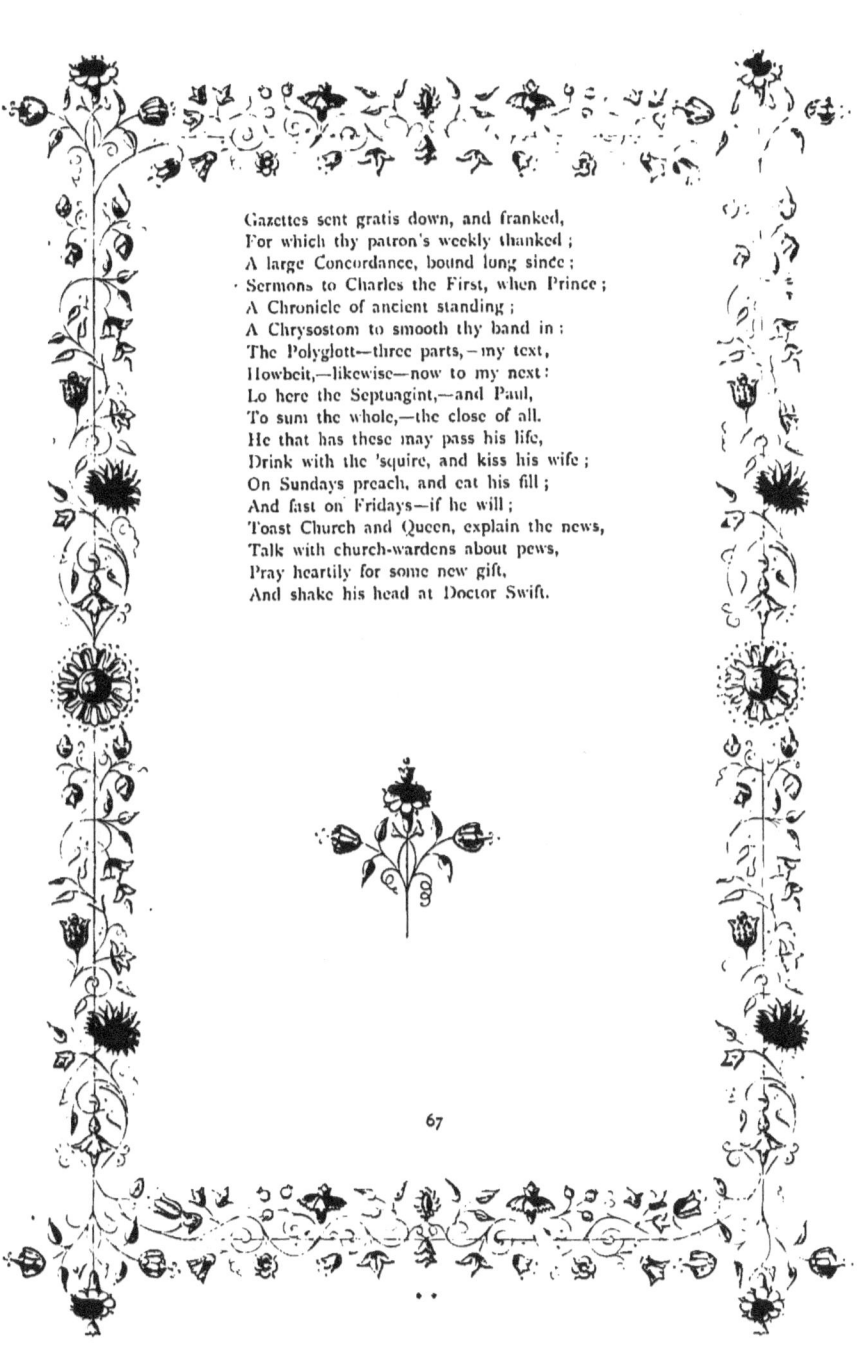

AMBROSE PHILIPS
1675—1749.

THIS butt of the wits could, as we see below, be occasionally simple, pretty, and unaffected.

To MISS CHARLOTTE PULTENEY, in her MOTHER'S ARMS, 1 *May*, 1724.

Timely blossom, infant fair,
Fondling of a happy pair,
Every morn and every night
Their solicitous delight,
Sleeping, waking, still at ease,
Pleasing, without skill to please;
Little gossip, lithe and hale,
Tattling many a broken tale,
Singing many a tuneless song,
Lavish of a heedless tongue;
Simple maiden, void of art,
Babbling out the very heart,
Yet abandoned to thy will,
Yet imagining no ill,
Yet too innocent to blush;
Like the linnet in the bush,
To the mother-linnet's note
Moduling her slender throat;
Chirping forth thy petty joys,
Wanton in the change of toys,
Like the linnet green, in May
Flitting to each bloomy spray;
Wearied then and glad of rest,
Like the linnet in the nest :—
This thy present happy lot,
This, in time, will be forgot:
Other pleasures, other cares,
Ever-busy Time prepares;
And thou shalt in thy daughter see,
This picture, once, resembled thee.

THE LITTLE GOSSIP.

COLLEY CIBBER.

1671—1757.

THE old beau and good actor was an admirable prose writer, and an opponent who did not quail even before the lance of Pope. The Medusa's head of satire had no terrors for this healthy man of the world. There is both nature and pathos in the poem we have selected.

THE BLIND BOY.

O say! what is that thing called Light,
    Which I must ne'er enjoy?
What are the blessings of the sight?
    O tell your poor blind boy!

You talk of wondrous things you see,
    You say the sun shines bright;
I feel him warm, but how can he
    Or make it day or night?

My day or night myself I make
    Whene'er I sleep or play;
And could I ever keep awake
    With me 'twere always day.

With heavy sighs I often hear
    You mourn my hapless woe;
But sure with patience I can bear
    A loss I ne'er can know.

Then let not what I cannot have
    My cheer of mind destroy:
Whilst thus I sing, I am a king,
    Although a poor blind boy.

WILLIAM OLDYS.

1696—1761.

OLDYS had the care of Lord Oxford's library, and was employed to select and edit the "*Harleian Miscellany*." His verse is so gaily thoughtful that we wish he had written more.

SONG,

MADE EXTEMPORE BY A GENTLEMAN, OCCASIONED BY A FLY
DRINKING OUT OF HIS CUP OF ALE.

Busy, curious, thristy fly,
Drink with me, and drink as I;
Freely welcome to my cup,
Couldst thou sip and sip it up.
Make the most of life you may;
Life is short, and wears away.

Both alike are mine and thine,
Hastening quick to their decline:
Thine's a summer, mine no more,
Though repeated to threescore;
Threescore summers, when they're gone,
Will appear as short as one.

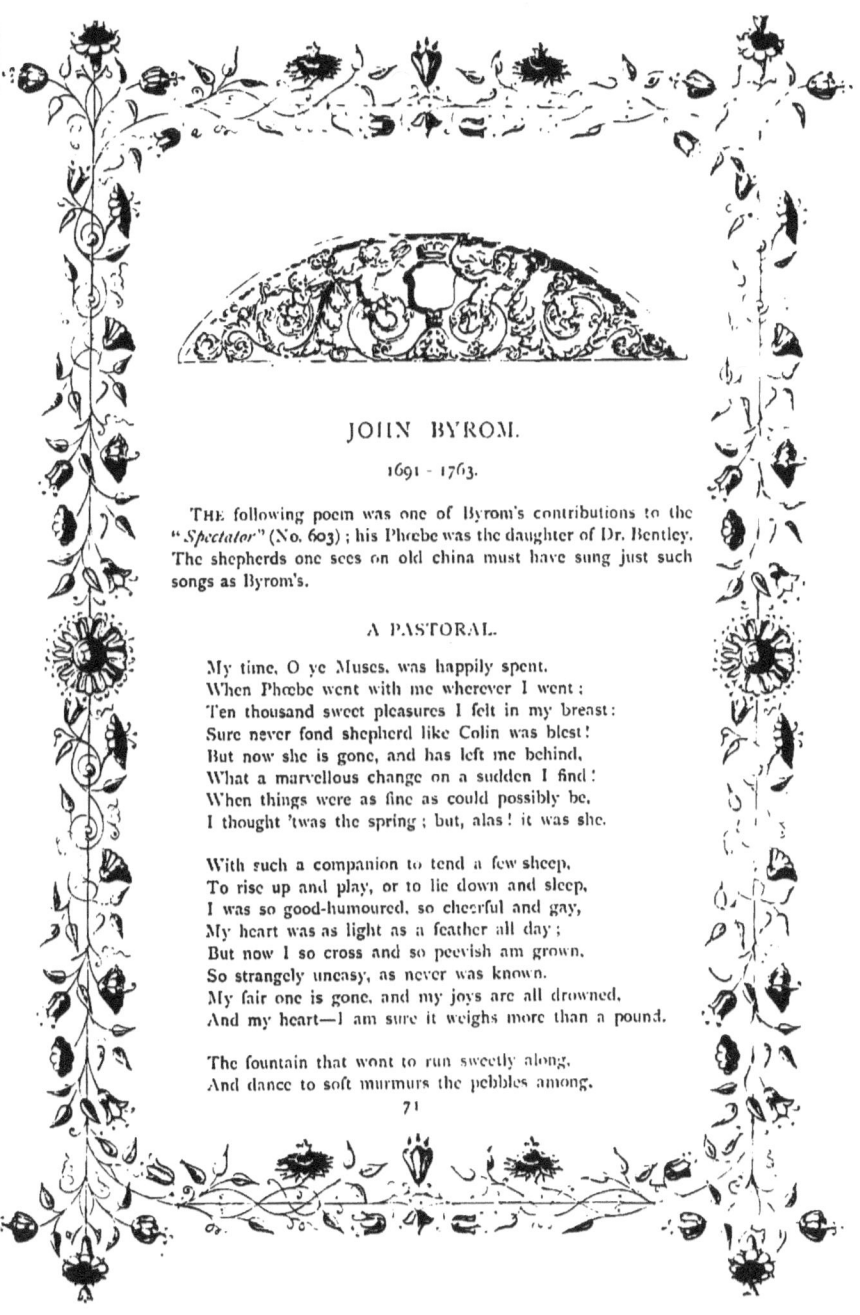

JOHN BYROM.

1691 - 1763.

THE following poem was one of Byrom's contributions to the "*Spectator*" (No. 603); his Phœbe was the daughter of Dr. Bentley. The shepherds one sees on old china must have sung just such songs as Byrom's.

A PASTORAL.

My time, O ye Muses, was happily spent,
When Phœbe went with me wherever I went;
Ten thousand sweet pleasures I felt in my breast:
Sure never fond shepherd like Colin was blest!
But now she is gone, and has left me behind,
What a marvellous change on a sudden I find!
When things were as fine as could possibly be,
I thought 'twas the spring; but, alas! it was she.

With such a companion to tend a few sheep,
To rise up and play, or to lie down and sleep,
I was so good-humoured, so cheerful and gay,
My heart was as light as a feather all day;
But now I so cross and so peevish am grown,
So strangely uneasy, as never was known.
My fair one is gone, and my joys are all drowned,
And my heart—I am sure it weighs more than a pound.

The fountain that wont to run sweetly along,
And dance to soft murmurs the pebbles among.

Thou know'st, little Cupid, if Phœbe was there,
'Twas pleasure to look at, 'twas music to hear:
But now she is absent, I walk by its side,
And still, as it murmurs, do nothing but chide;
Must you be so cheerful, while I go in pain?
Peace there with your bubbling, and hear me complain.

My lambkins around me would oftentimes play,
And Phœbe and I were as joyful as they;
How pleasant their sporting, how happy their time,
When Spring, Love, and Beauty, were all in their prime;
But now, in their frolics, when by me they pass,
I fling at their fleeces a handful of grass;
Be still, then, I cry, for it makes me quite mad,
To see you so merry while I am so sad.

My dog I was ever well pleasèd to see
Come wagging his tail to my fair one and me;
And Phœbe was pleased too, and to my dog said,
"Come hither, poor fellow!" and patted his head.
But now, when he's fawning, I, with a sour look,
Cry "Sirrah," and give him a blow with my crook:
And I'll give him another; for why should not Tray
Be as dull as his master when Phœbe's away?

When walking with Phœbe what sights have I seen!
How fair was the flower, how fresh was the green!
What a lovely appearance the trees and the shade,
The corn-fields and hedges, and everything made!
But now she has left me, though all are still there,
They none of them now so delightful appear:
'Twas naught but the magic, I find, of her eyes,
Made so many beautiful prospects arise.

Sweet music went with us both all the wood through,
The lark, linnet, throstle, and nightingale too;
Winds over us whispered, flocks by us did bleat,
And chirp went the grasshopper under our feet.
But now she is absent, though still they sing on,
The woods are but lonely, the melody's gone:
Her voice in the concert, as now I have found,
Gave everything else its agreeable sound.

Rose, what is become of thy delicate hue?
And where is the violet's beautiful blue?
Does ought of its sweetness the blossom beguile?
That meadow, those daisies, why do they not smile?
Ah! rivals, I see what it was that you drest,
And made yourself fine for—a place in her breast:
You put on your colours to pleasure her eye,
To be plucked by her hand, on her bosom to die.

How slowly Time creeps till my Phœbe return!
While amidst the soft zephyr's cool breezes I burn;
Methinks, if I knew whereabouts he would tread,
I could breathe on his wings, and 'twould melt down the lead.
Fly swifter, ye minutes, bring hither my dear,
And rest so much longer for't when she is here.
Ah, Colin! old Time is full of delay,
Nor will budge one foot faster for all thou canst say.

Will no pitying power that hears me complain,
Or cure my disquiet, or soften my pain?
To be cured, thou must, Colin, thy passion remove;
But what swain is so silly to live without love!
No, deity, bid the dear nymph to return,
For ne'er was poor shepherd so sadly forlorn.
Ah! what shall I do? I shall die with despair;
Take heed, all ye swains, how ye part with your fair.

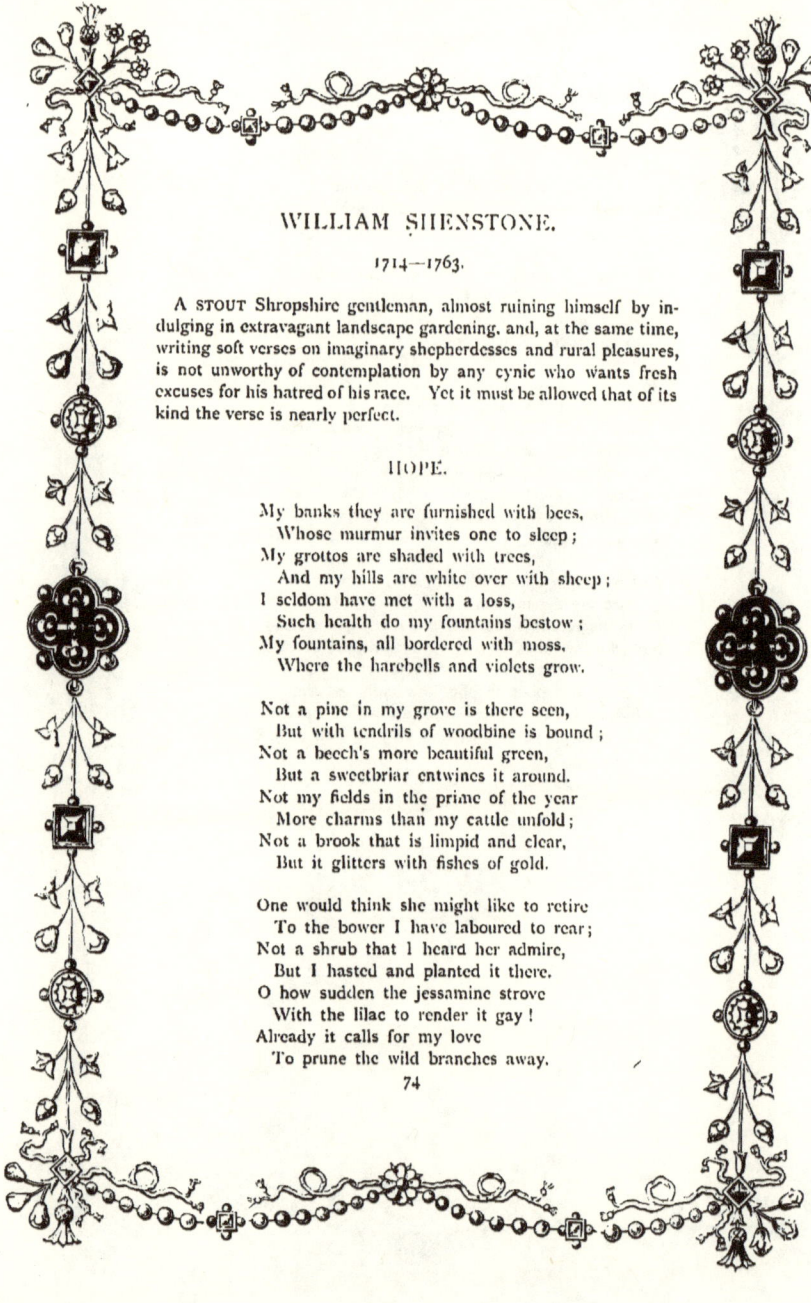

WILLIAM SHENSTONE.

1714—1763.

A STOUT Shropshire gentleman, almost ruining himself by indulging in extravagant landscape gardening, and, at the same time, writing soft verses on imaginary shepherdesses and rural pleasures, is not unworthy of contemplation by any cynic who wants fresh excuses for his hatred of his race. Yet it must be allowed that of its kind the verse is nearly perfect.

HOPE.

My banks they are furnished with bees,
    Whose murmur invites one to sleep;
My grottos are shaded with trees,
    And my hills are white over with sheep;
I seldom have met with a loss,
    Such health do my fountains bestow;
My fountains, all bordered with moss,
    Where the harebells and violets grow.

Not a pine in my grove is there seen,
    But with tendrils of woodbine is bound;
Not a beech's more beautiful green,
    But a sweetbriar entwines it around.
Not my fields in the prime of the year
    More charms than my cattle unfold;
Not a brook that is limpid and clear,
    But it glitters with fishes of gold.

One would think she might like to retire
    To the bower I have laboured to rear;
Not a shrub that I heard her admire,
    But I hasted and planted it there.
O how sudden the jessamine strove
    With the lilac to render it gay!
Already it calls for my love
    To prune the wild branches away.

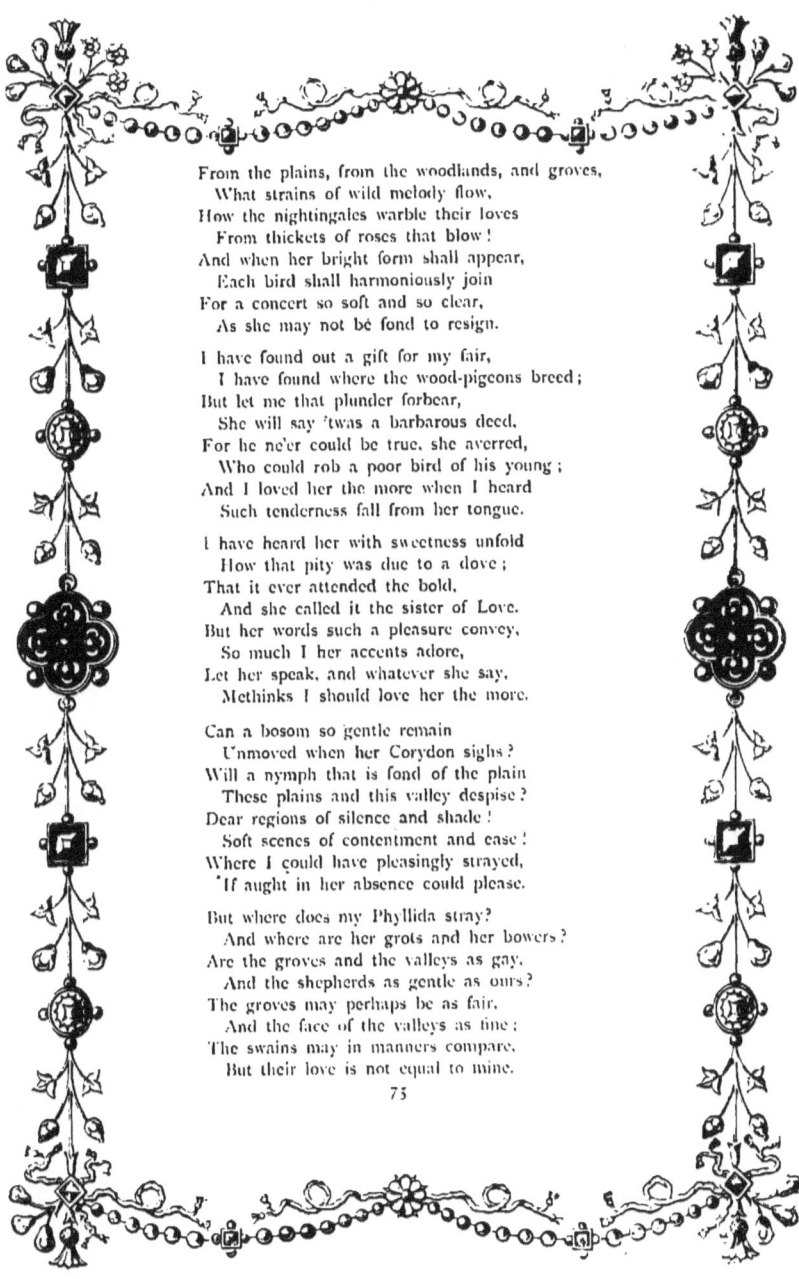

From the plains, from the woodlands, and groves,
  What strains of wild melody flow,
How the nightingales warble their loves
  From thickets of roses that blow!
And when her bright form shall appear,
  Each bird shall harmoniously join
For a concert so soft and so clear,
  As she may not be fond to resign.

I have found out a gift for my fair,
  I have found where the wood-pigeons breed;
But let me that plunder forbear,
  She will say 'twas a barbarous deed,
For he ne'er could be true, she averred,
  Who could rob a poor bird of his young;
And I loved her the more when I heard
  Such tenderness fall from her tongue.

I have heard her with sweetness unfold
  How that pity was due to a dove;
That it ever attended the bold,
  And she called it the sister of Love.
But her words such a pleasure convey,
  So much I her accents adore,
Let her speak, and whatever she say,
  Methinks I should love her the more.

Can a bosom so gentle remain
  Unmoved when her Corydon sighs?
Will a nymph that is fond of the plain
  These plains and this valley despise?
Dear regions of silence and shade!
  Soft scenes of contentment and ease!
Where I could have pleasingly strayed,
  If aught in her absence could please.

But where does my Phyllida stray?
  And where are her grots and her bowers?
Are the groves and the valleys as gay,
  And the shepherds as gentle as ours?
The groves may perhaps be as fair,
  And the face of the valleys as fine;
The swains may in manners compare,
  But their love is not equal to mine.

ROBERT DODSLEY.

1703—1764.

THIS amiable man, originally a stocking weaver, became next a footman, and lastly a poet and a publisher. We are indebted to Dodsley's Collection of old plays for the revival of the taste for Elizabethan literature, as we are to Dr. Percy for those immortal old ballads that let in a current of fresh air and sunshine upon our literature from which the Lake poets derived so much of their vitality.

THE PARTING KISS.

One kind wish before we part,
    Drop a tear, and bid adieu :
Though we sever, my fond heart,
    Till we meet, shall pant for you.

Yet, yet weep not so, my love,
    Let me kiss that falling tear ;
Though my body must remove,
    All my soul will still be here.

All my soul, and all my heart,
    And every wish shall pant for you ;
One kind kiss, then, ere we part,*
    Drop a tear, and bid adieu.

* "Ae ond kiss and then we sever."
                              Burns.

JOHN GILBERT COOPER.

1723—1769.

THE supposed writer of this poem was a Nottinghamshire magistrate, and a promoter of the "Society for the Encouragement of Arts and Manufactures." Dr. Percy published the verses believing them to be *ancient British*, save the mark! The worthy, but in this case, misguided, Doctor justly praises the poem as "a beautiful address to conjugal love—a subject too much neglected by the libertine muses."

AWAY! LET NOUGHT TO LOVE DISPLEASING.

Away! let nought to love displeasing,
My Winifreda, move your care;
Let nought delay the heavenly blessing,
Nor squeamish pride, nor gloomy fear.

What though no grants of royal donors,
With pompous titles grace our blood?
We'll shine in more substantial honours,
And, to be noble, we'll be good.

Our name while virtue thus we tender,
Will sweetly sound where'er 'tis spoke;
And all the great ones, they shall wonder
How they respect such little folk.

What though, from Fortune's lavish bounty,
No mighty treasures we possess?
We'll find within our pittance plenty,
And be content without excess.

Still shall each kind returning season
Sufficient for our wishes give;
For we will live a life of reason,
And that's the only life to live.

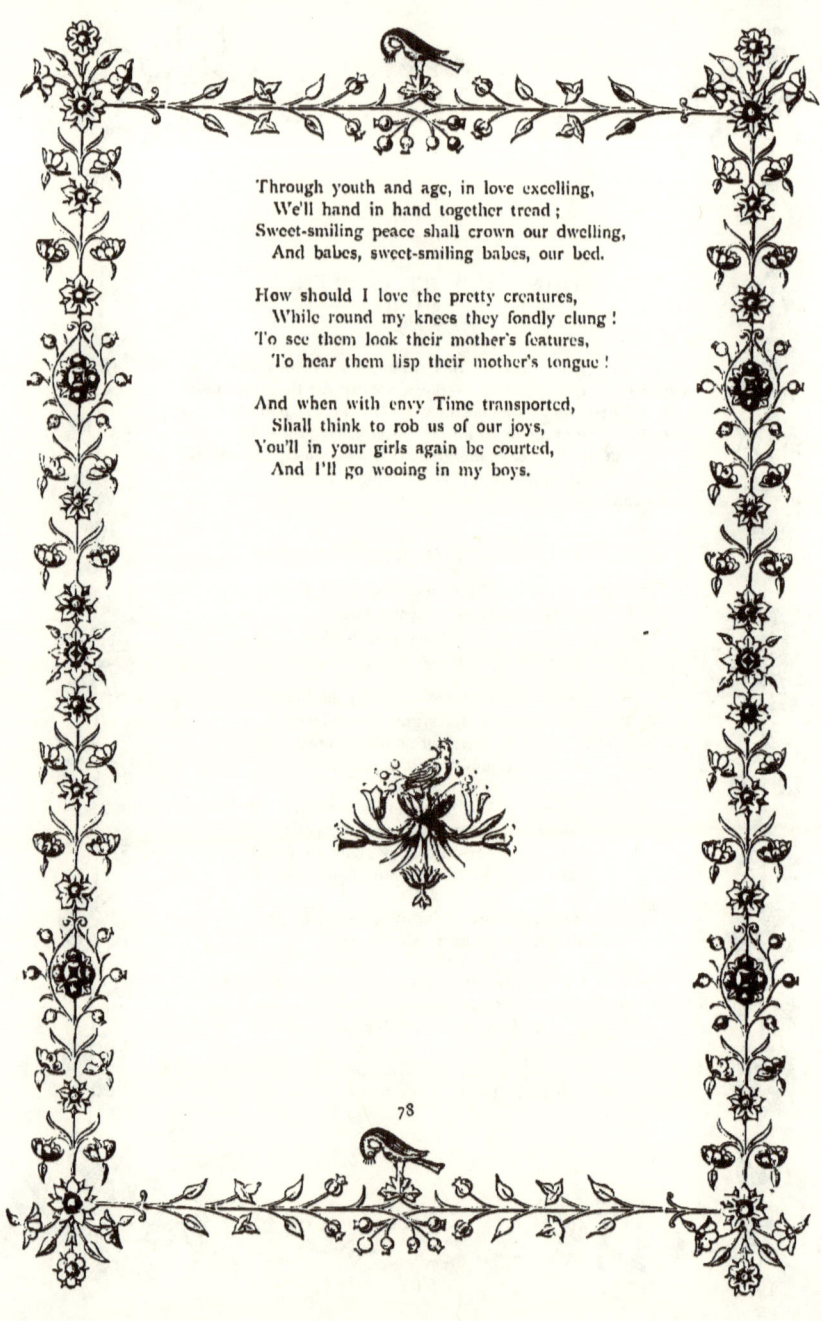

Through youth and age, in love excelling,
  We'll hand in hand together tread;
Sweet-smiling peace shall crown our dwelling,
  And babes, sweet-smiling babes, our bed.

How should I love the pretty creatures,
  While round my knees they fondly clung!
To see them look their mother's features,
  To hear them lisp their mother's tongue!

And when with envy Time transported,
  Shall think to rob us of our joys,
You'll in your girls again be courted,
  And I'll go wooing in my boys.

THOMAS GRAY.

1716—1771.

GRAY, like Milton, was, the son of a scrivener. A stiff and rather disagreeable College Don, he sometimes condescended to be playful, but not always with the happiest results.

ON THE DEATH OF A FAVOURITE CAT,

DROWNED IN A TUB OF GOLD FISHES.

'Twas on a lofty vase's side,
Where China's gayest art had dyed
   The azure flowers that blow,
Demurest of the tabby kind,
The pensive Selima, reclined,
   Gazed on the lake below.

Her conscious tail her joy declared:
The fair round face, the snowy beard,
   The velvet of her paws,
Her coat, that with the tortoise vies,
Her ears of jet, and emerald eyes,
   She saw, and purred applause.

Still had she gazed; but 'midst the tide
Two angel forms were seen to glide,
   The Genii of the stream:
Their scaly armour's Tyrian hue,
Though richest purple to the view,
   Betrayed a golden gleam.

The hapless nymph with wonder saw:
A whisker first, and then a claw,
    With many an ardent wish,
She stretched in vain, to reach the prize.
What female heart can gold despise?
    What cat's averse to fish?

Presumptuous maid! with looks intent
Again she stretched, again she bent.
    Nor knew the gulf between.
(Malignant Fate sat by, and smiled)
The slippery verge her feet beguiled,
    She tumbled headlong in.

Eight times emerging from the flood
She mewed to every watery god
    Some speedy aid to send;
No dolphin came, no Nereid stirr'd;
Nor cruel Tom nor Susan heard;
    A favourite has no friend.

From hence, ye beauties, undeceived,
Know, one false step is ne'er retrieved,
    And be with caution bold;
Not all that tempts your wandering eyes
And heedless hearts is lawful prize,
    Nor all that glitters gold.

TOBIAS GEORGE SMOLLETT.

(1721–1771.)

SMOLLETT'S love of his native country was a redeeming trait in the character of a soured and fretful man. There is tremendous vigour in his more serious verse. His Ode to Independence, "Lord of the lion heart and eagle eye!" begins with the rush of Pindar.

ODE TO LEVEN WATER.

On Leven's banks while free to rove,
And tune the rural pipe to love,
I envied not the happiest swain
That ever trod the Arcadian plain.
Pure stream, in whose transparent wave
My youthful limbs I wont to lave;
No torrents stain thy limpid source,
No rocks impede thy dimpling course,
That sweetly warbles o'er its bed,
With white, round, polished pebbles spread;
While, lightly poised, the scaly brood
In myriads cleave thy crystal flood;
The springing trout in speckled pride;
The salmon, monarch of the tide;
The ruthless pike, intent on war;
The silver eel and mottled par.
Devolving from thy parent lake,
A charming maze thy waters make,
By bowers of birch and groves of pine,
And edges flowered with eglantine.
Still on thy banks so gaily green
May numerous herds and flocks be seen:
And lasses chanting o'er the pail,
And shepherds piping in the dale;
And ancient faith that knows no guile,
And industry embrowned with toil;
And hearts resolved, and hands prepared,
The blessings they enjoy to guard!

PAUL WHITEHEAD.
1710—1774.

THIs not very remarkable poet was first a mercer's apprentice, and then a barrister. He wrote a satire on "Manners," another on "Pugilism;" and was a lounger, and a not very reputable trifler at the Prince of Wales's house in Leicester Fields.

HUNTING SONG.

The sun from the east tips the mountains with gold ;
The meadows all spangled with dew-drops behold !
Hear, the lark's early matin proclaims the new day,
And the horn's cheerful summons rebukes our delay.
Chorus. With the sports of the field there's no pleasure can vie,
While jocund we follow the hounds in full cry.

Let the drudge of the town make riches his sport ;
The slave of the state hunt the smiles of a court :
No care and ambition our pastime annoy,
But innocence still gives a zest to our joy.
With the sports, &c.

Mankind are all hunters in various degree ;
The priest hunts a living—the lawyer a fee,
The doctor a patient—the courtier a place,
Though often, like us, he's flung out in the chase.
With the sports, &c.

The cit hunts a plum—while the soldier hunts fame,
The poet a dinner—the patriot a name ;
And the practised coquette, though she seems to refuse,
In spite of her airs, still her lover pursues.
With the sports, &c.

Let the bold and the busy hunt glory and wealth ;
All the blessing we ask is the blessing of health,
With hound and with horn through the woodlands to roam,
And, when tired abroad, find contentment at home.
With the sports, &c.

THE WHIPPER-IN

OLIVER GOLDSMITH.

1724-1774.

GOLDSMITH is always delightful: and his satire is harmless as summer lightning. He was not the man to hurt even a wasp, much less a fly. His playfulness is graceful. We regret he did not sketch the intrusiveness and servility of Boswell.

STANZAS ON WOMAN.

From Vicar of Wakefield, Chap. xxiv.

When lovely woman stoops to folly,
  And finds too late that men betray,
What charm can soothe her melancholy,
  What art can wash her guilt away?

The only art her guilt to cover,
  To hide her shame from every eye,
To give repentance to her lover,
  And wring his bosom, is—to die.

THE HAUNCH OF VENISON.

A POETICAL EPISTLE TO LORD CLARE.

Thanks, my Lord, for your venison, for finer or fatter
Never ranged in a forest, or smoked in a platter:
The haunch was a picture for painters to study—
The fat was so white, and the lean was so ruddy.
Though my stomach was sharp, I could scarce help regretting
To spoil such a delicate picture by eating:
I had thoughts in my chamber to place it in view
To be shown to my friends as a piece of virtu;
As in some Irish houses, where things are so-so,
One gammon of bacon hangs up for a show
But, for eating a rasher of what they take pride in,
They'd as soon think of eating the pan it is fried in.
But hold—let me pause—don't I hear you pronounce
This tale of the bacon's a damnable bounce:

Well, suppose it a bounce—sure a poet may try
By a bounce now and then to get courage to fly.
But, my Lord, it's no bounce: I protest in my turn,
It's a truth—and your Lordship may ask Mr. Burn.
    To go on with my tale: as I gazed on the haunch,
I thought of a friend that was trusty and staunch—
So I cut it, and sent it to Reynolds undrest,
To paint it, or eat it, just as he liked best.
Of the neck and the breast I had next to dispose—
'Twas a neck and a breast that might rival Monroe's—
But in parting with these I was puzzled again
With the how, and the who, and the where, and the when:
There's Howard, and Coley, and Hogarth, and Hiff—
I think they love venison—I know they love beef;
There's my countryman Higgins—oh! let him alone
For making a blunder or picking a bone.
But, hang it!—to poets, who seldom can eat,
Your very good mutton's a very good treat;
Such dainties to them their health it might hurt,
It's like sending them ruffles when wanting a shirt.
While thus I debated, in reverie centred,
An acquaintance, a friend as he called himself, entered;
An underbred, fine-spoken fellow was he,
And he smiled as he looked at the venison and me.
"What have we got here? Why, this is good eating!
Your own I suppose—or is it in waiting?"
"Why, whose should it be?" cried I, with a flounce;
"I get these things often"—but that was a bounce;
"Some lords, my acquaintance, that settle the nation,
Are pleased to be kind—but I hate ostentation."
"If that be the case, then," cried he, very gay,
"I'm glad I have taken this house in my way.
To-morrow you take a poor dinner with me:
No words—I insist on't—precisely at three.
We'll have Johnson and Burke; all the wits will be there;
My acquaintance is slight, or I'd ask my Lord Clare.
And now that I think on't, as I am a sinner!
We wanted this venison to make out the dinner.
What say you—a pasty! it shall and it must,
And my wife, little Kitty, is famous for crust.
Here, porter—this venison with me to Mile End;
No stirring, I beg—my dear friend—my dear friend!"

Thus snatching his hat, he brushed off like the wind,
And the porter and eatables followed behind.
    Left alone to reflect, having emptied my shelf,
And "nobody with me at sea but myself,"
Though I could not help thinking my gentlemen hasty,
Yet Johnson, and Burke, and a good venison-pasty,
Were things that I never disliked in my life—
Though clogged with a coxcomb and Kitty his wife;
So next day, in due splendour to make my approach,
I drove to his door in my own hackney-coach.
    When come to the place where we all were to dine—
A chair-lumbered closet just twelve feet by nine—
My friend bade me welcome, but struck me quite dumb
With tidings that Johnson and Burke could not come;
"For I knew it," he cried, "both eternally fail,
The one with his speeches, and t'other with Thrale:
But no matter, I'll warrant we'll make up the party
With two full as clever, and ten times as hearty.
The one is a Scotchman, and the other a Jew,
They're both of them merry, and authors like you;
The one writes the Snarler, the other the Scourge;
Some think he writes Cinna—he owns to Panurge."
While thus he described them by trade and by name,
They entered, and dinner was served as they came.
    At the top a fried liver and bacon were seen;
At the bottom was tripe in a swinging tureen;
At the sides there was spinach and pudding made hot;
In the middle a place where the pasty was not.
Now, my Lord, as for tripe, it's my utter aversion,
And your bacon I hate like a Turk or a Persian;
So there I sat stuck like a horse in a pound,
While the bacon and liver went merrily round.
But what vexed me most was that damned Scottish rogue,
With his long-winded speeches, his smiles, and his brogue.
And, "Madam," quoth he, "may this bit be my poison,
A prettier dinner I never set eyes on;
Pray, a slice of your liver, though may I be curst,
But I've eat of your tripe till I'm ready to burst."
"The tripe," quoth the Jew, with his chocolate cheek.
"I could dine on this tripe seven days in a week:
I like these here dinners so pretty and small—
But your friend there, the doctor, eats nothing at all."

85

"Oh, oh!" quoth my friend, "he'll come in a trice,
He's keeping a corner for something that's nice:
There's a pasty"——"A pasty!" repeated the Jew;
"I don't care if I keep a corner for't too."
"What the de'il, mon, a pasty!" re-echoed the Scot;
"Though splitting, I'll still keep a corner for that."
"We'll all keep a corner," the lady cried out;
"We'll all keep a corner," was echoed about.
While thus we resolved, and the pasty delayed,
With looks that quite petrified, entered the maid;
A visage so sad, and so pale with affright,
Waked Priam, in drawing his curtains by night.
But we quickly found out—for who could mistake her?—
That she came with some terrible news from the baker;
And so it fell out, for that negligent sloven
Had shut out the pasty on shutting his oven.
Sad Philomel thus—but let similes drop—
And now that I think on't the story may stop.
To be plain, my good Lord, it's but labour misplaced
To send such good verses to one of your taste.
You've got an odd something,—a kind of discerning—
A relish, a taste, sickened over by learning—
At least it's your temper, as very well known,
That you think very slightly of all that's your own;
So, perhaps, in your habits of thinking amiss,
You may make a mistake, and think slightly of this.

SIR GILBERT ELLIOT.

— 1777.

SIR GILBERT, father of the first Earl of Minto, was Treasurer of the Navy, Keeper of the Signet in Scotland, and an eloquent speaker in Parliament. He introduced the use of the German flute into Scotland. The pastoral is rather a hopeless style of composition, and generally seems artificial and faded ; but Sir Gilbert's song is a pleasant specimen of the style.*

AMYNTA.

My sheep I neglected, I broke my sheep-hook,
And all the gay haunts of my youth I forsook ;
No more for Amynta fresh garlands I wove ;
For ambition, I said, would soon cure me of love.

Oh, what had my youth with ambition to do?
Why left I Amynta? Why broke I my vow?
Oh, give me my sheep, and my sheep-hook restore,
And I'll wander from love and Amynta no more.

Through regions remote in vain do I rove,
And bid the wide ocean secure me from love !
O fool ! to imagine that aught could subdue
A love so well founded, a passion so true !

Alas ! 'tis too late at thy fate to repine ;
Poor shepherd, Amynta can never be thine :
Thy tears are all fruitless, thy wishes are vain,
The moments neglected return not again.

* See Scott's "Lay of the Last Minstrel," Ch. I. s. 27, and Note.

DR. JOHN LANGHORNE.

1735—1779.

THIS amiable and warm-hearted man was a Prebend of Wells. In his "Country Justice," he anticipated the sober truthfulness and pathos of Crabbe. They both painted in the Dutch manner, but without its coarseness.

TO A REDBREAST.

Little bird, with bosom red,
Welcome to my humble shed!
Courtly domes of high degree
Have no room for thee and me.
Pride and pleasure's fickle throng
Nothing mind an idle song.

Daily near my table steal,
While I pick my scanty meal.
Doubt not, little though there be,
But I'll cast a crumb to thee;
Well rewarded, if I spy
Pleasure in thy glancing eye,
See thee, when thou'st ate thy fill,
Plume thy breast and wipe thy bill.

Come, my feathered friend, again,
Well thou know'st the broken pane.
Ask of me thy daily store;
Go not near Avaro's door:
Once within his iron hall,
Woful end shall thee befall.
Savage!—he would soon divest
Of its rosy plumes thy breast;
Then, with solitary joy,
Eat thee, bones and all, my boy!

DR. SAMUEL JOHNSON.

1709—1784.

As it amused Adam to see the elephant gambol before him and twining his lithe proboscis, it may amuse our readers to see the great lexicographer penning amatory verses, and rolling his cyclopean head to the dainty but attenuated music of a spinnet. It is pleasant to watch the great moralist bound like Hercules to a spinning wheel, and writing playful verses for arch and clever Mrs. Piozzi.

TO MRS. THRALE,
ON HER COMPLETING HER THIRTY-FIFTH YEAR.
AN IMPROMPTU.

Oft in danger, yet alive,
We are come to thirty-five;
Long may better years arrive,
Better years than thirty-five!
Could philosophers contrive
Life to stop at thirty-five,
Time his hours should never drive
O'er the bounds of thirty-five.
High to soar and deep to dive
Nature gives at thirty-five.
Ladies, stock and tend your hive,
Trifle not at thirty-five;

For howe'er we boast and strive,
Life declines from thirty-five.
He that ever hopes to thrive
Must begin by thirty-five;
And all who wisely wish to wive
Must look on Thrale at thirty-five.

TO MISS HICKMAN PLAYING ON THE SPINNET.

Bright Stella, formed for universal reign,
Too well you know to keep the slaves you gain;
When in your eyes resistless lightnings play,
Awed into love our conquered hearts obey,
And yield reluctant to despotic sway:
But when your music soothes the raging pain
We bid propitious Heaven prolong your reign,
We bless the tyrant and we hug the chain.
When old Timotheus struck the vocal string,
Ambition's fury fired the Grecian king:
Unbounded projects labouring in his mind,
He pants for room in one poor world confined.
Thus waked to rage by music's dreadful power,
He bids the sword destroy, the flame devour.
Had Stella's gentle touches moved the lyre,
Soon had the monarch felt a nobler fire;
No more delighted with destructive war,
Ambitious only now to please the fair;
Resigned his thirst of empire to her charms,
And found a thousand worlds in Stella's arms.

THE SPINNET

JOHN LOGAN.

1748—1788.

THERE is an unhappy confusion about Logan's poems. Logan, a Scotch Clergyman, falling into dissipated habits, came to London and turned Author on a small scale. Many of his poems are supposed to have been stolen from the papers of his friend, Michael Bruce, a poetical young schoolmaster, who died of consumption in very early life. Burke admired this Cuckoo poem, and the elder D'Israeli calls it magical for " picture, melody, and sentiment."

TO THE CUCKOO.

Hail! beauteous stranger of the grove,
  Thou messenger of Spring!
Now Heaven repairs thy rural seat,
  And woods thy welcome sing.

What time the daisy decks the green
  Thy certain voice we hear;
Hast thou a star to guide thy path,
  Or mark the rolling year?

Delightful visitant! with thee
  I hail the time of flowers,
And hear the sound of music sweet
  From birds among the bowers.

The schoolboy, wandering through the wood
  To pull the primrose gay,
Starts, the new voice of Spring to hear,
  And imitates thy lay.

What time the pea puts on the bloom
  Thou fliest thy vocal vale,
An annual guest in other lands,
  Another Spring to hail.

Sweet bird! thy bower is ever green.
  Thy sky is ever clear;
Thou hast no sorrow in thy song,
  No winter in thy year!

Oh, could I fly, I'd fly with thee!
  We'd make, with joyful wing,
Our annual visit o'er the globe,
  Companions of the Spring.

THOMAS WARTON.

1728—1790.

THIS grave poet was the son of a Professor of Poetry at Oxford. Wordsworth imitated his sonnets, and their quiet meditative tone suited the genius of the Lake poet.

WRITTEN ON A BLANK LEAF OF DUGDALE'S "MONASTICON."

Deem not devoid of elegance the sage,
By Fancy's genuine feelings unbeguiled
Of painful pedantry, the poring child,
Who turns of these proud domes the historic page
Now sunk by Time, and Henry's fiercer rage.
Think'st thou the warbling muses never smiled
On his lone hours? Ingenious views engage
His thoughts on themes unclassic falsely styled,
Intent. While cloistered piety displays
Her mouldering roll, the piercing eye explores
New manners, and the pomp of elder days,
Whence culls the pensive bard his pictured stores.
Not rough nor barren are the winding ways
Of hoar antiquity, but strewn with flowers.

ON REVISITING THE RIVER LODDON.

Oh! what a weary race my feet have run
Since first I trod thy banks, with alders crowned,
And thought my way was all through fairy ground,
Beneath the azure sky and golden sun—
When first my muse to lisp her notes begun!
While pensive memory traces back the round
Which fills the varied interval between;
Much pleasure, more of sorrow, marks the scene.
Sweet native stream! those skies and suns so pure
No more return to cheer my evening road!
Yet still one joy remains, that not obscure
Nor useless all my vacant days have flowed
From youth's gay dawn to manhood's prime mature,
Nor with the Muse's laurel unbestowed.

THOMAS BLACKLOCK.

1721—1791.

This poet, who was born blind, was the son of a Cumberland bricklayer who had settled in Dumfriesshire; he became a clergyman, but the parishioners objecting with a rather brutish intolerance to a blind minister, he settled in Edinburgh, and lived by taking lodgers. He seems to have been a happy and amiable man, and cheerful, in spite of his deprivation. He was an early and generous admirer of the genius of Burns.

ODE TO AURORA ON MELISSA'S BIRTH-DAY.

    Of Time and Nature eldest born,
    Emerge, thou rosy-fingered Morn;
    Emerge, in purest dress arrayed,
    And chase from heaven Night's envious shade,
    That I once more may pleased survey,
    And hail Melissa's natal-day.

    Of Time and Nature eldest born,
    Emerge, thou rosy-fingered Morn;
    In order at the eastern gate
    The hours to draw thy chariot wait;
    Whilst Zephyr, on his balmy wings,
    Mild Nature's fragrant tribute brings,
    With odours sweet to strew thy way,
    And grace the bland revolving day.

    But, as thou lead'st the radiant sphere
    That gilds its birth and marks the year,
    And as his stronger glories rise,
    Diffused around the expanded skies,
    Till, clothed with beams serenely bright,
    All heaven's vast concave flames with light;

Melissa still pursues her way,
Her virtues with thy splendour vie,
Increasing to the mental eye ;
Though less conspicuous, not less dear,
Long may they Bion's prospect cheer ;
So shall his heart no more repine,
Blessed with her rays, though robbed of thine.

SAMUEL BISHOP.
1731—1795.

LITTLE is known of this writer, except that he was a clergyman, and Master of Merchant Taylors' School. He could not have been a severe disciplinarian to have written such amiable verses. The poets in general have not been eloquent on the unromantic theme of love after marriage.

TO MRS. BISHOP,
ON THE ANNIVERSARY OF HER WEDDING-DAY, WHICH WAS ALSO HER BIRTH-DAY, WITH A RING.

'Thee, Mary, with this ring I wed'—
So, fourteen years ago, I said.
Behold another ring!—'For what!'
To wed thee o'er again! Why not?

With that first ring I married youth,
Grace, beauty, innocence, and truth;
Taste long admired, sense long revered,
And all my Molly then appeared.

If she, by merit since disclosed,
Prove twice the woman I supposed,
I plead that double merit now,
To justify a double vow.

Here, then, to-day—with faith as sure,
With ardour as intense, as pure,
As when, amidst the rites divine,
I took thy troth and plighted mine—

To thee, sweet girl, my second ring
A token and a pledge I bring:
With this I wed, till death us part,
Thy riper virtues to my heart;

Those virtues which, before untried,
The wife has added to the bride;
Those virtues, whose progressive claim,
Endearing wedlock's very name,

My soul enjoys, my song approves,
For conscience' sake as well as love's!
And why?—They shew me every hour
Honour's high thought, Affection's power,
Discretion's deed, sound Judgment's sentence,
And teach me all things—but repentance.

ROBERT BURNS.

1759—1796.

How Genius can transform men, and confer titles beyond any registered in human courts! The Ayrshire ploughman earned a fame (in spite of all his disfiguring vices) eternal and unshakable as Ben Lomond. Let his faults be forgotten and his virtues live! Great power from God had fallen on this peasant, and his poems, as long as Scotland remains Scotland, will live in the national heart and there be cherished.

OF A' THE AIRTS THE WIND CAN BLAW.

Of a' the airts* the wind can blaw
I dearly like the West,
For there the bonnie lassie lives,
The lassie I lo'e best:
There wild woods grow, and rivers row,
And mony a hill between;
But day and night my fancy's flight
Is ever wi' my Jean.

I see her in the dewy flowers,
I see her sweet and fair:
I hear her in the tunefu' birds,
I hear her charm the air:
There's not a bonnie flower that springs
By fountain, shaw, or green,
There's not a bonnie bird that sings
But minds me o' my Jean.

O blaw ye westlin' winds, blaw saft
Amang the leafy trees;
Wi' balmy gale frae hill and dale
Bring hame the laden bees;
And bring the lassie back to me
That's aye sae neat and clean;
Ae smile o' her wad banish care,
Sae charming is my Jean.

* Points of the compass

What sighs and vows amang the knowes
    Hae passed atween us twa!
How fond to meet, how wae to part
    That night she gaed awa!
The Powers aboon can only ken,
    To whom the heart is seen,
That nane can be sae dear to me
    As my sweet lovely Jean!

A ROSEBUD BY MY EARLY WALK.

A rose-bud by my early walk,
Adown a corn-enclosèd bawk,*
Sae gently bent its thorny stalk,
    All on a dewy morning.

Ere twice the shades o' dawn are fled,
In a' its crimson glory spread,
And drooping rich the dewy head,
    It scents the early morning.

Within the bush, her covert nest
A little linnet fondly prest,
The dew sat chilly on her breast
    Sae early in the morning.

She soon shall see her tender brood,
The pride, the pleasure o' the wood,
Amang the fresh green leaves bedewed,
    Awake the early morning.

So thou, dear bird, young Jeanie fair!
On trembling string or vocal air
Shall sweetly pay the tender care
    That tends thy early morning.

So thou, sweet rose-bud, young and gay,
Shall beauteous blaze upon the day,
And bless the parent's evening ray
    That watched thy early morning.

* An untilled ridge in a corn-field.

WILLIAM COWPER.

1731 1800.

Who can read the poet's delightful Letters to Lady Hesketh without loving the writer? So gentle and good—so tender and so witty, he pours forth his heart in all simplicity and love, without restraint, affectation, or even one selfish thought.

THE POPLAR FIELD.

The poplars are felled: farewell to the shade,
And the whispering sound of the cool colonnade;
The winds play no longer and sing in the leaves,
Nor Ouse on his bosom their image receives.

Twelve years have elapsed since I last took a view
Of my favourite field and the bank where they grew;
And now in the grass behold they are laid,
And the tree is my seat that once lent me a shade.

The blackbird has fled to another retreat,
Where the hazels afford him a screen from the heat,
And the scene where his melody charmed me before
Resounds with his sweet-flowing ditty no more.

My fugitive years are all hasting away,
And I must ere long lie as lowly as they,
With a turf on my breast, and a stone at my head,
Ere another such grove shall arise in its stead.

The change both my heart and my fancy employs;
I reflect on the frailty of man and his joys;
Short-lived as we are, yet our pleasures, we see,
Have a still shorter date, and die sooner than we.

THE ROSE.

The rose had been washed, just washed in a shower,
  Which Mary to Anna conveyed,
The plentiful moisture encumbered the flower,
  And weighed down its beautiful head.

The cup was all filled, and the leaves were all wet,
  And it seemed, to a fanciful view,
To weep for the buds it had left with regret
  On the flourishing bush where it grew.

I hastily seized it, unfit as it was
  For a nosegay, so dripping and drowned,
And swinging it rudely, too rudely, alas!
  I snapped it, it fell to the ground.

And such, I exclaimed, is the pitiless part
  Some act by the delicate mind,
Regardless of wringing and breaking a heart
  Already to sorrow resigned.

This elegant rose, had I shaken it less,
  Might have bloomed with its owner awhile,
And the tear that is wiped with a little address
  May be followed perhaps by a smile.

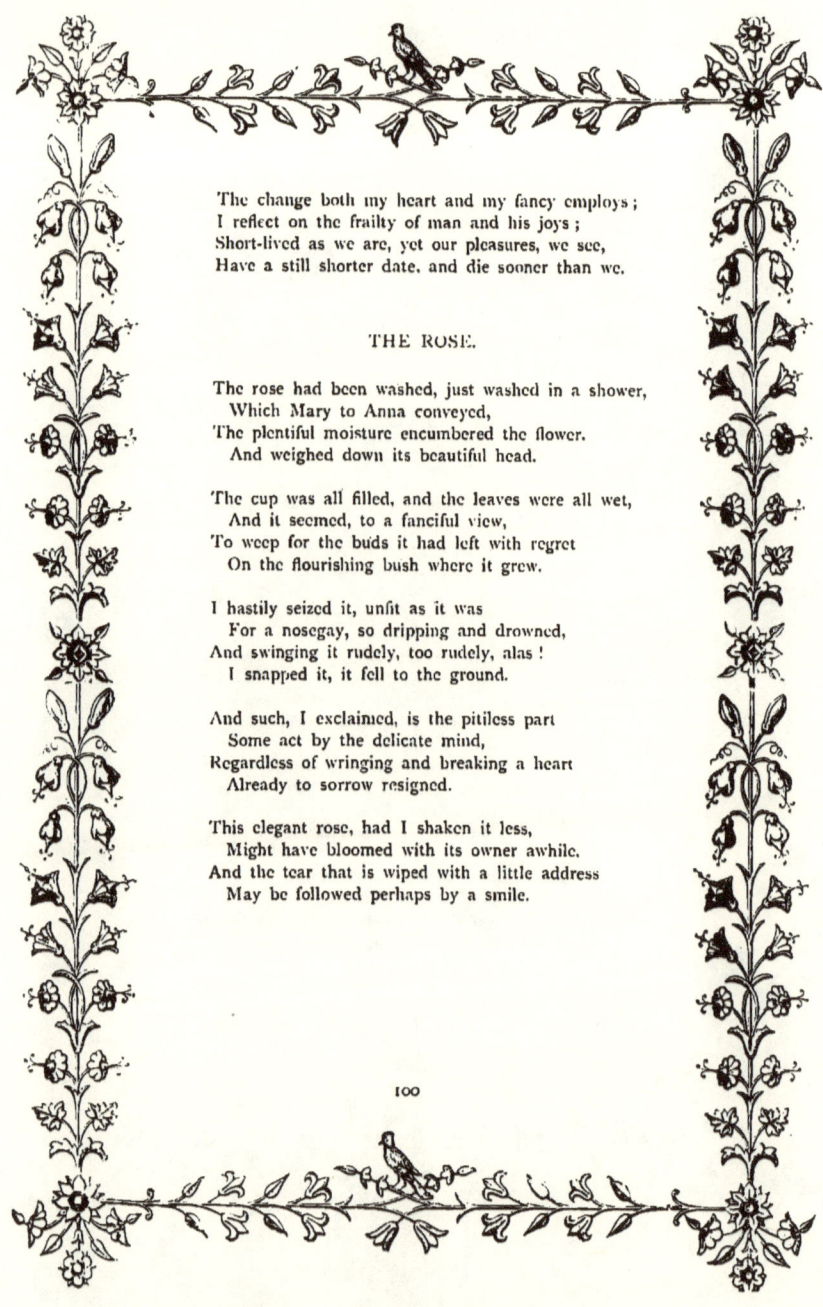

DR. ERASMUS DARWIN.

1731 1802.

THIS almost forgotten poet was a fashionable physician in Lichfield, who attempted, like Cowley, in smooth and glittering verse to lecture on Science in rhyme. Cowper admired him, and Campbell began by imitating him. Street reciters are, even now, sometimes to be heard reciting the Doctor's "Death of Eliza," which is very rhetorically effective, and not without a certain pompous sentiment.

SONG TO MAY.

Born in yon blaze of orient sky,
Sweet May! thy radiant form unfold :
Unclose thy blue voluptuous eye,
And wave thy shadowy locks of gold.

For thee the fragrant zephyrs blow,
For thee descends the sunny shower;
The rills in softer murmurs flow,
And brighter blossoms gem the bower.

Light graces, decked in flowery wreaths
And tiptoe joys, their hands combine ;
And Love his sweet contagion breathes,
And, laughing, dances round thy shrine.

Warm with new life, the glittering throng
On quivering fin and rustling wing,
Delighted join their votive song,
And hail thee Goddess of the Spring!

From the ' Loves of the Plants."

HENRY KIRKE WHITE.

1785—1806.

TENNYSON describes, in his "Will Waterproof," the violet blooming
"Among the chops and steaks."

In Kirke White's case, a butcher's son became a poet. His poetry is rather colourless, but it is pure and simple, and was, it must be remembered, the work of a very young man.

TO AN EARLY PRIMROSE.

Mild offspring of a dark and sullen sire!.
Whose modest form, so delicately fine,
    Was nursed in whirling storms
    And cradled in the winds.

Thee, when young Spring first question'd Winter's sway
And dared the sturdy blusterer to the fight,
    Thee on this bank he threw
    To mark his victory

In this low vale, the promise of the year,
Serene, thou openest to the nipping gale,
    Unnoticed and alone,
    Thy tender elegance.

So virtue blooms, brought forth amid the storms
Of chill adversity; in some lone walk
    Of life she rears her head,
    Obscure and unobserved;

While every bleaching breeze that on her blows
Chastens her spotless purity of breast,
    And hardens her to bear
    Serene the ills of life.

MRS. CHARLOTTE SMITH.

1749—1806.

This amiable and unfortunate lady, the victim of an ill-assorted marriage, wrote some admirable Sonnets. She was a friend of Hayley; and Sir Walter Scott mentions her sweet, mournful poems with a measured praise.

HOPE: A RONDEAU.

Just like Hope is yonder bow
That from the centre bends so low,
Where bright prismatic colours show
How gems of heavenly radiance glow,
        Just like Hope!

Yet if, to the illusion new,
The pilgrim should the arch pursue,
Farther and farther from his view
It flies, then melts in chilling dew,
        Just like Hope!

Ye fade, ethereal hues, for ever!
While, cold Reason, thy endeavour
Soothes not that sad heart which never
        Glows with Hope!

DR. THOMAS PERCY.

1721—1811.

The Bishop of Dromore was one of Dr. Johnson's best friends. We ought to be grateful to him for his publication of those fine old ballads which lit up again the Gothic spirit, and tended to foster the genius of Scott. A love of nature and simplicity rose like the Nile with them to fertilize our then somewhat arid literature.

O NANCY, WILT THOU GO WITH ME?

O Nancy, wilt thou go with me,
  Nor sigh to leave the flaunting town;
Can silent glens have charms for thee,
  The lowly cot and russet gown?
No longer dressed in silken sheen,
  No longer decked with jewels rare,
Say, canst thou quit each courtly scene
  Where thou wert fairest of the fair?

O Nancy! when thou'rt far away,
  Wilt thou not cast a wish behind?
Say, canst thou face the parching ray,
  Nor shrink before the wintry wind?
O! can that soft and gentle mien
  Extremes of hardship learn to bear,
Nor, sad, regret each courtly scene
  Where thou wert fairest of the fair?

O Nancy! canst thou love so true,
  Through perils keen with me to go,
Or when thy swain mishap shall rue,
  To share with him the pang of woe?
Say, should disease or pain befall,
  Wilt thou assume the nurse's care;
Nor wistful those gay scenes recall
  Where thou wert fairest of the fair?

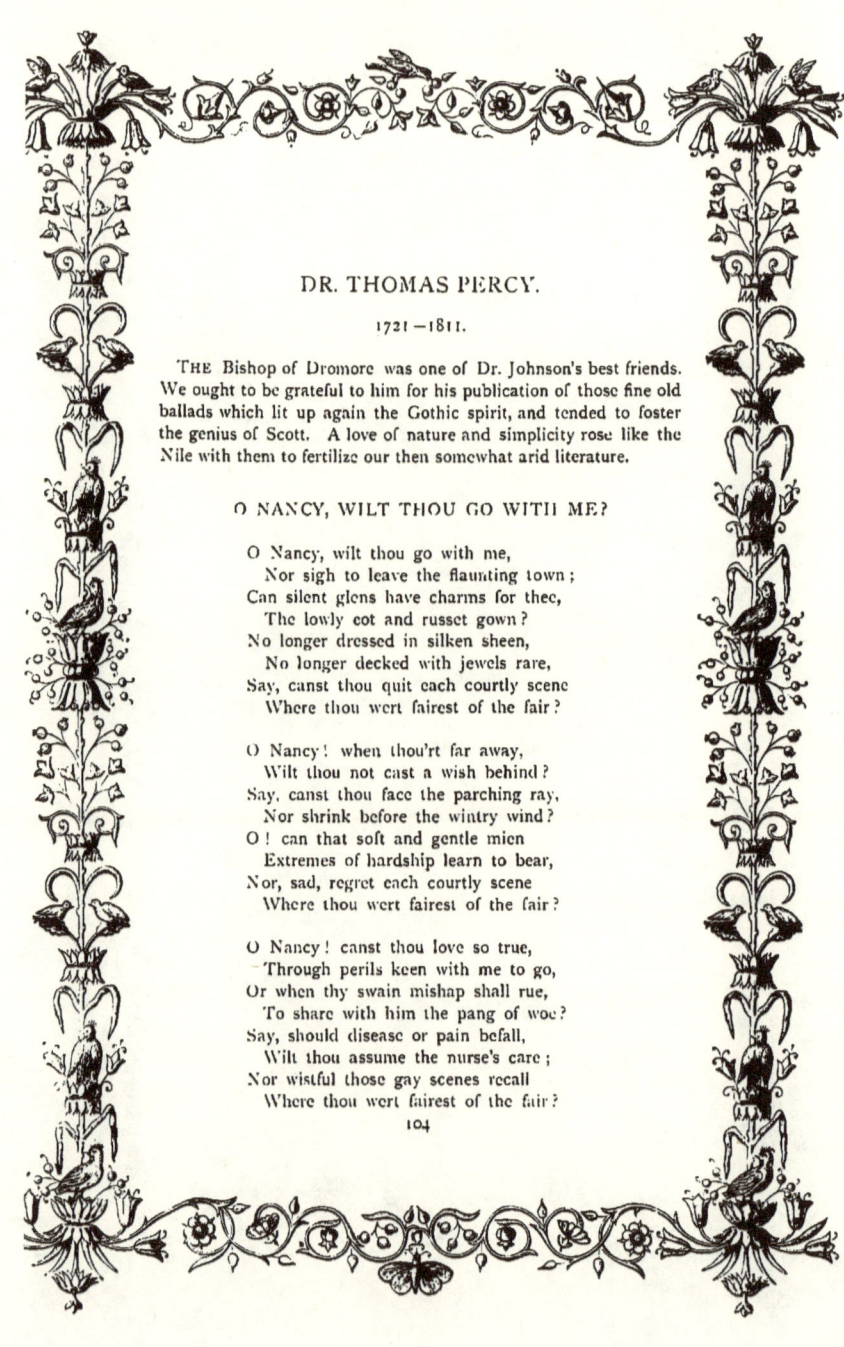

And when at last thy love shall die,
　Wilt thou receive his parting breath?
Wilt thou repress each struggling sigh,
　And cheer with smiles the bed of death?
And wilt thou o'er his breathless clay
　Strew flowers and drop the tender tear?
Nor *then* regret those scenes so gay
　Where thou wert fairest of the fair?*

---

* Burns says in reference to the above, "It is too barefaced to take Dr. Percy's charming song, and by means of transposing a few English words into Scots, to offer to pass it for a Scots song."—BURNS, *Remarks on Scottish Songs and Ballads.*

R. B. SHERIDAN.*

1751—1816.

SHERIDAN was more a wit than a poet, but we give his songs rather as specimens of his manner than in admiration of their excellence. An elaborate manufacturer of wit, and taking as much trouble to facet a joke as a jeweller does to cut a diamond, he had not the impulses from which true poetry springs.

ON FEMALE INFLUENCE.

In female hearts did sense and merit rule,
The lover's mind would ask no other school;
Shamed into sense, the scholars of your eyes,
Our beaux from gallantry would soon be wise;
Would gladly light, their homage to improve,
The lamp of knowledge at the torch of love.

TO —— ——.

Dear object of my late and early prayer,
Source of my joy and solace of my care,
Whose gentle friendship such a charm can give
As makes me wish, and tells me how to live;
To thee the Muse with grateful hand would bring
These first fair flowers of the doubtful Spring.
Oh, may they, fearless of the varying sky,
Bloom on thy breast and smile beneath thine eye,
In fairer lights their vivid blue display,
And sweeter breathe their little lives away.

TO

The stricken deer that in his velvet side
  Feels at each step the trembling arrow play,
In shades of thickest covert loves to hide,
  And from the cruel hunter speeds away.
But I, more wounded than the stricken deer,
  Scarce wish from my destroyer's aim to fly—
I weep, but 'tis, alas! too soft a tear,
  And e'en my groans are mingled with a sigh.

ON A CHILD.

In some rude spot where vulgar herbage grows,
  If chance a violet rear its purple head,
The careful gardener moves it ere it blows
  To thrive and flourish in a nobler bed.
    Such was thy fate, dear child!
    Thy opening such!
Pre-eminence in early bloom was shown;
    For earth too good, perhaps,
    And loved too much
Heaven saw and early marked thee for its own.

FROM THE "DUENNA."

I ne'er could any lustre see
In eyes that would not look on me;
I ne'er saw nectar on a lip
But where mine own did hope to sip.
Has the maid who touched my heart
Cheeks of rose untouched by art?
I will own the colour true
When yielding blushes aid their hue.

Is her hand so soft and pure?
I must press it, to be sure;
Nor can I be certain then
Till it, grateful, press again.
Must I with attentive eye
Watch her heaving bosom sigh?
I will do so when I see
That heaving bosom sigh for me.

HAD I A HEART FOR FALSEHOOD FRAMED.

Had I a heart for falsehood framed,
  I ne'er could injure you;
For though your tongue no promise claimed,
  Your charms would make me true.
To you no soul shall bear deceit,
  No stranger offer wrong;
But friends in all the aged you'll meet,
  And lovers in the young.

But when they learn that you have blest
  Another with your heart,
They'll bid aspiring passion rest,
  And act a brother's part:
Then, lady, dread not here deceit,
  Nor fear to suffer wrong;
For friends in all the aged you'll meet,
  And brothers in the young.

JOHN KEATS.

1795 1821.

KEATS was the son of a livery stable keeper, who apprenticed him to a chemist, till by his own genius the poet cut the thongs that held him to the counter. Beginning with an ambitious poem full of imperfections, gross affectations, and sterile conceits, he rose in power till he produced that fine torso, the "Hyperion." His smaller poems are full of beautiful observations of nature, and show fresh and exhaustless fancy.

ROBIN HOOD.

TO A FRIEND.

No! those days are gone away,
And their hours are old and gray,
And their minutes buried all
Under the down-trodden pall
Of the leaves of many years:
Many times have Winter's shears,
Frozen North and chilling East
Sounded tempests to the feast
Of the forests whispering fleeces,
Since men knew nor rent nor leases.
　No, the bugle sounds no more,
And the twanging bow no more;
Silent is the ivory shrill
Past the heath and up the hill;
There is no mid-forest laugh,
Where lone Echo gives the half
To some wight amazed to hear
Jesting deep in forest drear.
　On the fairest time of June
You may go, with sun or moon,
Or the seven stars to light you,
Or the polar ray to right you;

But you never may behold
Little John or Robin bold;
Never one of all the clan
Thrumming on an empty can
Some old hunting ditty, while
He doth his green way beguile
To fair hostess Merriment,
Down beside the pasture Trent;
For he left the merry tale,
Messenger for spicy ale.

   Gone, the merry morris din;
Gone, the song of Gamelyn;
Gone, the tough-belted outlaw
Idling in the "grenè shawe;"
All are gone away and past!
And if Robin should be cast
Sudden from his tufted grave,
And if Marian should have
Once again her forest days,
She would weep and he would craze:
He would swear, for all his oaks,
Fall'n beneath the dock-yard strokes,
Have rotted on the briny seas;
She would weep that her wild bees
Sang not to her—strange! that honey
Can't be got without hard money.

   So it is; yet let us sing
Honour to the old bow-string!
Honour to the bugle-horn!
Honour to the woods unshorn!
Honour to the Lincoln green!
Honour to the archer keen!
Honour to tight Little John,
And the horse he rode upon!
Honour to bold Robin Hood
Sleeping in the underwood!
Honour to Maid Marian,
And to all the Sherwood clan!
Though their days have hurried by,
Let us two a burden try

FANCY.

Ever let the Fancy roam!
Pleasure never is at home:
At a touch sweet Pleasure melteth,
Like to bubbles when rain pelteth;
Then let wingèd Fancy wander
Through the thought still spread beyond her;
Open wide the mind's cage door,
She'll dart forth, and cloudward soar.
O sweet Fancy! let her loose:
Summer's joys are spoilt by use,
And the enjoying of the Spring
Fades as does its blossoming:
Autumn's red-lipped fruitage too
Blushing through the mist and dew
Cloys with tasting: what do then?
Sit thee by the ingle, when
The sear faggot blazes bright,
Spirit of a winter's night;
When the soundless earth is muffled,
And the cakèd snow is shuffled
From the ploughboy's heavy shoon;
When the Night doth meet the Noon
In a dark conspiracy
To banish Even from her sky.
— Sit thee there, and send abroad
With a mind self-overawed
Fancy, high-commissioned :— send her!
She has vassals to attend her:
She will bring, in spite of frost,
Beauties that the earth hath lost;
She will bring thee, all together,
All delights of summer weather;
All the buds and bells of May
From dewy sward or thorny spray;
All the heapèd Autumn's wealth,
With a still, mysterious stealth;
She will mix these pleasures up
Like three fit wines in a cup,
And thou shalt quaff it ;—thou shalt hear
Distant harvest-carols clear;

Rustle of the reapèd corn;
Sweet birds antheming the morn:
And in the same moment—hark!
'Tis the early April lark.
Or the rooks, with busy caw
Foraging for sticks and straw.
Thou shalt, at one glance, behold
The daisy and the marigold;
White-plumed lilies, and the first
Hedge-grown primrose that hath burst;
Shaded hyacinth, alway
Sapphire queen of the mid-May;
And every leaf, and every flower
Pearlèd with the self-same shower.
Thou shalt see the field-mouse peep
Meagre from its cellèd sleep;
And the snake all winter-thin
Cast on sunny bank its skin;
Freckled nest eggs thou shalt see
Hatching in the hawthorn-tree,
When the hen-bird's wing doth rest
Quiet on her mossy nest;
Then the hurry and alarm
When the bee-hive casts its swarm;
Acorns ripe down-pattering
While the autumn breezes sing.
  O sweet Fancy! let her loose;
Everything is spoilt by use:
Where's the cheek that doth not fade,
Too much gazed at? Where's the maid
Whose lip mature is ever new?
Where's the eye, however blue,
Doth not weary? Where's the face
One would meet in every place?
Where's the voice, however soft,
One would hear so very oft?
At a touch sweet Pleasure melteth
Like to bubbles when rain pelteth.
Let then wingèd Fancy find
Thee a mistress to thy mind:
Dulcet-eyed as Ceres' daughter,
Ere the God of Torment taught her

How to frown and how to chide;
With a waist and with a side
White as Hebe's, when her zone
Slipt its golden clasp, and down
Fell her kirtle to her feet,
While she held the goblet sweet,
And Jove grew languid.—Break the mesh
Of the Fancy's silken leash;
Quickly break her prison-string.
And such joys as these she'll bring:
—Let the wingèd Fancy roam!
Pleasure never is at home.

IN A DREAR-NIGHTED DECEMBER.

In a drear-nighted December,
Too happy, happy Tree,
Thy branches ne'er remember
Their green felicity:
The north cannot undo them
With a sleety whistle through them,
Nor frozen thawings glue them
From budding at the prime.

In a drear-nighted December,
Too happy, happy Brook,
Thy bubblings ne'er remember
Apollo's summer look;
But with a sweet forgetting
They stay their crystal fretting,
Never, never petting
About the frozen time.

Ah, would 'twere so with many
A gentle girl and boy!
But were there ever any
Writhed not at passèd joy?
To know the change and feel it,
When there is none to heal it,
Nor numbèd sense to steal it
Was never said in rhyme.

PERCY BYSSHE SHELLEY.

1792—1822.

THIS great genius, so early doomed, so cruelly exiled for errors that time and experience would have removed, is the greatest of our Anglo-Italian poets whose natures have grown sweeter and fairer under a richer sun than that of England. Shelley's pure mind delighted to shape creatures from the elements, and to infuse the fire from Heaven into those spirits of his own fashioning. Never since the times of Æschylus have such choruses been written as those of his Prometheus Unbound; and no one, with the exception of a young poet (Mr. Swinburne, in our own day), has more completely caught the Greek feeling.

LINES TO AN INDIAN AIR.

I arise from dreams of thee
In the first sweet sleep of night,
When the winds are breathing low,
And the stars are shining bright:
I arise from dreams of thee,
And a spirit in my feet
Has led me—who knows how?
To thy chamber window, sweet!

The wandering airs they faint
On the dark, the silent stream—
The champak odours fail
Like sweet thoughts in a dream;

The nightingale's complaint,
It dies upon her heart,
As I must on thine,
Beloved as thou art!

O lift me from the grass!
I die, I faint, I fail!
Let thy love in kisses rain
On my lips and eyelids pale.
My cheek is cold and white, alas!
My heart beats loud and fast,
Oh! press it close to thine again,
Where it will break at last.

LOVE'S PHILOSOPHY.

The fountains mingle with the river,
And the rivers with the ocean,
The winds of heaven mix for ever
With a sweet emotion;
Nothing in the world is single;
All things by a law divine
In one another's being mingle—
Why not I with thine?

See the mountains kiss high heaven,
And the waves clasp one another;
No sister flower would be forgiven
If it disdained its brother;
And the sunlight clasps the earth,
And the moonbeams kiss the sea,
What are all these kissings worth,
If thou kiss not me?

DIRGE FOR THE YEAR.

Orphan hours, the year is dead,
Come and sigh, come and weep!
Merry hours, smile instead,
For the year is but asleep.

See, it smiles as it is sleeping,
Mocking your untimely weeping.

As an earthquake rocks a corse
  In its coffin in the clay,
So White Winter, that rough nurse,
  Rocks the death-cold year to-day;
Solemn hours! wail aloud
For your mother in her shroud.

As the wild air stirs and sways
  The tree-swung cradle of a child,
So the breath of these rude days
  Rocks the year:—be calm and mild,
Trembling hours, she will arise
With new love within her eyes.

January grey is here,
  Like a sexton by her grave;
February bears the bier,
  March with grief doth howl and rave,
And April weeps,—but, O ye hours,
Follow with May's fairest flowers!

LORD BYRON.

1788—1824.

THIS great genius and most unhappy man began life by writing the verses to be expected of a young "man of quality," till suddenly he found the talisman, and rose among the eagles of the higher order. Abandoned in morals, a voluntary exile, the victim of his own vices and his own gigantic vanity, wallowing in the lowest vices of Venice, Byron, in the last years of his life, laid aside his cynical and ribald poem to give his heart and soul to Greece, and to die in her cause. He did not merely *pose* himself for a patriot: he was one truly; and he left the world glorified by that single self-sacrifice.

SHE WALKS IN BEAUTY.*

She walks in beauty, like the night
   Of cloudless climes and starry skies,
And all that's best of dark and bright
   Meets in her aspect and her eyes.
Thus mellowed to that tender light
   Which heaven to gaudy day denies.

One shade the more, one ray the less
   Had half impaired the nameless grace
Which waves in every raven tress
   Or softly lightens o'er her face,
Where thoughts serenely sweet express
   How pure, how dear their dwelling-place.

And on that cheek, and o'er that brow
   So soft, so calm, yet eloquent,
The smiles that win, the tints that glow
   But tell of days in goodness spent,-
A mind at peace with all below,
   A heart whose love is innocent.

* Written on returning from a ball where Lady Wilmot Horton had appeared in mourning, with numerous spangles on her dress.

MAID OF ATHENS, ERE WE PART.

Maid of Athens, ere we part,
Give, oh give me back my heart!
Or, since that has left my breast,
Keep it now, and take the rest!
Hear my vow before I go,
Ζώη μοῦ, σἁς ἀγαπῶ.

By those tresses unconfined
Wooed by each Ægean wind;
By those lids whose jetty fringe
Kiss thy soft cheeks' blooming tinge;
By those wild eyes like the roe,
Ζώη μοῦ, σἁς ἀγαπῶ.

By that lip I long to taste;
By that zone-encircled waist;
By all the token-flowers that tell
What words can never speak so well;
By love's alternate joy and woe,
Ζώη μοῦ, σἁς ἀγαπῶ.

Maid of Athens! I am gone:
Think of me, sweet! when alone.
Though I fly to Istamboul,
Athens holds my heart and soul:
Can I cease to love thee? No!
Ζώη μοῦ, σἁς ἀγαπῶ.

STANZAS FOR MUSIC.

There be none of Beauty's daughters
  With a magic like thee ;
And like music on the waters
  Is thy sweet voice to me :
When, as if its sound were causing
The charmèd ocean's pausing,
The waves lie still and gleaming,
And the lullèd winds seem dreaming :

And the midnight moon is weaving
  Her bright chain o'er the deep,
Whose breast is gently heaving
  As an infant's asleep :
So the spirit bows before thee
To listen and adore thee ;
With a full but soft emotion,
Like the swell of Summer's ocean.

MRS. BARBAULD.

1743–1825.

This excellent and amiable woman was the daughter of Dr. Aikin. She married a French Protestant Dissenting Minister, who kept a school at Palgrave, in Suffolk. Charles James Fox was a great admirer of her songs.

LIFE.

Life! I know not what thou art,
But know that thou and I must part;
And when, or how, or where we met
I own to me's a secret yet.
   Life! we've been long together
Through pleasant and through cloudy weather;
'Tis hard to part when friends are dear—
Perhaps 'twill cost a sigh, a tear;
—Then steal away, give little warning,
   Choose thine own time;
Say not Good Night,—but in some brighter clime
   Bid me Good Morning.

LORD THURLOW.

1781—1829.

WHO could expect an owl to sing like a thrush?—and yet here we have a judge, who looked, as it was said, wiser than any one ever was, writing very graceful and natural verse even in an artificial and unnatural age.

SONG TO MAY.

May! queen of blossoms
   And fulfilling flowers,
With what pretty music
   Shall we charm the hours?
Wilt thou have pipe and reed
Blown in the open mead,
Or to the lute give heed
   In the green bowers?

Thou hast no need of us
   Or pipe or wire,
That hast the golden bee
   Ripened with fire;
And many thousand more
Songsters that thee adore,
Filling earth's grassy floor
   With new desire.

Thou hast thy mighty herds,
  Tame, and free livers;
Doubt not, thy music too
  In the deep rivers;
And the whole plumy flight,
Warbling the day and night—
Up at the gates of light,
  See, the lark quivers!

When with the jacinth
  Coy fountains are tressed;
And for the mournful bird
  Green woods are dressed,
That did for Tereus pine;
Then shall our songs be thine
To whom our hearts incline:
  May, be thou blessed!

CAPTAIN MORRIS.

(Date unknown.)

THIS Welsh wit was one of the gayest *bon vivants* of his time. There are traditions still existing of his carouses in Covent Garden taverns. His songs were for the most part objectionable, but those that were written by him in his capacity as a gentleman equal Tom Moore's verses for rythm, fire, and spontaneity. There is a tradition, that when the original of Thackeray's Costigan died, and was buried under the window at Offley's, Captain Morris read a disgraceful mock funeral service from the window above, and then poured a crown bowl of punch upon the grave of the poor clever vagabond who had so often been his boon companion.

A REASON FAIR TO FILL MY GLASS.

I've oft been asked by prosing souls
  And men of sober tongue,
What joys there are in draining bowls
  And tippling all night long?
But though these cautious knaves I scorn,
  For once I'll not disdain
To tell them why I drink till morn
  And fill my glass again.

'Tis by the glow my bumper gives
  Life's picture's mellow made;
The fading light then brightly lives,
  And softly sinks the shade:
Some happier tint still rises there
  With every drop I drain,
And that I think's a reason fair
  To fill my glass again.

My muse, too, when her wings are dry,
  No frolic flight will take,
But round the bowl she'll dip and fly
  Like swallows round a lake:

Then if the nymphs will have their share
　Before they'll bless their swain,
Why that I think's a reason fair
　To fill my glass again.

In life I've rung all changes through,
　Run every pleasure down,
'Mid each extreme of folly, too,
　And lived with half the town;
For me there's nothing new or rare
　Till wine deceives my brain,
And that I think's a reason fair
　To fill my glass again.

There's many a lad I knew is dead,
　And many a lass grown old,
And as the lesson strikes my head
　My weary heart grows cold;
But wine awhile drives off despair,
　Nay, bids a hope remain,
Why that I think's a reason fair
　To fill my glass again.

I find too when I stint my glass
　And sit with sober air,
I'm posed by some dull reasoning ass
　Who treads the path of care;
Or, harder still, am doomed to bear
　Some coxcomb's fribbling strain,
And that I'm sure's a reason fair
　To fill my glass again.

Though hipped and vexed at England's fate
　In these convulsive days,
I can't endure the ruined state
　My sober eye surveys;
But through the bottle's dazzling glare
　The gloom is seen less plain,
And that I think's a reason fair
　To fill my glass again.

THE TOWN AND THE COUNTRY.

In London I never know what to be at,
Enraptured with this, and enchanted with that;
I am wild with the sweets of Variety's plan,
And life seems a blessing too happy for man.

But the Country, Lord help me! sets all matters right,
So calm and composing from morning till night;
Oh! it settles the spirits, though nothing is seen,
But an ass on a common, or goose on a green!

In Town, if it rain, why it bars not our hope,
The eye has its range, and the fancy its scope;
Still the same, though it pour all night and all day,
It spoils not our prospects, it stops not our way.

In the Country, how blest when it rains in the fields
To feast on the transports which shuttlecock yields!
Or go crawling from window to window to see
A hog on a dunghill, or crow on a tree!

In London how easy we visit and meet,
Gay pleasure's the theme, and sweet smiles are our treat;
Our morning's a round of good humour, delight,
And we rattle in comfort to pleasure at night.

In the Country how charming your visits to make,
Through ten miles of mud, for formality's sake;
With the coachman quite drunk, and the moon in a fog,
And no thoughts in your head but a ditch or a bog.

In London, if folks ill together are put,
A beau may be dropped, or a quiz may be cut;
We change without end, and if happy or ill,
Our wants are at hand, and our wishes at will.

In the Country you're nailed like a pale in your park,
To some stick of a neighbour, as old as the ark;
And if you are sick, or in fits tumble down,
You meet Death ere the doctor can reach you from Town.

'Tis true, if in fishing you take much delight,
In a boat you may shiver from morning till night;
But though blessed with the patience which Job had of old,
The devil of a thing can you catch—but a cold!

Then how often you've screwed to your chairs fist to fist,
All stupidly yawning, o'er sixpenny whist;
And although you may lose, 'tis no less true than strange,
You have nothing to pay!—the good folks have no change.

I've oft heard that love in a cottage is sweet,
When two hearts in one link of soft sympathy meet;
I know not of that, for alas! I'm a swain,
Who require, I own it, more links to my chain.

Your jays and your magpies may chatter in trees,
And whisper soft nonsense in groves, if they please;
But a house is much more to my mind than a tree,
And for groves! oh, a sweet grove of chimnies for me!

Then in Town let me live, and in Town let me die,
For I own I can't relish the Country, not I.
If I must have a villa in summer to dwell,
Oh, give me the sweet shady side of Pall Mall!

SIR WALTER SCOTT.

1771—1832.

Scott had too great a grasp of invention, and was too intent on large canvasses, too fond of making money and buying land, to write many verses suitable to our purpose.

SONG IN QUENTIN DURWARD.

Ah! County Guy, the hour is nigh,
   The sun has left the lea,
The orange flower perfumes the bower,
   The breeze is on the sea.
The lark, his lay who thrilled all day,
   Sits hushed his partner nigh;
Breeze, bird, and flower confess the hour,
   But where is County Guy?

The village maid steals through the shade
   Her shepherd's suit to hear;
To beauty shy, by lattice high,
   Sings high-born Cavalier.
The star of Love, all stars above,
   Now reigns o'er earth and sky;
And high and low the influence know—
   But where is County Guy?

SERENADE FROM THE "PIRATE."

Farewell! Farewell! the voice you hear
   Has left its last soft tone with you,—
Its next must join the seaward cheer,
   And shout among the shouting crew.

The accents which I scarce could form
   Beneath your frown's controlling check,
Must give the word, above the storm,
   To cut the mast, and clear the wreck.

The timid eye I dared not raise,—
   The hand that shook when pressed to thine
Must point the guns upon the chase,—
   Must bid the deadly cutlass shine.

To all I love, or hope, or fear,—
Honour, or own, a long adieu!
To all that life has soft and dear,
Farewell! save memory of you!

SONG IN "WOODSTOCK."

An hour with thee!—When earliest day
Dapples with gold the eastern grey,
Oh, what can frame my mind to bear
The toil and turmoil, cark and care,
New griefs, which coming hours unfold,
And sad remembrance of the old?—
                      One hour with thee!

One hour with thee!—When burning June
Waves his red flag at pitch of noon;
What shall repay the faithful swain
His labour on the sultry plain;
And, more than cave or sheltering bough,
Cool feverish blood and throbbing brow?—
                      One hour with thee!

One hour with thee!—When sun is set,
Oh, what can teach me to forget
The thankless labours of the day;
The hopes, the wishes flung away;
The increasing wants and lessening gains,
The master's pride who scorns my pains?—
                      One hour with thee!

TO A LADY,

WITH FLOWERS FROM THE ROMAN WALL.

Take these flowers which, purple waving,
   On the ruined rampart grew,
Where, the sons of freedom braving,
   Rome's imperial standards flew.

Warriors from the breach of danger
   Pluck no longer laurels there;
They but yield the passing stranger
   Wild-flower wreaths for Beauty's hair.

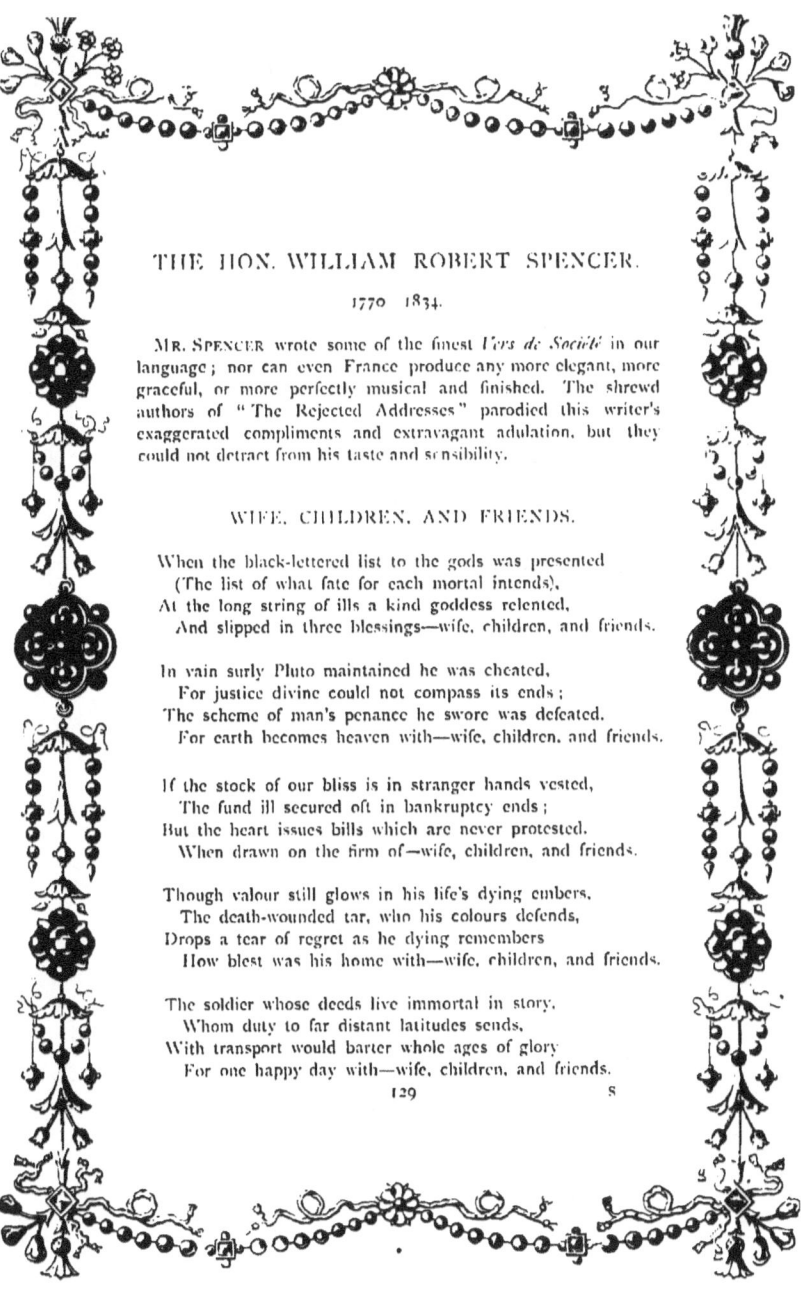

THE HON. WILLIAM ROBERT SPENCER.

1770 1834.

MR. SPENCER wrote some of the finest *Vers de Société* in our language; nor can even France produce any more elegant, more graceful, or more perfectly musical and finished. The shrewd authors of "The Rejected Addresses" parodied this writer's exaggerated compliments and extravagant adulation, but they could not detract from his taste and sensibility.

WIFE, CHILDREN, AND FRIENDS.

When the black-lettered list to the gods was presented
    (The list of what fate for each mortal intends),
At the long string of ills a kind goddess relented,
    And slipped in three blessings—wife, children, and friends.

In vain surly Pluto maintained he was cheated,
    For justice divine could not compass its ends;
The scheme of man's penance he swore was defeated,
    For earth becomes heaven with—wife, children, and friends.

If the stock of our bliss is in stranger hands vested,
    The fund ill secured oft in bankruptcy ends;
But the heart issues bills which are never protested,
    When drawn on the firm of—wife, children, and friends.

Though valour still glows in his life's dying embers,
    The death-wounded tar, who his colours defends,
Drops a tear of regret as he dying remembers
    How blest was his home with—wife, children, and friends.

The soldier whose deeds live immortal in story,
    Whom duty to far distant latitudes sends,
With transport would barter whole ages of glory
    For one happy day with—wife, children, and friends.

Though spice-breathing gales on his caravan hover,
  Though for him Arabia's fragrance ascends,
The merchant still thinks of the woodbines that cover
  The bower where he sat with—wife, children, and friends.

The dayspring of youth still unclouded by sorrow
  Alone on itself for enjoyment depends;
But drear is the twilight of age if it borrow
  No warmth from the smile of—wife, children, and friends.

Let the breath of renown ever freshen and nourish
  The laurel which o'er the dead favourite bends;
O'er me wave the willow, and long may it flourish,
  Bedewed with the tears of—wife, children, and friends.

Let us drink, for my song, growing graver and graver,
  To subjects too solemn insensibly tends;
Let us drink, pledge me high, love and virtue shall flavour
  The glass which I fill to—wife, children, and friends.

TO LADY ANNE HAMILTON.

Too late I stayed—forgive the crime;
  Unheeded flew the hours;
How noiseless falls the foot of Time
  That only treads on flowers!

What eye with clear account remarks
  The ebbing of the glass,
When all its sands are diamond-sparks
  That dazzle as they pass?

Oh! who to sober measurement
  Time's happy swiftness brings,
When birds of Paradise have lent
  Their plumage for his wings?

SAMUEL TAYLOR COLERIDGE.

1772—1834.

COLERIDGE was like Michael Angelo in this, that his greatest works were but torsos. His life passed in glorious dreams, in planning the title-pages of future books, and in trying to build up a system of philosophy on the mud shoals of German theory. With such powers, how can we ever enough lament that Coleridge wrote so little!

LOVE.

All thoughts, all passions, all delights,
Whatever stirs this mortal frame,
All are but ministers of Love,
And feed his sacred flame.

Oft in my waking dreams do I
Live o'er again that happy hour,
When midway on the mount I lay
Beside the ruined tower.

The moonshine stealing o'er the scene
Had blended with the lights of eve;
And she was there, my hope, my joy,
My own dear Genevieve:

She leaned against the armèd man,
The statue of the armèd knight;
She stood and listened to my lay,
Amid the lingering light.

Few sorrows hath she of her own,
My hope! my joy! my Genevieve!
She loves me best, whene'er I sing
    The songs that make her grieve.

I played a soft and doleful air,
I sang an old and moving story—
An old rude song, that suited well
    That ruin wild and hoary.

She listened with a flitting blush,
With downcast eyes and modest grace;
For well she knew, I could not choose
    But gaze upon her face.

I told her of the Knight that wore
Upon his shield a burning brand;
And that for ten long years he wooed
    The Lady of the Land.

I told her how he pined: and ah!
The deep, the low, the pleading tone
With which I sang another's love
    Interpreted my own.

She listened with a flitting blush,
With downcast eyes and modest grace;
And she forgave me, that I gazed
    Too fondly on her face.

But when I told the cruel scorn
That crazed that bold and lovely Knight,
And that he crossed the mountain-woods,
    Nor rested day nor night;

That sometimes from the savage den,
And sometimes from the darksome shade,
And sometimes starting up at once
    In green and sunny glade,

There came and looked him in the face
An angel beautiful and bright;
And that he knew it was a fiend,
    This miserable Knight!

And that, unknowing what he did,
He leaped amid a murderous band,
And saved from outrage worse than death
    The Lady of the Land;

And how she wept, and clasped his knees;
And how she tended him in vain;
And ever strove to expiate
    The scorn that crazed his brain;

And that she nursed him in a cave,
And how his madness went away,
When on the yellow forest leaves
    A dying man he lay;

—His dying words—but when I reached
That tenderest strain of all the ditty,
My faltering voice and pausing harp
    Disturbed her soul with pity!

All impulses of soul and sense
Had thrilled my guileless Genevieve;
The music and the doleful tale,
    The rich and balmy eve;

And hopes, and fears that kindle hope,
An undistinguishable throng,
And gentle wishes long subdued,
    Subdued and cherished long!

She wept with pity and delight,
She blushed with love and virgin shame;
And like the murmur of a dream,
    I heard her breathe my name.

Her bosom heaved—she stept aside,
As conscious of my look she stept—
Then suddenly, with timorous eye,
    She fled to me and wept.

She half enclosed me with her arms,
She pressed me with her meek embrace;
And, bending back her head, looked up,
    And gazed upon my face.

'Twas partly love, and partly fear,
And partly 'twas a bashful art
That I might rather feel than see
    The swelling of her heart.

I calmed her fears, and she was calm,
And told her love with virgin pride;
And so I won my Genevieve,
    My bright and beauteous Bride!

INSCRIPTION

FOR A FOUNTAIN ON A HEATH.

This Sycamore, oft musical with bees,—
Such tents the Patriarchs loved! O long unharmed
May all its aged boughs o'er-canopy
The small round basin, which this jutting stone
Keeps pure from falling leaves! Long may the Spring,
Quietly as a sleeping infant's breath,
Send up cold waters to the traveller
With soft and even pulse! Nor ever cease
Yon tiny cone of sand its soundless dance,
Which at the bottom, like a Fairy's page,
As merry and no taller, dances still,
Nor wrinkles the smooth surface of the Fount.
Here twilight is, and coolness: here is moss,
A soft seat, and a deep and ample shade.
Thou may'st toil far and find no second tree.
Drink, Pilgrim, here! Here rest! and if thy heart
Be innocent, here too shalt thou refresh
Thy spirit, listening to some gentle sound,
Or passing gale or hum of murmuring bees!

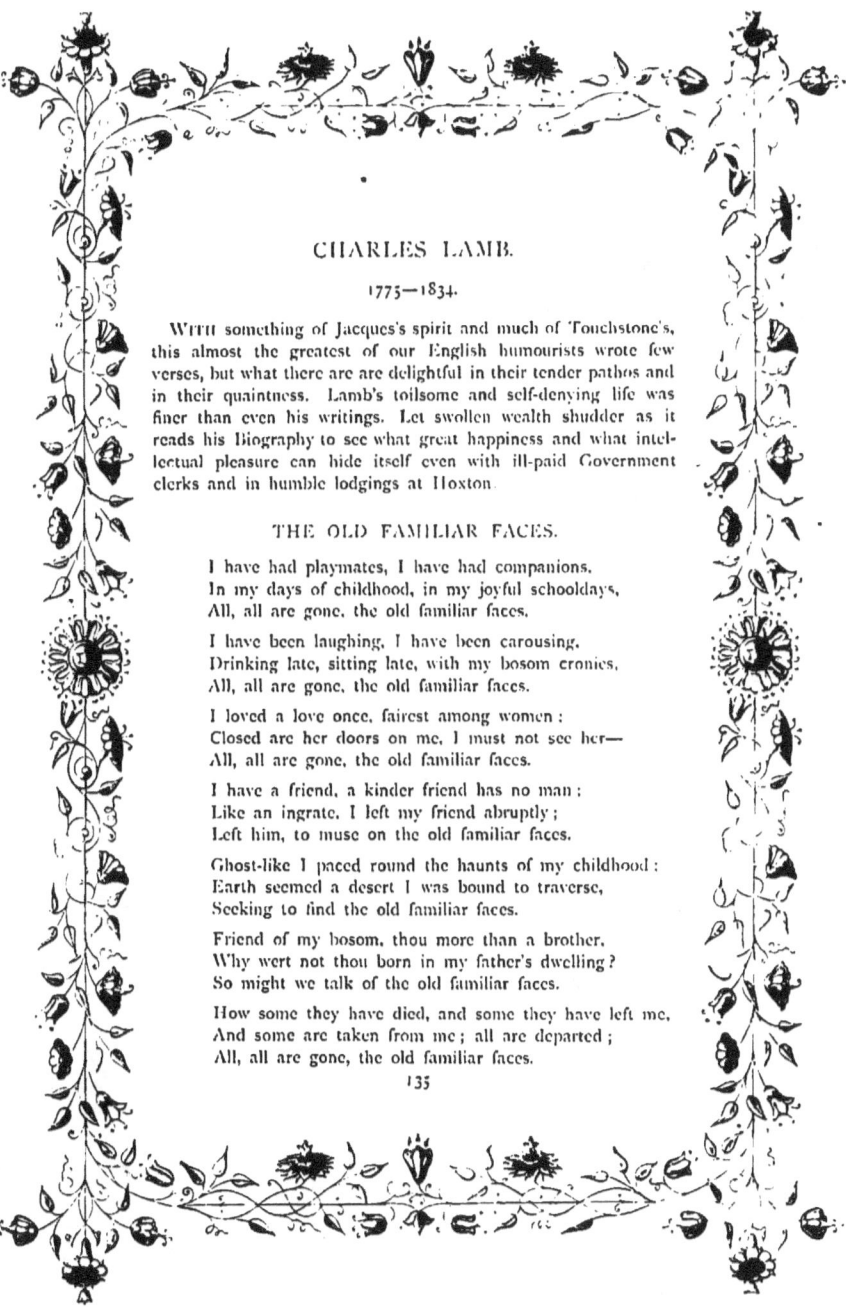

CHARLES LAMB.

1775—1834.

WITH something of Jacques's spirit and much of Touchstone's, this almost the greatest of our English humourists wrote few verses, but what there are are delightful in their tender pathos and in their quaintness. Lamb's toilsome and self-denying life was finer than even his writings. Let swollen wealth shudder as it reads his Biography to see what great happiness and what intellectual pleasure can hide itself even with ill-paid Government clerks and in humble lodgings at Hoxton.

THE OLD FAMILIAR FACES.

I have had playmates, I have had companions,
In my days of childhood, in my joyful schooldays,
All, all are gone, the old familiar faces.

I have been laughing, I have been carousing,
Drinking late, sitting late, with my bosom cronies,
All, all are gone, the old familiar faces.

I loved a love once, fairest among women;
Closed are her doors on me, I must not see her—
All, all are gone, the old familiar faces.

I have a friend, a kinder friend has no man;
Like an ingrate, I left my friend abruptly;
Left him, to muse on the old familiar faces.

Ghost-like I paced round the haunts of my childhood;
Earth seemed a desert I was bound to traverse,
Seeking to find the old familiar faces.

Friend of my bosom, thou more than a brother,
Why wert not thou born in my father's dwelling?
So might we talk of the old familiar faces.

How some they have died, and some they have left me,
And some are taken from me; all are departed;
All, all are gone, the old familiar faces.

HESTER.*

When maidens such as Hester die
Their place ye may not well supply.
Though ye among a thousand try
    With vain endeavour.

A month or more hath she been dead,
Yet cannot I by force be led
To think upon the wormy bed
    And her together.

A springy motion in her gait,
A rising step, did indicate
Of pride and joy no common rate
    That flushed her spirit.

I know not by what name beside
I shall it call:—if 'twas not pride.
It was a joy to that allied
    She did inherit.

Her parents held the Quaker rule
Which doth the human feeling cool;
But she was trained in Nature's school,
    Nature had blest her.

A waking eye, a prying mind,
A heart that stirs, is hard to bind ;
A hawk's keen sight ye cannot blind,
    Ye could not Hester.

My sprightly neighbour! gone before
To that unknown and silent shore,
Shall we not meet, as heretofore,
    Some summer morning—

When from thy cheerful eyes a ray
Hath struck a bliss upon the day
A bliss that would not go away,
    A sweet fore-warning?

JAMES HOGG.

1772—1835.

THIS kind, thoughtless man began life as a cowherd till the inspiration came upon him, and he rose into the cloudland of song. His "Kilmeny" is one of the most beautiful dreams of Fairyland ever penned by poet, and some of his songs are truly beautiful.

THE SKYLARK.

Bird of the wilderness,
Blithesome and cumberless,
Sweet be thy matin o'er moorland and lea!
Emblem of happiness,
Blest is thy dwelling-place,
O to abide in the desert with thee!

Wild is thy lay and loud,
Far in the downy cloud,
Love gives it energy, love gave it birth.
Where on thy dewy wing,
Where art thou journeying?
Thy lay is in heaven, thy love is on earth.

O'er fell and fountain sheen,
O'er moor and mountain green,
O'er the red streamer that heralds the day,
Over the cloudlet dim,
Over the rainbow's rim,
Musical cherub, soar, singing, away!

Then, when the gloaming comes,
Low in the heather blooms
Sweet will thy welcome and bed of love be!
Emblem of happiness,
Blest is thy dwelling-place,
O to abide in the desert with thee!

WHEN THE KYE COMES HAME.

Come all ye jolly shepherds
    That whistle through the glen,
I'll tell ye of a secret
    That courtiers dinna ken;
What is the greatest bliss
    That the tongue o' man can name?
'Tis to woo a bonny lassie
    When the kye comes hame.

Chorus.

When the kye comes hame,
    When the kye comes hame,
'Tween the gloamin' and the mirk,
    When the kye comes hame.

'Tis not beneath the coronet,
    Nor canopy of state,
'Tis not on couch of velvet,
    Nor arbour of the great—
'Tis beneath the spreading birk
    In the glen without the name,
Wi' a bonny, bonny lassie,
    When the kye comes hame.

There the blackbird bigs his nest
    For the mate he lo'es to see,
And on the topmost bough,
    O, a happy bird is he!
Then he pours his melting ditty,
    And love is a' the theme;
And he'll woo his bonny lassie
    When the kye comes hame.

When the blewart bears a pearl,
    And the daisy turns a pea,
And the bonny luckan gowan
    Has fauldit up her e'e,

Then the laverock frae the blue lift
Draps down, and thinks nae shame
To woo his bonny lassie
　When the kye comes hame.

See yonder pawky shepherd
　That lingers on the hill,
His yowes are in the fauld,
　And his lambs are lying still;
Yet he downa gang to bed,
　For his heart is in a flame
To meet his bonny lassie
　When the kye comes hame.

When the little wee bit heart
　Rises high in the breast,
And the little wee bit starn
　Rises red in the east,
O there's a joy sae dear
　That the heart can hardly frame,
Wi' a bonny, bonny lassie,
　When the kye comes hame.

Then since all nature joins
　In this love without alloy,
O, wha wad prove a traitor
　To nature's dearest joy?
O wha wad choose a crown
　Wi' its perils and its fame,
And miss his bonny lassie
　When the kye comes hame.

　　When the kye comes hame,
　　　When the kye comes hame,
　　'Tween the gloamin' and the mirk,
　　　When the kye comes hame.

FELICIA D. HEMANS.

1793—1835.

This amiable poetess wrote much agreeable verse, always pervaded by tenderness of feeling, and a pure religious sentiment, however wanting in condensation and vigour.

TO MY OWN PORTRAIT.

How is it that before mine eyes,
    While gazing on thy mien,
All my past years of life arise,
    As in a mirror seen?
What spell within thee hath been shrined,
To image back my own deep mind?

Even as a song of other times
    Can trouble memory's springs;
Even as a sound of vesper-chimes
    Can wake departed things;
Even as a scent of vernal flowers
Hath records fraught with vanished hours:—

Such power is thine!—they come, the dead,
   From the grave's bondage free,
And smiling back the changed are led
   To look in love on thee;
And voices that are music flown
Speak to me in the heart's full tone:

Till crowding thoughts my soul oppress—
   The thoughts of happier years,
And a vain gush of tenderness
   O'erflows in child-like tears;
A passion which I may not stay,
A sudden fount that must have way.

But thou, the while—oh! almost strange,
   Mine imaged self! it seems
That on *thy* brow of peace no change
   Reflects my own swift dreams;
Almost I marvel not to trace
Those lights and shadows in *thy* face.

To see *thee* calm, while powers thus deep,—
   Affection—memory—grief—
Pass o'er my soul as winds that sweep
   O'er a frail aspen-leaf!
O that the quiet of thine eye
Might sink there when the storm goes by!

Yet look thou still serenely on,
   And if sweet friends there be
That when my song and soul are gone
   Shall seek my form in thee,—
Tell them of one for whom 'twas best
To flee away and be at rest!

GEORGE COLMAN, JUNIOR.

1762–1836.

COLMAN was eminent as a writer of comedies, a *bon vivant*, and a wit. Sheridan was his friend, and George IV. his boon companion. One good action of that king (some say the only one) was to rescue Colman from difficulties, and appoint him dramatic censor. The man without principles henceforward became impatient of patriotism, and the ribald talker erased the slightest adjuration with a Pharisaical shudder.

LODGINGS FOR SINGLE GENTLEMEN.

Who has e'er been in London, that overgrown place,
Has seen ' Lodgings to let' stare him full in the face ;
Some are good and let dearly ; while some, 'tis well known,
Are so dear, and so bad, they are best let alone.

Will Waddle, whose temper was studious and lonely,
Hired lodgings that took single gentlemen only ;
But Will was so fat he appeared like a tun,
Or like two single gentlemen rolled into one.

He entered his rooms, and to bed he retreated,
But all the night long he felt fever'd and heated ;
And, though heavy to weigh as a score of fat sheep,
He was not by any means heavy to sleep.

Next night 'twas the same ; and the next, and the next ;
He perspired like an ox ; he was nervous and vexed ;
Week passed after week, till by weekly succession
His weakly condition was past all expression.

In six months his acquaintance began much to doubt him,
For his skin "like a lady's loose gown" hung about him.
He sent for a doctor, and cried like a ninny,
" I have lost many pounds—make me well—there's a guinea."

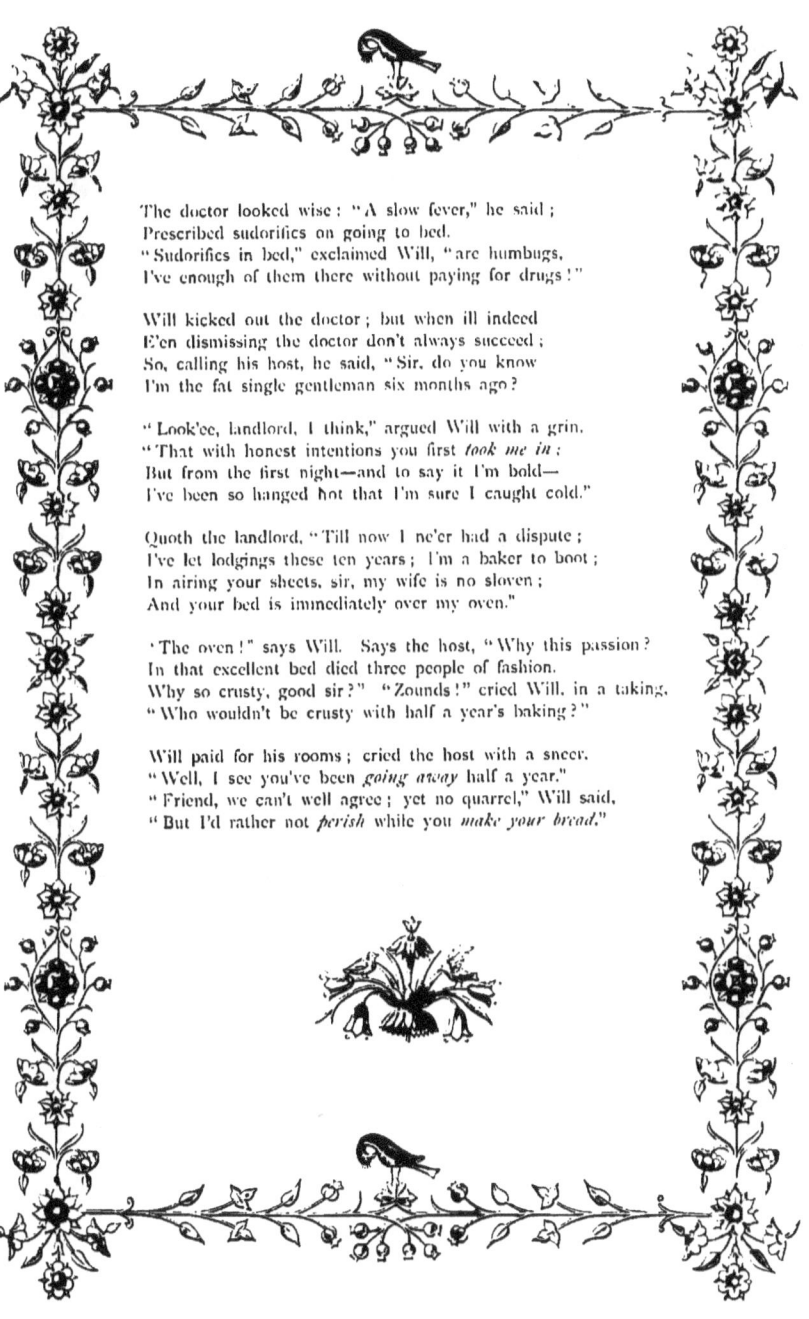

The doctor looked wise: "A slow fever," he said;
Prescribed sudorifics on going to bed.
"Sudorifics in bed," exclaimed Will, "are humbugs,
I've enough of them there without paying for drugs!"

Will kicked out the doctor; but when ill indeed
E'en dismissing the doctor don't always succeed;
So, calling his host, he said, "Sir, do you know
I'm the fat single gentleman six months ago?

"Look'ee, landlord, I think," argued Will with a grin,
"That with honest intentions you first *took me in*;
But from the first night—and to say it I'm bold—
I've been so hanged hot that I'm sure I caught cold."

Quoth the landlord, "Till now I ne'er had a dispute;
I've let lodgings these ten years; I'm a baker to boot;
In airing your sheets, sir, my wife is no sloven;
And your bed is immediately over my oven."

"The oven!" says Will. Says the host, "Why this passion?
In that excellent bed died three people of fashion.
Why so crusty, good sir?" "Zounds!" cried Will, in a taking,
"Who wouldn't be crusty with half a year's baking?"

Will paid for his rooms; cried the host with a sneer,
"Well, I see you've been *going away* half a year."
"Friend, we can't well agree; yet no quarrel," Will said,
"But I'd rather not *perish* while you *make your bread*."

LETITIA LANDON.

1802—1838.

L. E. L. whose unhappy death secured for her a fame that otherwise her poetry might not have obtained, was a woman of quick sensibilities, impulsive and imprudent. At a time when Byron's influence still prevailed she wrote poems which are more remarkable for sentiment than imagination.

SONG.

Oh never another dream can be
   Like that early dream of ours,
When the fairy Hope lay down to sleep,
   Like a child, among the flowers.

But Hope has wakened since, and wept,
   Like a rainbow, itself away;
And the flowers have faded and fallen around—
   We have none for a wreath to-day.

Now wisdom wakes in the place of hope,
   And our hearts are like winter hours:
Ah! after-life has been little worth
   That early dream of ours.

JAMES SMITH.

1775—1839.

THE two Smiths were sons of a solicitor to the Board of Ordnance. James Smith was the perfection of a diner-out; as a club wit he had no rival; and of all the parodies of the world there are few to equal or even to compare with the "Rejected Addresses." James Smith wrote the greater part of the Entertainments for Charles Matthews the elder.

BRIGHTON.

(Solvitur acris hyems grata vice veris.)

Now fruitful Autumn lifts his sun-burnt head,
   The slighted Park few cambric muslins whiten,
The dry machines revisit Ocean's bed,
   And Horace quits awhile the town for Brighton.

The cit foregoes his box at Turnham Green,
   To pick up health and shells with Amphitrite.
Pleasure's fair daughters trip along the Steyne,
   Led by the dame the Greeks call Aphrodite.

Phœbus, the tanner, plies his fiery trade;
   The graceful nymphs ascend Judea's ponies.
Scale the West Cliff, or visit the Parade,
   While poor papa in town a patient drone is.

Loose trousers snatch the wreath from pantaloons;
   Nankeen of late were worn the sultry weather in;
But now (so will the Prince's Light Dragoons)
   White jean have triumphed o'er their Indian brethren.

Here with choice food earth smiles and ocean yawns,
   Intent alike to please the London glutton,
This, for our breakfast proffers shrimps and prawns,
   That, for our dinner Southdown lamb and mutton.

Yet here, as elsewhere, Death impartial reigns.
  Visits alike the cot and the Pavilion,
And for a bribe, with equal scorn disdains
  My half a crown, and Baring's half a million.

Alas! how short the span of human pride!
  Time flies, and hope's romantic schemes are undone;
Cosweller's coach, that carries four inside,
  Waits to take back th' unwilling bard to London.

Ye circulating novelists, adieu!
  Long envious cords my black portmanteau tighten;
Billiards, begone! avaunt, illegal loo!
  Farewell, old Ocean's bauble, glittering Brighton!

Long shalt thou laugh thine enemies to scorn,
  Proud as Phœnicia, queen of watering places!
Boys yet unbreeched and virgins yet unborn
  On thy bleak downs shall tan their blooming faces.

CHIGWELL:
OR, "PRÆTERITOS ANNOS."

School, that in Burford's honoured time
Reared me to youth's elastic prime
    From childhood's airy slumbers—
School, at whose antique shrine I bow,
Sexagenarian pilgrim now,
    Accept a poet's numbers.

Those yew-trees never seem to grow:
The village stands *in statu quo*,
    Without a single new house;
But, heavens! how shrunk! how very small!
'Tis a mere step from Urmstone's wall,
    "Up town," to Morgan's brewhouse.

There in yon rough-cast mansion dwelt
Sage Denham, Galen's son, who dealt
    In squills and cream of tartar;
Fronting the room where now I dine
Beneath thy undulating sign,
    Peak-bearded Charles the Martyr!

Pent in by beams of mouldering wood
The parish stocks stand where they stood—
   Did ever drunkard rue 'em?
I dive not in parochial law,
Yet this I know I never saw
   Two legs protruded through 'em.

Here, to the right, rose hissing proofs
Of skill to solder horses' hoofs,
   Formed in the forge of Radley;
And there, the almshouses beyond,
Half-way before you gain the Pond,
   Lived wry-mouthed Martin Hadley.

Does Philby still exist? Where now
Are Willis, Wilcox, Green, and Howe?
   Ann Wright, the smart and handy?
Hillman alone a respite steals
From Fate; and *vice* Hadley deals
   In tea and sugar-candy.

Can I my school-friend Belson track?
Where hides him Chamberlaine? where Black,
   Intended for the altar?
Does life-blood circulate in Bates?
Where are Jack Cumberlege and Yates?
   The Burrells, Charles and Walter?

There, at your ink-bespattered shrine,
Cornelius Nepos first was mine;
   Here fagged I hard at Plutarch:
Found Ovid's mighty pleasant ways,
While Plato's metaphysic maze
   Appeared like Pluto—too dark.

Here usher Ireland sat—and there
Stood Bolton, Cowel, Parker, Ware,
   Medley the pert and witty;
And here—crack station, near the fire—
Sat Roberts, whose Haymarket sire
   Sold oil and spermaceti.

Yon pew the gallery below
Held Nancy, pride of Chigwell Row,
   Who set all hearts a-dancing:
In bonnet white, divine brunette,
O'er Burnet's field I see thee yet
   To Sunday church advancing.

Seek we the churchyard; there the yew
Shades many a swain whom once I knew,
   Now nameless and forgotten;
Here towers Sir Edward's marble bier,
Here lies stern Vickery, and here,
   My father's friend, Tom Cotton.

The common herd serenely sleep,
Turf-bound, "in many a mouldering heap"
   Pent in by bands of osier;
While at the altar's feet is laid
The founder of the school, arrayed
   In mitre and in crosier.

'Tis nature's law: wave urges wave:
The coffined grandsire seeks the grave;
   The babe that feeds by suction
Finds with his ancestor repose:
Life ebbs, and dissolution sows
   The seeds of reproduction.

World, in thy ever-busy mart
I've acted no unnoticed part—
   Would I resume it? oh no!
Four acts are done, the jest grows stale;
The waning lamps burn dim and pale,
   And reason asks—*Cui bono?*

I've met with no "affliction sore;"
But hold! methinks, "long time I *bore;*"
   Here ends my lucubration—
Content, with David's son, to know
That all is vanity below,
   Though not quite all vexation.

WINTHROP MACKWORTH PRAED.

1802—1839.

At Eton Praed distinguished himself by his share in a Magazine to which Macaulay and Moultrie both contributed. In later years, when he became the delight of the society which he adorned, he still continued to write highly polished and skilful verse, full of subtle and delicate observation, and pleasant refined humour. Such poems as the "Vicar" and "Quince" are like the cabinet pictures of Metzu or Terburg, with an infusion of the courtliness of Vandyke and the humour of Wilkie. The perfumed air of the drawing-room steals round us while we read. It was Praed who first raised the Charade to the rank of a poem. It was perhaps a waste of time and a misplacing of talent. It was like jewelling an étui or a knee-buckle; but Praed delighted to please and amuse those among whom he lived, and he has obtained a fame which he did not seek, and which he did not expect. His "Vicar," certainly his *chef d'œuvre*, is finished with the care of an inlaid Indian box.

CHARADE,

ON THE POET CAMPBELL.

Come from my First, ay, come!
 The battle dawn is nigh;
And the screaming trump and the thundering drum
 Are calling thee to die!
 Fight as thy father fought,
 Fall as thy father fell,
Thy task is taught, thy shroud is wrought;
 So forward! and farewell!

Toll ye my Second, toll!
Fling high the flambeau's light!
And sing the hymn for a parted soul,
Beneath the silent night!
The wreath upon his head,
The cross upon his breast,
Let the prayer be said, and the tear be shed:
So take him to his rest!

Call ye my Whole, ay, call!
The lord of lute and lay;
And let him greet the sable pall
With a noble song to-day;
Go, call him by his name;
No fitter hand may crave
To light the flame of a soldier's fame
On the turf of a soldier's grave.

In certain moods Praed's verses resemble Hood's; they may not have the depth and tenderness of Hood, but they have the same whimsical surprises, and the same startling, sparkling play of words. How light, graceful, and fluent the following verses run, on springs as elastic as those of a West End barouche!—

THE VICAR.

Some years ago, ere Time and Taste
Had turned our parish topsy-turvy,
When Darnel Park was Darnel Waste,
And roads as little known as scurvy,
The man who lost his way between
Saint Mary's Hill and Sandy Thicket
Was always shown across the green,
And guided to the Parson's wicket.

Back flew the bolt, of lissom lath;
Fair Margaret in her tidy kirtle
Led the lorn traveller up the path,
Through clean-clipt rows of box and myrtle;

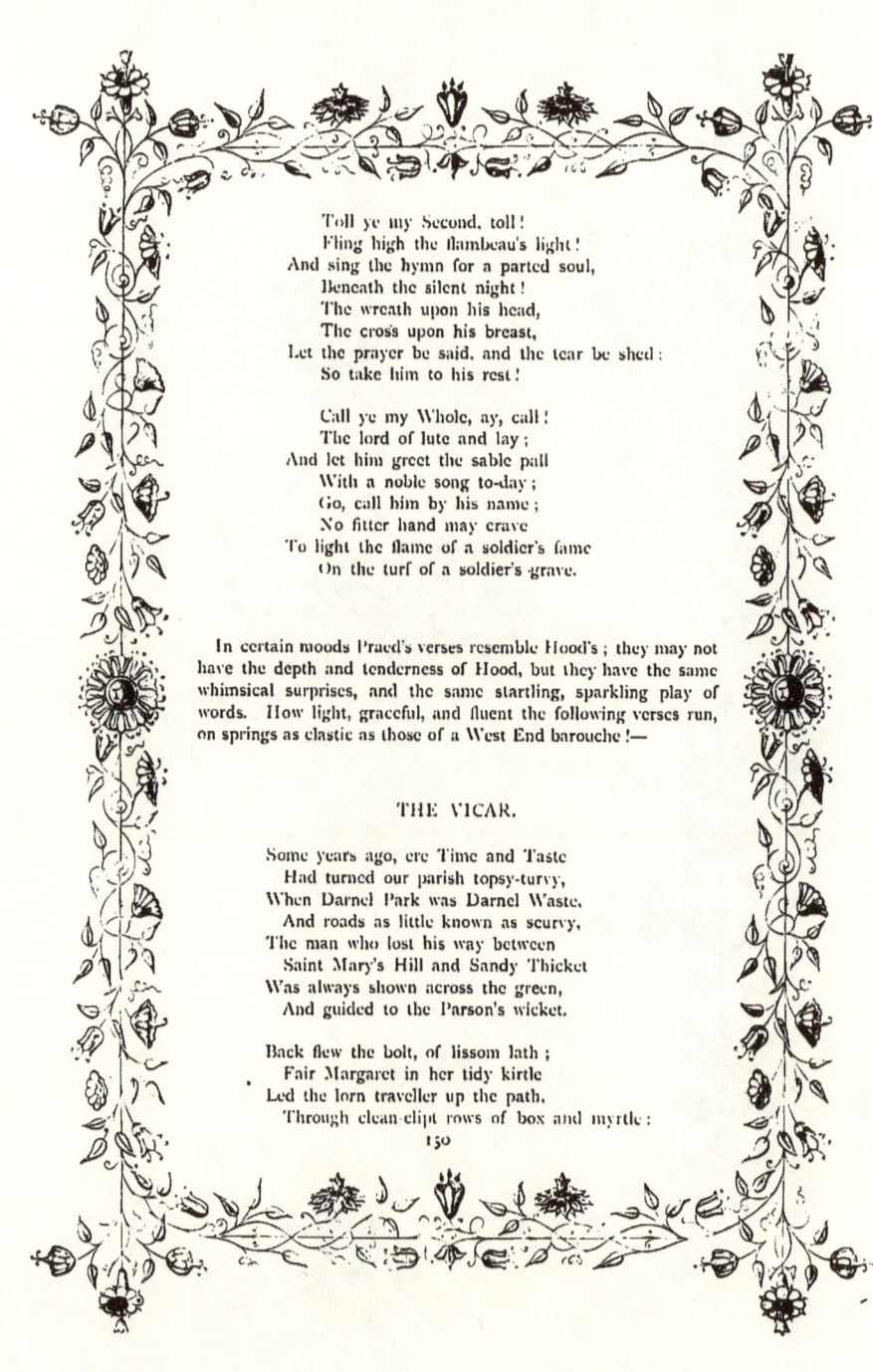

And Don and Sancho, Tramp and Tray,
  Upon the parlour steps collected,
Wagged all their tails, and seemed to say,
  "Our master knows you; you're expected!"

Uprose the Reverend Dr. Brown,
  Uprose the Doctor's "winsome marrow;"
The lady laid her knitting down,
  Her husband clasped his ponderous Barrow;
Whate'er the stranger's caste or creed,
  Pundit or papist, saint or sinner,
He found a stable for his steed,
  And welcome for himself, and dinner.

If, when he reached his journey's end,
  And warmed himself in court or college,
He had not gained an honest friend,
  And twenty curious scraps of knowledge;—
If he departed as he came,
  With no new light on love or liquor:—
Good sooth, the traveller was to blame,
  And not the Vicarage or the Vicar.

His talk was like a stream which runs
  With rapid change from rock to roses:
It slipped from politics to puns:
  It passed from Mahomet to Moses:
Beginning with the laws which keep
  The planets in their radiant courses,
And ending with some precept deep,
  For dressing eels or shoeing horses.

He wrote, too, in a quiet way
  Small treatises and smaller verses;
And sage remarks on chalk and clay,
  And hints to noble lords and nurses;
True histories of last year's ghost,
  Lines to a ringlet or a turban,
And trifles for the *Morning Post*,
  And nothings for Sylvanus Urban.

He did not think all mischief fair,
  Although he had a knack of joking:

He did not make himself a bear;
   Although he had a taste for smoking;
And when religious sects ran mad,
   He held, in spite of all his learning,
That, if a man's belief is bad,
   It will not be improved by burning.

And he was kind, and loved to sit
   In the low hut or garnished cottage,
And praise the farmer's homely wit,
   And share the widow's homelier pottage:
At his approach complaint grew mild,
   And when his hand unbarred the shutter,
The clammy lips of fever smiled
   The welcome which they could not utter.

He always had a tale for me
   Of Julius Cæsar or of Venus;
From him I learned the rule of three,
   Cat's cradle, leap-frog, and *quæ genus;*
I used to singe his powdered wig,
   To steal the staff he put such trust in;
And make the puppy-dance a jig
   When he began to quote Augustine.

Alack the change! in vain I look
   For haunts in which my boyhood trifled;
The level lawn, the trickling brook,
   The trees I climbed, the beds I rifled:
The church is larger than before;
   You reach it by a carriage entry:
It holds three hundred people more;
   And pews are fitted up for gentry.

Sit in the Vicar's seat, you'll hear
   The doctrine of a gentle Johnian,
Whose hand is white, whose tone is clear
   Where phrase is very Ciceronian.
Where is the old man laid?—look down,
   And construe on the slab before you,
Hic jacet GULIELMUS BROWN,
   Vir nullâ non Donandus Lauru.

One of his pleasantest little poems on his schoolfellows (for
Praed never forgot Eton) is the following: —

SCHOOL AND SCHOOLFELLOWS.

    Twelve years ago I made a mock
      Of filthy trades and traffics;
    I wondered what they meant by "stock;"
      I wrote delightful sapphics;
    I knew the streets of Rome and Troy;
      I supped with Fates and Furies;
    Twelve years ago I was a boy,
      A happy boy, at Drury's.

    Twelve years ago!—how many a thought
      Of faded pains and pleasures,
    Those whispered syllables have brought
      From memory's hoarded treasures!
    The fields, the forms, the beasts, the books,
      The glories and disgraces,
    The voices of dear friends, the looks
      Of old familiar faces.

    Now stopping Harry Vernon's ball
      That rattled, like a rocket;
    Now hearing Wentworth's "fourteen all!"
      And striking for the pocket;
    Now feasting on a cheese and flitch,—
      Now drinking from the pewter;
    Now leaping over Chalvey Ditch,
      Now laughing at my tutor.

    Where are my friends?—I am alone,
      No playmate shares my beaker—
    Some lie beneath the church-yard stone,
      And some before the Speaker;
    And some compose a tragedy,
      And some compose a rondo;
    And some draw sword for liberty,
      And some draw pleas for John Doe.

Tom Mill was used to blacken eyes,
  Without the fear of sessions;
Charles Medler loathed false quantities
  As much as false professions;
Now Mill keeps order in the land,
  A magistrate pedantic;
And Medler's feet repose unscanned
  Beneath the wide Atlantic.

Wild Nick, whose oaths made such a din,
  Does Dr. Martext's duty;
And Mullion, with that monstrous chin,
  Is married to a beauty;
And Darrel studies, week by week,
  His Mant, and not his Manton;
And Ball, who was but poor at Greek,
  Is very rich at Canton.

And I am eight-and-twenty now—
  The world's cold chain has bound me;
And darker shades are on my brow—
  And sadder scenes around me:
In Parliament I fill my seat
  With many other noodles;
And lay my head in Jermyn Street,
  And sip my hock at Boodle's.

But often when the cares of life
  Have set my temples aching,
When visions haunt me of a wife,
  When duns await my waking,
When Lady Jane is in a pet,
  Or Hoby in a hurry,
When Captain Hazard wins a bet,
  Or Beaulieu spoils a curry;

For hours and hours I think and talk
  Of each remember'd hobby;
I long to lounge in Poet's Walk—
  To shiver in the Lobby;

I wish that I could run away
 From House and Court and Levée,
Where bearded men appear to-day,
 Just Eton boys grown heavy :

That I could bask in childhood's sun,
 And dance o'er childhood's roses ;
And find huge wealth in one pound one,
 Vast wit in broken noses ;
And play Sir Giles at Datchet Lane,
 And call the milk-maids Houris ;
That I could be a boy again,
 A happy boy, at Drury's !

There is no great profundity of thought in these verses ; but how exquisitely the lines are turned ! and with delicate art the Drawing room Poet hides his real feeling under a mask of playfulness.

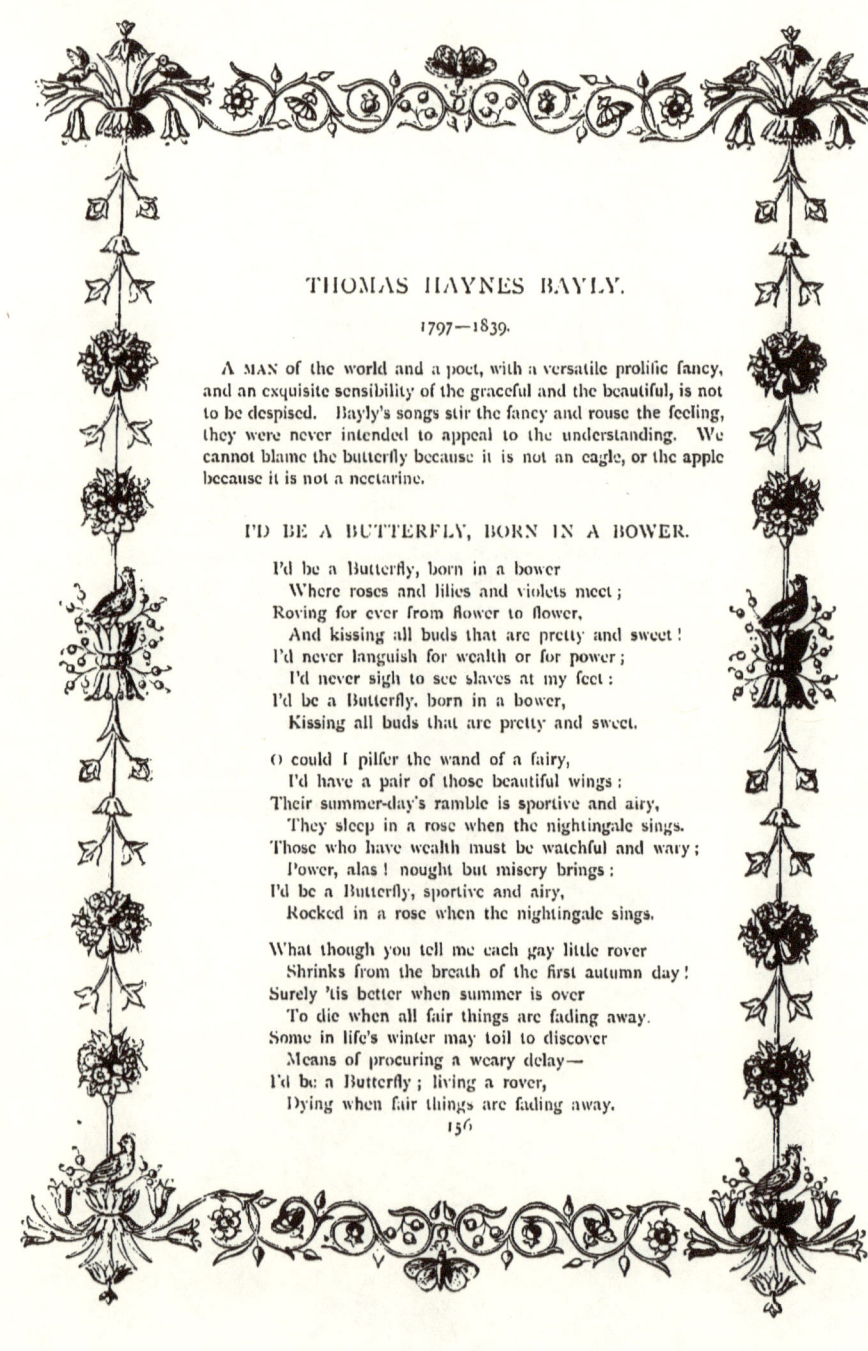

THOMAS HAYNES BAYLY.

1797—1839.

A MAN of the world and a poet, with a versatile prolific fancy, and an exquisite sensibility of the graceful and the beautiful, is not to be despised. Bayly's songs stir the fancy and rouse the feeling, they were never intended to appeal to the understanding. We cannot blame the butterfly because it is not an eagle, or the apple because it is not a nectarine.

I'D BE A BUTTERFLY, BORN IN A BOWER.

I'd be a Butterfly, born in a bower
    Where roses and lilies and violets meet;
Roving for ever from flower to flower,
    And kissing all buds that are pretty and sweet!
I'd never languish for wealth or for power;
    I'd never sigh to see slaves at my feet:
I'd be a Butterfly, born in a bower,
    Kissing all buds that are pretty and sweet.

O could I pilfer the wand of a fairy,
    I'd have a pair of those beautiful wings:
Their summer-day's ramble is sportive and airy,
    They sleep in a rose when the nightingale sings.
Those who have wealth must be watchful and wary;
    Power, alas! nought but misery brings:
I'd be a Butterfly, sportive and airy,
    Rocked in a rose when the nightingale sings.

What though you tell me each gay little rover
    Shrinks from the breath of the first autumn day!
Surely 'tis better when summer is over
    To die when all fair things are fading away.
Some in life's winter may toil to discover
    Means of procuring a weary delay—
I'd be a Butterfly; living a rover,
    Dying when fair things are fading away.

THE OLD BACHELOR.

When I was a schoolboy, aged ten,
   Oh, mighty little Greek I knew;
With my short striped trousers, and now and then
   With stripes upon my jacket too!
When I saw other boys to the playground run,
   I threw my old "Gradus" by,
And I left the task I had scarce begun,
   There'll be time enough for that, said I.

When I was at college, my pride was dress,
   And my groom and my bit of blood;
But as for my study, I must confess
   That I was content with my stud.
I was deep in my tradesmen's books, I'm afraid,
   Though not in my own, by the by;
And when rascally tailors came to be paid,
   There'll be time enough for that, said I.

I was just nineteen when I first fell in love,
   And I scribbled a deal of rhyme;
And I talked to myself in a shady grove,
   And I thought I was quite sublime;
I was torn from my love! 'twas a dreadful blow,
   And the lady she wiped her eye;
But I didn't die of grief, oh, dear me, no!
   There'll be time enough for that, said I.

The next was a lady of rank, a dame
   With blood in her veins, you see;
With the leaves of the Peerage she fanned the flame
   That was now consuming me.
But though of her great descent she spoke,
   I found she was still very high,
And I thought looking up to a wife no joke,
   There'll be time enough for that, said I.

My next *penchant* was for one whose face
   Was her fortune, she was so fair!
Oh! she spoke with an air of enchanting grace,—
   But a man cannot live upon air;

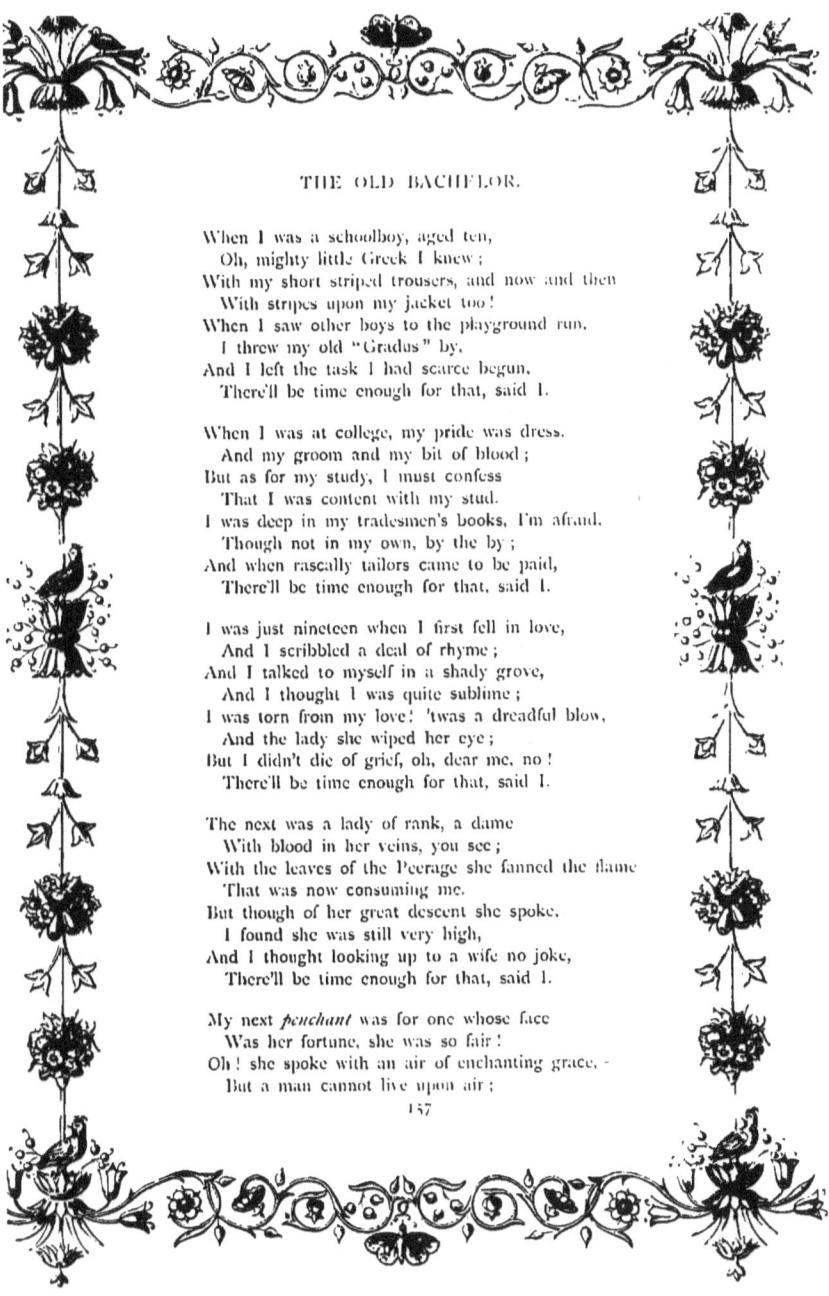

And when poverty enters the door young Love
  Will out of the casement fly;
The truth of the proverb I'd no wish to prove,
  There'll be time enough for that, said I.

My next was a lady who loved romance,
  And wrote very splendid things;
And she said with a sneer, when I asked her to dance,
  "Sir, I ride upon a horse with wings."
There was ink on her thumb when I kissed her hand,
  And she whispered, "If you should die
I'll write you an epitaph, gloomy and grand;"
  There'll be time enough for that, said I.

I left her, and sported my figure and face
  At opera, party, and ball;
I met pretty girls at every place,
  But I found a defect in all!
The first did not suit me, I cannot tell how,
  The second I cannot say why;
And the third, bless me! I will not marry now,
  There'll be time enough for that, said I.

I looked in the glass, and I thought I could trace
  A sort of a wrinkle or two;
So I made up my mind that I'd make up my face,
  And come out as good as new.
To my hair I imparted a little more jet,
  And I scarce could suppress a sigh;
But I cannot be quite an old Bachelor yet—
  No, there's time enough for that, said I.

I was now fifty-two, yet I still did adopt
  All the airs of a juvenile beau;
But, somehow, whenever a question I popped
  The girls with a laugh said "No!"
I am sixty to-day, not a very young man,
  And a bachelor doomed to die;
So, youth, be advised, and marry while you can,
  There's no time to be lost, say I.

BEAU BRUMMELL.

1778—1840.

THERE was a certain sense of poetical grace about the old dandy, as the subjoined verses show. A heartless life led with him to a miserable death; a beggar in a foreign country, to the last poor Brummell aped the highflown and artificial courtesy that had been the ideal of his life.

THE BUTTERFLY'S FUNERAL.

Oh ye! who so lately were blithesome and gay,
At the Butterfly's banquet carousing away;
Your feasts and your revels of pleasure are fled,
For the soul of the banquet, the Butterfly's dead!

No longer the Flies and the Emmets advance
To join with their friend in the Grasshopper's dance;
For see his thin form o'er the favourite bend,
And the Grasshopper mourns for the loss of his friend.

And hark! to the funeral dirge of the Bee,
And the Beetle, who follows as solemn as he;
And see where so mournful the green rushes wave,
The Mole is preparing the Butterfly's grave.

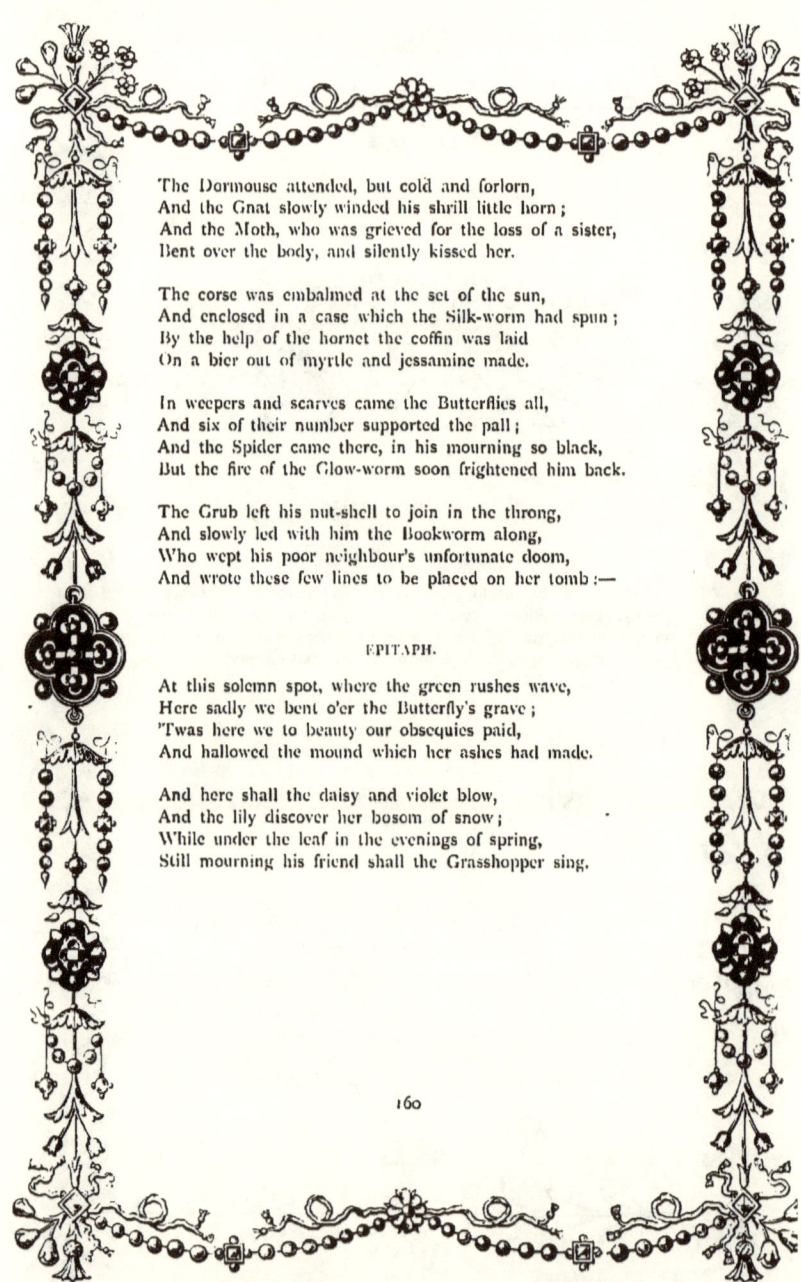

The Dormouse attended, but cold and forlorn,
And the Gnat slowly winded his shrill little horn;
And the Moth, who was grieved for the loss of a sister,
Bent over the body, and silently kissed her.

The corse was embalmed at the set of the sun,
And enclosed in a case which the Silk-worm had spun;
By the help of the hornet the coffin was laid
On a bier out of myrtle and jessamine made.

In weepers and scarves came the Butterflies all,
And six of their number supported the pall;
And the Spider came there, in his mourning so black,
But the fire of the Glow-worm soon frightened him back.

The Grub left his nut-shell to join in the throng,
And slowly led with him the Bookworm along,
Who wept his poor neighbour's unfortunate doom,
And wrote these few lines to be placed on her tomb:—

EPITAPH.

At this solemn spot, where the green rushes wave,
Here sadly we bent o'er the Butterfly's grave;
'Twas here we to beauty our obsequies paid,
And hallowed the mound which her ashes had made.

And here shall the daisy and violet blow,
And the lily discover her bosom of snow;
While under the leaf in the evenings of spring,
Still mourning his friend shall the Grasshopper sing.

THEODORE E. HOOK.

1788—1842.

THE poetry of Hook consists of little but excellent farcical rhymes and buffoonery in verse. It is only lightened here and there by such lines as these we quote. This brilliant man, after a gay but wasted life, died hopelessly in debt, neglected and deserted by the herd that he had wasted his extraordinary talent in amusing.

LINES FROM THE HEART.

Sweet is the vale where virtue dwells,
  The vale where honest love invites,
By margined brook or moss-grown cells,
  To taste its joys, its soft delights.
Sweet is the vale where oft I've strayed
  Through tangled brake or meadow green ;
Sweet are its groves, and sweet its shade,
  The verdant vale of Taunton Dean.

If friends the wayworn stranger seeks
  Whose kindness comfort can impart,
Here every tongue a welcome speaks,
  A home he finds in every heart.
Nay, when I hear the cynic cry
  "No friendship in the world is seen,"
My fleeting thoughts to Taunton fly,
  For friendship dwells in Taunton Dean.

The bandage once from Cupid's eyes
  By reason and by prudence drawn,
The wanton god to Taunton flies
  To revel on its daisied lawn.
For oh! 'tis sure where Beauty plays
  Love in its ecstasy is seen ;
His sight restored he onward strays :
  She holds her court in Taunton Dean.

And if amid the brilliant throng
   One angel girl appears most fair,
After his flight would Love be wrong
   To claim her heart, and settle there?
My Rosa's eye, her peach-bloom cheek,
   Her smile divine, her look serene,
Command the god—he dares not speak,
   But owns her sway in Taunton Dean.

Grant me a cot wherein to live
   With such a girl, with friends so rare,
No greater boon need Fortune give,
   Save what my wants might warrant there.
'Tis all I hope,—'tis all I seek,
   For there all bliss, all joy is seen;
In one short prayer, my wishes speak,
   To live, to die, in Taunton Dean.

ALLAN CUNNINGHAM.

1784—1842.

This vigorous and excellent ballad writer was the son of a builder in Dumfriesshire. He came to London, connected himself with the newspaper press, and became clerk of the works to Chantrey the sculptor. It is a great misfortune to his fame that some of his best works were passed off as *bonâ fide* old Galloway and Nithsdale ballads. It is not too much to say that these counterfeit ballads are as full of pathos, tenderness, and rough vigour, as the poems that they imitate.

THE POET'S BRIDAL-DAY SONG.

O! my love's like the stedfast sun,
Or streams that deepen as they run;
Nor hoary hairs, nor forty years,
Nor moments between sighs and tears,
Nor nights of thought, nor days of pain,
Nor dreams of glory dreamed in vain,
Nor mirth, nor sweetest song which flows
To sober joys and soften woes,
Can make my heart or fancy flee
One moment, my sweet wife, from thee.

Even while I muse, I see thee sit
In maiden bloom and matron wit—
Fair, gentle as when first I sued,
Ye seem, but of sedater mood;
Yet my heart leaps as fond for thee
As when, beneath Arbigland Tree,
We strayed and wooed, and thought the moon
Set on the sea an hour too soon;
Or lingered 'mid the falling dew,
When looks were fond and words were few.

Though I see smiling at thy feet
Five sons and a fair daughter sweet
And time, and care, and birth-time woes
Have dimmed thine eye and touched thy rose;
To thee, and thoughts of thee, belong
All that charms me of tale or song;
When words come down like dews unsought,
With gleams of deep enthusiast thought,
And fancy in her heaven flies free—
They come, my love, they come from thee.

O, when more thought we gave of old
To silver than some give to gold;
'Twas sweet to sit and ponder o'er
What things should deck our humble bower!
'Twas sweet to pull in hope with thee
The golden fruit from Fortune's tree;
And sweeter still to chose and twine
A garland for these locks of thine—
A song-wreath which may grace my Jean,
While rivers flow and woods are green.

At times there come, as come there ought,
Grave moments of sedater thought—
When Fortune frowns, nor lends our night
One gleam of her inconstant light;
And Hope, that decks the peasant's bower,
Shines like the rainbow through the shower,
O, then I see, while seated nigh,
A mother's heart shine in thine eye;
And proud resolve and purpose meek,
Speak of thee more than words can speak:
I think the wedded wife of mine
The best of all that's not divine.

DOCTOR MAGINN.

1794—1842.

POOR reckless vagabond Maginn was one of those men of genius who started "Bentley's Miscellany" in 1837. An extraordinary linguist, Maginn could adapt Greek and even Hebrew to the most distorted English metres. Idle and dissipated, Maginn died at last in hopeless poverty, ending very prematurely an ill-spent and wasted life.

MY SOLDIER-BOY.

I give my soldier-boy a blade,
  In fair Damascus fashioned well;
Who first the glittering falchion swayed,
  Who first beneath its fury fell,
I know not, but I hope to know
  That for no mean or hireling trade,
To guard no feeling base or low,
  I give my soldier-boy a blade.

Cool, calm, and clear the lucid flood
  In which its tempering work was done;
As calm, as clear, as cool of mood,
  Be thou whene'er it sees the sun.
For country's claim, at honour's call,
  For outraged friend, insulted maid,
At mercy's voice to bid it fall,
  I give my soldier-boy a blade.

The eye which marked its peerless edge,
  The hand that weighed its balanced poise,
Anvil and pincers, forge and wedge,
  Are gone, with all their flame and noise—
And still the gleaming sword remains;
  So when in dust I low am laid,
Remember, by these heart-felt strains,
  I gave my soldier-boy a blade.

ROBERT SOUTHEY.

1774—1843.

SOUTHEY wrote a great deal of diffuse poetry, now partially forgotten. He over-read himself, choking his imagination with books that contained other men's thoughts. There is great purity of feeling and learned imagination, though little dramatic power in Southey's poems.

THE HOLLY TREE.

O Reader! hast thou ever stood to see
    The Holly Tree?
The eye that contemplates it well perceives
    Its glossy leaves
Ordered by an intelligence so wise
As might confound the Atheist's sophistries.

Below a circling fence, its leaves are seen
    Wrinkled and keen,
No grazing cattle through their prickly round
    Can reach to wound,
But as they grow where nothing is to fear,
Smooth and unarmed the pointless leaves appear.

I love to view these things with curious eyes,
    And moralize;
And in the wisdom of the Holly Tree
    Can emblems see
Wherewith perchance to make a pleasant rhyme,
Such as may profit in the after-time.

So, though abroad perchance I might appear
    Harsh and austere;
To those who on my leisure would intrude,
    Reserved and rude;
Gentle at home amid my friends I'd be,
Like the high leaves upon the Holly Tree.

And should my youth, as youth is apt, I know,
    Some harshness show,
All vain asperities I day by day
    Would wear away,
Till the smooth temper of my age should be
Like the high leaves upon the Holly Tree.

And as when all the summer trees are seen
    So bright and green,
The Holly leaves their fadeless hues display
    Less bright than they;
But when the bare and wintry woods we see,
What then so cheerful as the Holly Tree?

So serious should my youth appear among
    The thoughtless throng,
So would I seem amid the young and gay
    More grave than they,
That in my age as cheerful I might be
As the green winter of the Holly Tree.

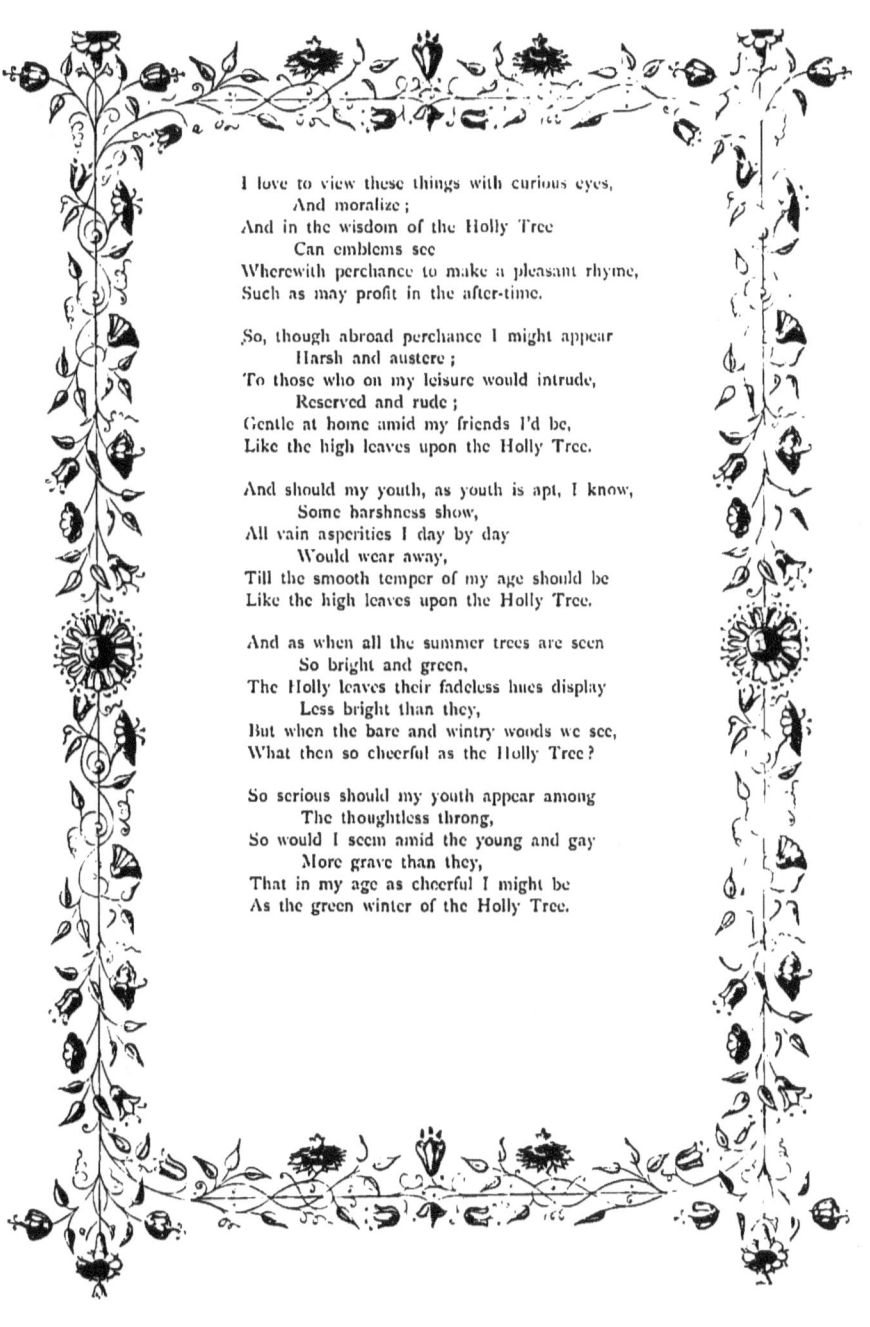

THOMAS CAMPBELL.

1777—1844.

CAMPBELL is always a puzzle to us. How could such a precise and trim man (Scotch too of all things) beginning with mechanical heroic verse, and big-wig metaphors of the old school, suddenly spring forth into the fire of "Hohenlinden," the thunder march of "Lochiel," and the exulting "Battle of the Baltic?" Above all, how, having written such poems, could he refrain from writing more? Probably for the same reason that a not very dissimilar genius, Gray, wrote so little—a prudish and almost pedantic desire for perfection, correcting and correcting till all "grew ripe and rotten."

FIELD FLOWERS.

Ye field flowers! the gardens eclipse you, 'tis true,
Yet, wildings of Nature, I dote upon you,
   For ye waft me to summers of old,
When the earth teemed around me with fairy delight,
And when daisies and buttercups gladdened my sight,
   Like treasures of silver and gold.

I love you for lulling me back into dreams
Of the blue Highland mountains and echoing streams,
   And of birchen glades breathing their balm,
While the deer was seen glancing in sunshine remote,
And the deep mellow crush of the wood-pigeon's note
   Made music that sweetened the calm.

Not a pastoral song has a pleasanter tune
Than ye speak to my heart, little wildings of June:
   Of old ruinous castles ye tell,
Where I thought it delightful your beauties to find,
When the magic of Nature first breathed on my mind,
   And your blossoms were part of her spell.

Even now what affections the violet awakes;
What loved little islands, twice seen in their lakes,
    Can the wild water-lily restore;
What landscapes I read in the primrose's looks,
And what pictures of pebbled and minnowy brooks
    In the vetches that tangled their shore!

Earth's cultureless buds, to my heart ye were dear
Ere the fever of passion or ague of fear
    Had scathed my existence's bloom;
Once I welcome you more, in life's passionless stage
With the visions of youth to revisit my age,
    And I wish you to grow on my tomb.

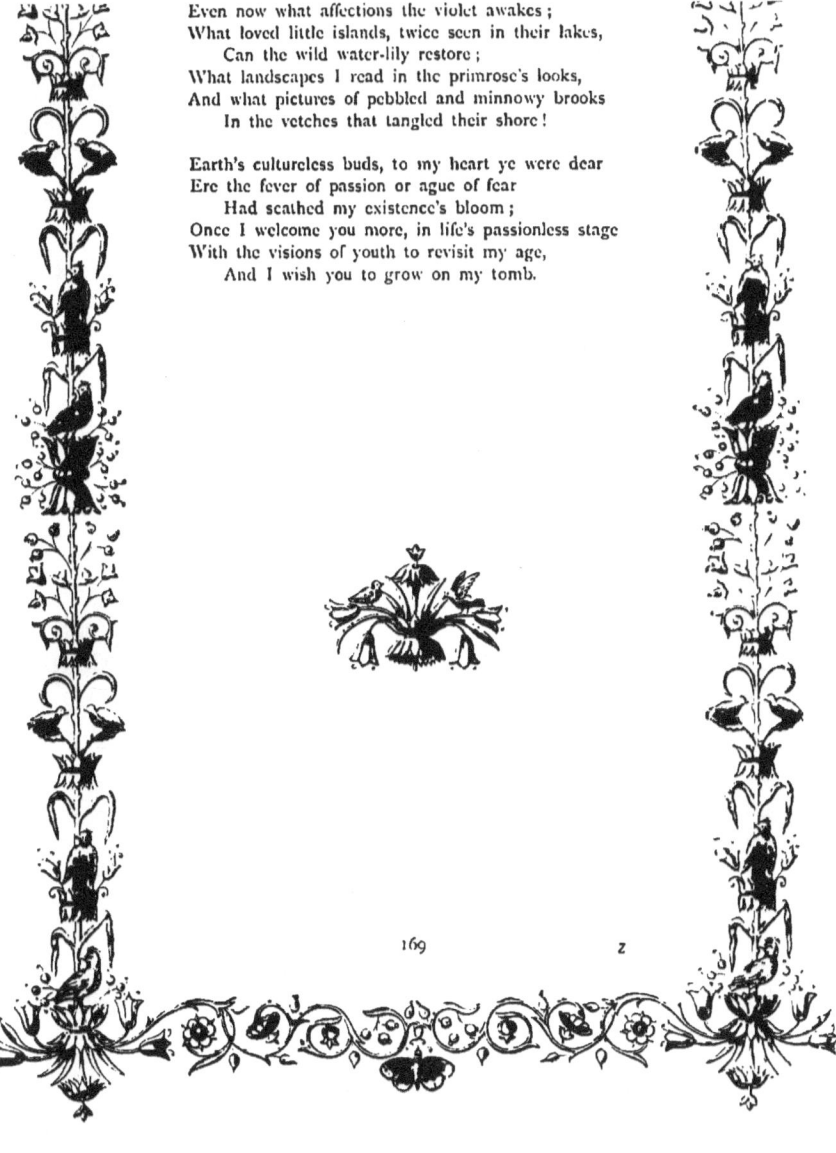

THOMAS HOOD.

1798—1845.

This exquisite humorist was the son of a London bookseller. Originally intended as a merchant's clerk, he first turned engraver, and finally author. With the gloom of chronic disease upon him, he toiled bravely and arduously for his family, lighting our murky London air with jokes that sparkled like the star sparks of fireworks. He excelled both in pathos and humour: his "Dream of Eugene Aram" is vigorous and passionate; his "Miss Kilmansegg" is irresistibly droll, and spangled with gems of exquisite and thoughtful nonsense. In his "Song of the Shirt," which appeared in *Punch*, Hood rose to a higher flight, and touched the deeper cords of the human heart. True to the finer utilitarianism of our age, the poet wished to have this line alone inscribed upon his grave,

"He wrote 'The Song of the Shirt.'"

Those who have themselves suffered can best sympathize with the miseries of the poor. An invalid for half his life as Hood was, it is not any wonder that thoughts upon physical suffering are frequent in his writings—unconsciously they crept in as some pang of pain followed the laugh that always came from the heart. An honest and industrious writer for daily bread (the nightingale perhaps requires the thorn at its breast), Hood had acquired an extraordinary command of words, his power of pleating and twisting phrases was miraculous; some of his poems he enclosed in crystal tear drops, while others he cut into as many facets as if they had been rose diamonds.

IT WAS NOT IN THE WINTER.

It was not in the winter
    Our loving lot was cast;
It was the time of Roses,—
    We plucked them as we passed!

That churlish season never frowned
 On early lovers yet :—
Oh, no—the world was newly crowned
 With flowers when first we met!

'Twas twilight, and I bade you go,
 But still you held me fast;
It was the time of Roses,—
 We plucked them as we passed.

What else could peer thy glowing cheek,
 That tears began to stud?
And when I asked the like of Love,
 You snatched a damask bud;

And oped it to the dainty core,
 Still glowing to the last.—
It was the time of Roses,
 We plucked them as we passed.

LAMAN BLANCHARD.

1803—1845.

IN the nourishing sunshine of success, this cultivated writer would certainly have done great things. With greater depth than Bayley, much of the fancy of Barry Cornwall, and with a command of language that is unusual, Mr. Blanchard wrote verses beautiful in their refinement, and springing from the true source.

THE POET'S HEART

'Tis like unto that dainty flower
That shuts by day its fragrance up,
And lifts unto a darkened hour
   Its little essence-cup.

'Tis as the grape on which it lives;
That pleasure-ripened heart must be
In sorrow crushed, or ere it gives
   The wine of poesy.

Or like some silver-wingèd fly,
By taper tempted from its flight,
It sparkles, faints, falls quiveringly,
   And mingles with the light.

And sure it bears a fortune such
As waits upon that graceful bird,
Whose music, mute to living touch,
   At death's dim porch is heard.

And still the dolphin's fate partakes:
Though bright the hue which pride hath given,
'Tis pain whose darling pencil wakes
   The master-tints of heaven.

A mine where many a living gem
In cell so deep lies casketed,
That man sends down a sigh for them,
  And turns away his head.

But not that dainty flower, the grape,
The insect's sufferance and devotion ;
The swan's life-ending song, and shape
  Diviner with emotion :—

And not the dolphin's sacrifice,
The mine's most rare and dazzling part—
O! not all these could pay its price,
  Or form one poet's heart.

REV. RICHARD HARRIS BARHAM.

1788—1845.

The "Ingoldsby Legends" are now classical; occasionally somewhat coarse and ribald, they are delightful for their superabundant fun, wonderful grotesque rhymes, and facile humour. We have taken Barham at somewhat more serious moments, and intent on a quieter fun.

SONG.

There sits a bird on yonder tree,
   More fond than cushat dove;
There sits a bird on yonder tree,
   And sings to me of love.
Oh! stoop thee from thine eyrie down,
   And nestle thee near my heart,
     For the moments fly,
     And the hour is nigh
When thou and I must part,
     My love!
When thou and I must part.

In yonder covert lurks a fawn,
   The pride of the sylvan scene;
In yonder covert lurks a fawn,
   And I am his only queen;

Oh! bound from thy secret lair,
   For the sun is below the west
     No mortal eye
     May our meeting spy.
   For all are closed in rest,
     My love!
   Each eye is closed in rest.

Oh! sweet is the breath of morn
   When the sun's first beams appear;
Oh! sweet is the shepherd's strain
   When it dies on the listening ear;
And sweet the soft voice which speaks
   The wanderer's welcome home;
     But sweeter far
     By yon pale mild star
   With our true love thus to roam,
     My dear!
   With our own true love to roam.

REFLECTIONS IN WESTMINSTER ABBEY.

A feeling sad came o'er me as I trod the sacred ground
Where Tudors and Plantagenets were lying all around:
I stepped with noiseless foot, as though the sound of mortal tread
Might burst the bands of the dreamless sleep that wraps the
   mighty dead!

The slanting rays of the evening sun shone through those cloisters
   pale
With fitful light on regal vest and warrior's sculptured mail;
As from the stained and storied pane it danced with quivering
   gleam,
Each cold and prostrate form below seemed quickening in the
   beam.

Now, sinking low, no more was heard the organ's solemn swell,
And faint upon the listening ear the last Hosanna fell:
It died—and not a breath did stir;—above each knightly stall
Unmoved the bannered blazonry hung waveless as a pall.

I stood alone!—a living thing 'midst those that were no more—
I thought on ages past and gone—the glorious deeds of yore—
On Edward's sable panoply, on Cressy's tented plain,
The fatal Roses twined at length, on great Eliza's reign.

I thought on Naseby—Marston Moor—on Worcester's 'crowning
   fight;'
When on mine ear a sound there fell—it chilled me with affright
As thus in low unearthly tones I heard a voice begin,
'—This here's the Cap of Giniral Monk!—Sir! please put
   summut in!'

AS I LAYE A-THYNKYNGE.

THE LAST LINES OF THOMAS INGOLDSBY.

As I laye a-thynkynge, a-thynkynge, a-thynkynge,
Merrie sang the Birde as she sat upon the spraye;
   There came a noble Knyghte,
   With his hauberke shynynge brighte,
   And his gallant heart was lyghte,
      Free and gay;
As I laye a-thynkynge, he rode upon his waye.

As I laye a-thynkynge, a-thynkynge, a-thynkynge,
Sadly sang the Birde as she sat upon the tree!
   There seemed a crimson plain
   Where a gallant Knyghte lay slayne,
   And a steed with broken rein
      Ran free,
As I laye a-thynkynge, most pitiful to see!

As I lay a-thynkynge, a-thynkynge, a-thynkynge,
Merrie sang the Birde as she sat upon the boughe;
   A lovely Mayde came by,
   And a gentil youth was nyghe,
   And he breathèd many a syghe
      And a vowe;
As I laye a-thynkynge, her hearte was gladsome now.

As I laye a-thynkynge, a-thynkynge, a-thynkynge,
Sadly sang the Birde as she sat upon the thorne;
    No more a youth was there,
    But a maiden rent her haire,
    And cried in sad despaire,
      'That I was borne!'
As I laye a-thynkynge, she perishèd forlorne.

As I laye a-thynkynge, a-thynkynge, a-thynkynge,
Sweetly sang the Birde as she sat upon the briar;
    There came a lovely Childe,
    And his face was meek and mild,
    Yet joyously he smiled
      On his sire;
As I lay a thynkynge, a Cherub mote admire.

But I lay a-thynkynge, a-thynkynge, a-thynkynge,
And sadly sang the Birde as it perched upon a bier;
    That joyous smile was gone,
    And the face was white and wan,
    As the downe upon the Swan
      Doth appear,
As I lay a-thynkynge—oh! bitter flowed the tear!

As I lay a-thynkynge, the golden sun was sinking,
O merrie sang the Birde as it glittered on her breast
    With a thousand gorgeous dyes,
    While soaring to the skies,
    'Mid the stars she seemed to rise,
      As to her nest;
As I lay a-thynkynge, her meaning was exprest:—

    'Follow, follow me away,
    It boots not to delay,'—
    'Twas so she seemed to saye,
      'HERE IS REST!'

THE MISSES BRONTË.

ANNE BRONTË (ACTON BELL). 1820—1849.

GENIUSES are like mushrooms, they spring up, unstudied and unheeded, in all sorts of quiet unobserved places. This wonderful family of a Yorkshire rector, nurtured with a gloomy severity in a lonely dull place, broke into blossom with the suddenness and lavishness of an Indian jungle. Their poetry does not equal their passionately earnest novels, but it still has a merit of its own.

HOME.

How brightly glistening in the sun
  The woodland ivy plays!
While yonder beeches from their barks
  Reflect his silver rays.

That sun surveys a lovely scene
  From softly smiling skies;
And wildly through unnumbered trees
  The wind of winter sighs.

Now loud, it thunders o'er my head,
  And now in distance dies.
But give me back my barren hills
  Where colder breezes rise;

Where scarce the scattered stunted trees
  Can yield an answering swell,
But where a wilderness of heath
  Returns the sound as well.

For yonder garden, fair and wide,
  With groves of evergreen,
Long winding walks and borders trim,
  And velvet lawns between;

Restore to me that little spot
With grey walls comp issed round.
Where knotted grass neglected lies,
And weeds usurp the ground.

Though all around this mansion high
Invites the foot to roam,
And though its halls are fair within—
Oh! give me back my HOME.

CHARLOTTE BRONTE (CURRER BELL). 1817—1855.

THE LETTER.

What is she writing? watch her now,
How fast her fingers move!
How eagerly her youthful brow
Is bent in thought above!
Her long curls drooping shade the light,
She puts them quick aside,
Nor knows that band of crystals bright
Her hasty touch untied.
It slips adown her silken dress,
Falls glittering at her feet;
Unmarked it falls, for she no less
Pursues her labour sweet.

The very loveliest hour that shines
Is in that deep blue sky;
The golden sun of June declines,
It has not caught her eye.
The cheerful lawn and unclosed gate,
The white road far away,
In vain for her light footsteps wait,
She comes not forth to-day.
There is an open door of glass
Close by that lady's chair,
From thence to slopes of mossy grass
Descends a marble stair.

Tall plants of bright and spicy bloom
 Around the threshold grow;
Their leaves and blossoms shade the room
 From that sun's deepening glow.
Why does she not a moment glance
 Between the clustering flowers,
And mark in heaven the radiant dance
 Of evening's rosy hours?
O look again! Still fixed her eye,
 Unsmiling, earnest, still,
And fast her pen and fingers fly
 Urged by her eager will.

Her soul is in the absorbing task;
 To whom then doth she write?
Nay, watch her still more closely, ask
 Her own eyes' serious light.
Where do they turn, as now her pen
 Hangs o'er the unfinished line?
Whence fell the tearful gleam that then
 Did in their dark spheres shine?
The summer-parlour looks so dark
 When from that sky you turn,
And from the expanse of that green park,
 You scarce may aught discern.

Yet o'er the piles of porcelain rare,
 O'er flower-stand, couch, and vase,
Sloped, as if leaning on the air,
 One picture meets the gaze.
'Tis there she turns; you may not see
 Distinct, what form defines
The clouded mass of mystery
 Yon broad gold frame confines.
But look again; inured to shade
 Your eyes now faintly trace
A stalwart form, a massive head,
 A firm determined face.

Black Spanish locks, a sunburnt cheek,
 A brow high, broad, and white,

Where every furrow seems to speak
  Of mind and moral might.
Is that her god? I cannot tell;
  Her eye a moment met
The impending picture, then it fell
  Darkened and dimmed and wet.
A moment more, her task is done,
  And sealed the letter lies;
And now towards the setting sun
  She turns her tearful eyes.

Those tears flow over, wonder not,
  For by the inscription see
In what a strange and distant spot
  Her heart of hearts must be!
Three seas and many a league of land
  That letter must pass o'er
Ere read by him to whose loved hand
  'Tis sent from England's shore.
Remote colonial wilds detain
  Her husband, loved though stern;
She 'mid that smiling English scene
  Weeps for his wished return.

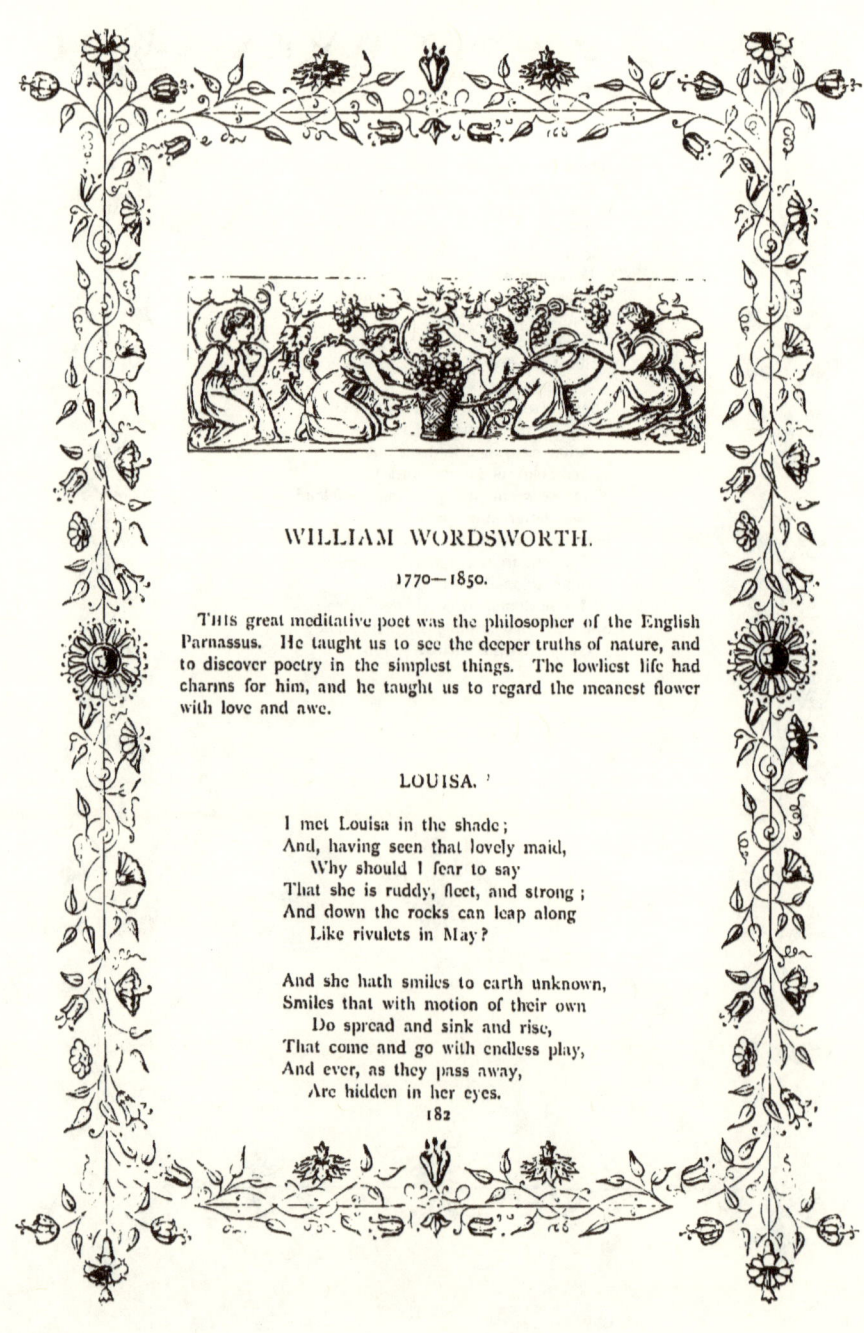

WILLIAM WORDSWORTH.

1770—1850.

THIS great meditative poet was the philosopher of the English Parnassus. He taught us to see the deeper truths of nature, and to discover poetry in the simplest things. The lowliest life had charms for him, and he taught us to regard the meanest flower with love and awe.

LOUISA.

I met Louisa in the shade;
And, having seen that lovely maid,
  Why should I fear to say
That she is ruddy, fleet, and strong;
And down the rocks can leap along
  Like rivulets in May?

And she hath smiles to earth unknown,
Smiles that with motion of their own
  Do spread and sink and rise,
That come and go with endless play,
And ever, as they pass away,
  Are hidden in her eyes.

She loves her fire, her cottage-home;
Yet o'er the moorland will she roam
  In weather rough and bleak;
And when against the wind she strains,
Oh! might I kiss the mountain rains
  That sparkle on her cheek!

Take all that's mine "beneath the moon,"
If I with her but half a noon
  May sit beneath the walls
Of some old cave or mossy nook,
When up she winds along the brook
  To hunt the waterfalls.

SHE DWELT AMONG THE UNTRODDEN WAYS.

She dwelt among the untrodden ways
  Beside the springs of Dove,
A maid whom there were none to praise,
  And very few to love.

A violet by a mossy stone
  Half hidden from the eye!—
Fair as a star, when only one
  Is shining in the sky.

She lived unknown, and few could know
  When Lucy ceased to be;
But she is in her grave, and, oh,
  The difference to me!

POOR SUSAN.

At the corner of Wood Street when daylight appears
There's a thrush that sings loud, it has sung for three years:
Poor Susan has passed by the spot, and has heard
In the silence of morning the song of the bird.

'Tis a note of enchantment; what ails her? She sees
A mountain ascending, a vision of trees;
Bright volumes of vapour through Lothbury glide,
And a river flows on through the vale of Cheapside.

She looks, and her heart is in Heaven : but they fade,
The mist and the river, the hill and the shade ;
The stream will not flow, and the hill will not rise,
And the colours have all passed away from her eyes.

SHE WAS A PHANTOM OF DELIGHT.

She was a phantom of delight
When first she gleamed upon my sight ;
A lovely apparition, sent
To be a moment's ornament ;
Her eyes as stars of Twilight fair ;
Like Twilight's, too, her dusky hair ;
But all things else about her drawn
From May-time and the cheerful dawn ;
A dancing shape, an image gay,
To haunt, to startle, and way-lay.

I saw her upon nearer view,
A spirit, yet a woman too!
Her household motions light and free,
And steps of virgin-liberty ;
A countenance in which did meet
Sweet records, promises as sweet ;
A creature not too bright or good
For human nature's daily food,
For transient sorrows, simple wiles,
Praise, blame, love, kisses, tears, and smiles.

And now I see with eye serene
The very pulse of the machine ;
A being breathing thoughtful breath,
A traveller betwixt life and death ;
The reason firm, the temperate will,
Endurance, foresight, strength, and skill :

A perfect woman, nobly planned
To warn, to comfort, and command;
And yet a spirit still, and bright
With something of an angel light.

YARROW UNVISITED.

From Stirling Castle we had seen
  The mazy Forth unravelled,
Had trod the banks of Clyde and Tay,
  And with the Tweed had travelled;
And when we came to Clovenford,
  Then said my "winsome marow,"
"Whate'er betide, we'll turn aside,
  And see the Braes of Yarrow."

"Let Yarrow folk, frae Selkirk town,
  Who have been buying, selling,
Go back to Yarrow, 'tis their own,
  Each maiden to her dwelling.
On Yarrow's banks let herons feed,
  Hares couch, and rabbits burrow,
But we will downwards with the Tweed,
  Nor turn aside to Yarrow.

"There's Galla Water, Leader Haughs,
  Both lying right before us;
And Dryburgh, where with chiming Tweed
  The lintwhites sing in chorus;
There's pleasant Teviotdale, a land
  Made blithe with plough and harrow:
Why throw away a needful day
  To go in search of Yarrow?

"What's Yarrow but a river bare
  That glides the dark hills under?
There are a thousand such elsewhere
  As worthy of your wonder."

—Strange words they seemed of slight and scorn;
  My true-love sighed for sorrow,
And looked me in the face, to think
  I thus could speak of Yarrow!

"O green," said I, "are Yarrow's holms,
  And sweet is Yarrow flowing!
Fair hangs the apple frae the rock,
  But we will leave it growing.
O'er hilly path and open strath
  We'll wander Scotland thorough;
But, though so near, we will not turn
  Into the dale of Yarrow.

" Let beeves and home-bred kine partake
  The sweets of Burn-mill meadow;
The swan on still Saint Mary's Lake
  Float double, swan and shadow!
We will not see them; will not go
  To-day, nor yet to-morrow;
Enough if in our hearts we know
  There's such a place as Yarrow.

" Be Yarrow stream unseen, unknown!
  It must, or we shall rue it;
We have a vision of our own,
  Ah! why should we undo it?
The treasured dreams of times long past,
  We'll keep them, winsome marrow!
For when we're there, although 'tis fair,
  'Twill be another Yarrow!

" If care with freezing years should come
  And wandering seem but folly,—
Should we be loth to stir from home,
  And yet be melancholy;
Should life be dull, and spirits low,
  'Twill soothe us in our sorrow
That earth has something yet to show,
  The bonny Holms of Yarrow!"

I WANDERED LONELY.

I wandered lonely as a cloud
That floats on high o'er vales and hills,
When all at once I saw a crowd,
A host of dancing daffodils,
Along the lake, beneath the trees,
Ten thousand dancing in the breeze.

The waves beside them danced, but they
Out-did the sparkling waves in glee :—
A Poet could not but be gay
In such a laughing company !
I gazed—and gazed—but little thought
What wealth the show to me had brought.

For oft, when on my couch I lie
In vacant or in pensive mood,
They flash upon that inward eye
Which is the bliss of solitude ;
And then my heart with pleasure fills,
And dances with the daffodils.

WILLIAM LISLE BOWLES.

1762—1850.

Bowles's Sonnets influenced the genius of Coleridge. His poetry is as elegant and correct as that of Rogers. There is a charm in his sober and truthful painting that is delightful in its quietude.

WATER-PARTY ON BEAULIEU RIVER,

IN THE NEW FOREST.

June, 1799.

I thought 'twas a toy of the fancy—a dream
  That leads with illusion the senses astray,
And I sighed with delight, as we stole down the stream,
  While Eve, as she smiled on our sail, seemed to say,
  "Rejoice in my light, ere it fade fast away!"

We left the loud rocking of ocean behind,
  And stealing along the clear current serene,
The 'Phædria' spread her white sails to the wind,
  And they who divided had many a day been,
  Gazed with added delight on the charms of the scene!

Each bosom one spirit of peace seemed to feel,
  We heard not the tossing, the stir, and the war
Of the ocean without; we heard but the keel,
  The keel that went whispering along the green shore,
  And the stroke, as it dipped, of the feathering oar.

Beneath the dark woods now as winding we go,
  What sounds of rich harmony burst on the ear;
Hark! cheerly the loud-swelling clarionets blow;
  Now the tones gently die, now more mellow we hear
  The horns through the high forest echoing clear.

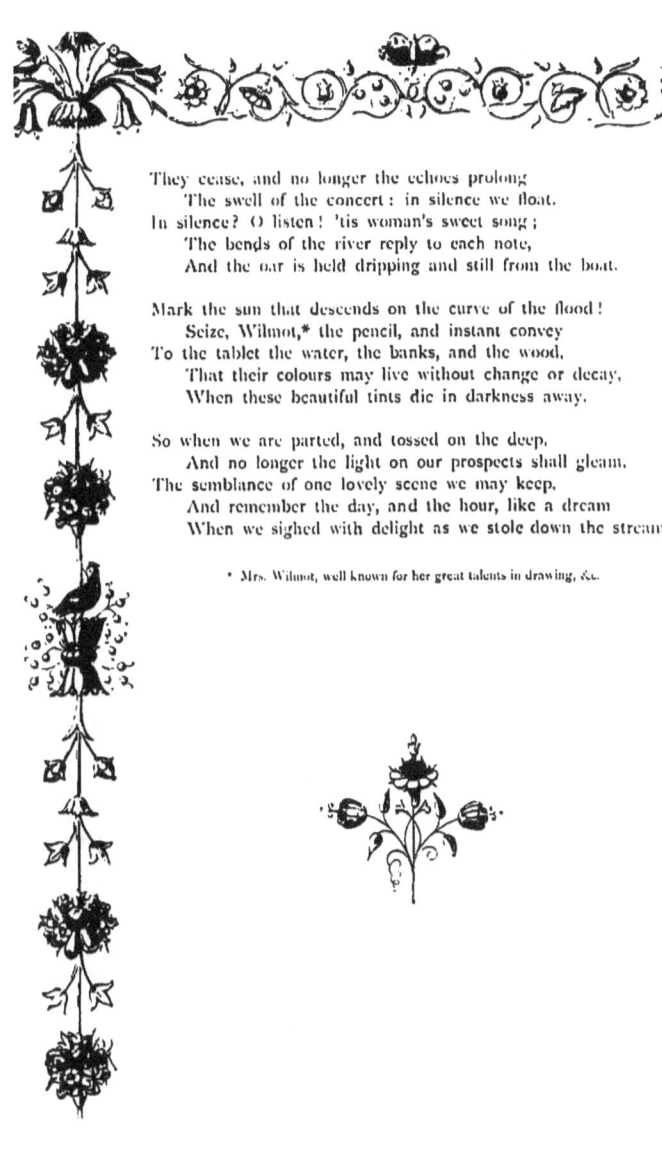

They cease, and no longer the echoes prolong
   The swell of the concert: in silence we float.
In silence? O listen! 'tis woman's sweet song;
   The bends of the river reply to each note,
And the oar is held dripping and still from the boat.

Mark the sun that descends on the curve of the flood!
   Seize, Wilmot,* the pencil, and instant convey
To the tablet the water, the banks, and the wood,
   That their colours may live without change or decay,
When these beautiful tints die in darkness away.

So when we are parted, and tossed on the deep,
   And no longer the light on our prospects shall gleam,
The semblance of one lovely scene we may keep,
   And remember the day, and the hour, like a dream
When we sighed with delight as we stole down the stream

    * Mrs. Wilmot, well known for her great talents in drawing, &c.

THOMAS MOORE.

1779—1852.

MOORE may be said to have remodelled the poetry of Ireland, rewrote its old songs, and remoulded the most tender and patriotic of its legends. From the "green isle" he wandered to Persia and Hindostan, seeking fresh regions over which his muse might wander. Somewhat too cloying with incessant sweetness, his verse is always melodious and refined.

TAKE BACK THE VIRGIN PAGE.

WRITTEN ON RETURNING A BLANK BOOK.

Take back the Virgin Page
   White and unwritten still;
Some hand more calm and sage
   The leaf must fill.
Thoughts came as pure as light—
   Pure as ev'n *you* require:
But oh! each word I write
   Love turns to fire.

Yet let me keep the book:
   Oft shall my heart renew,
When on its leaves I look,
   Dear thoughts of you.

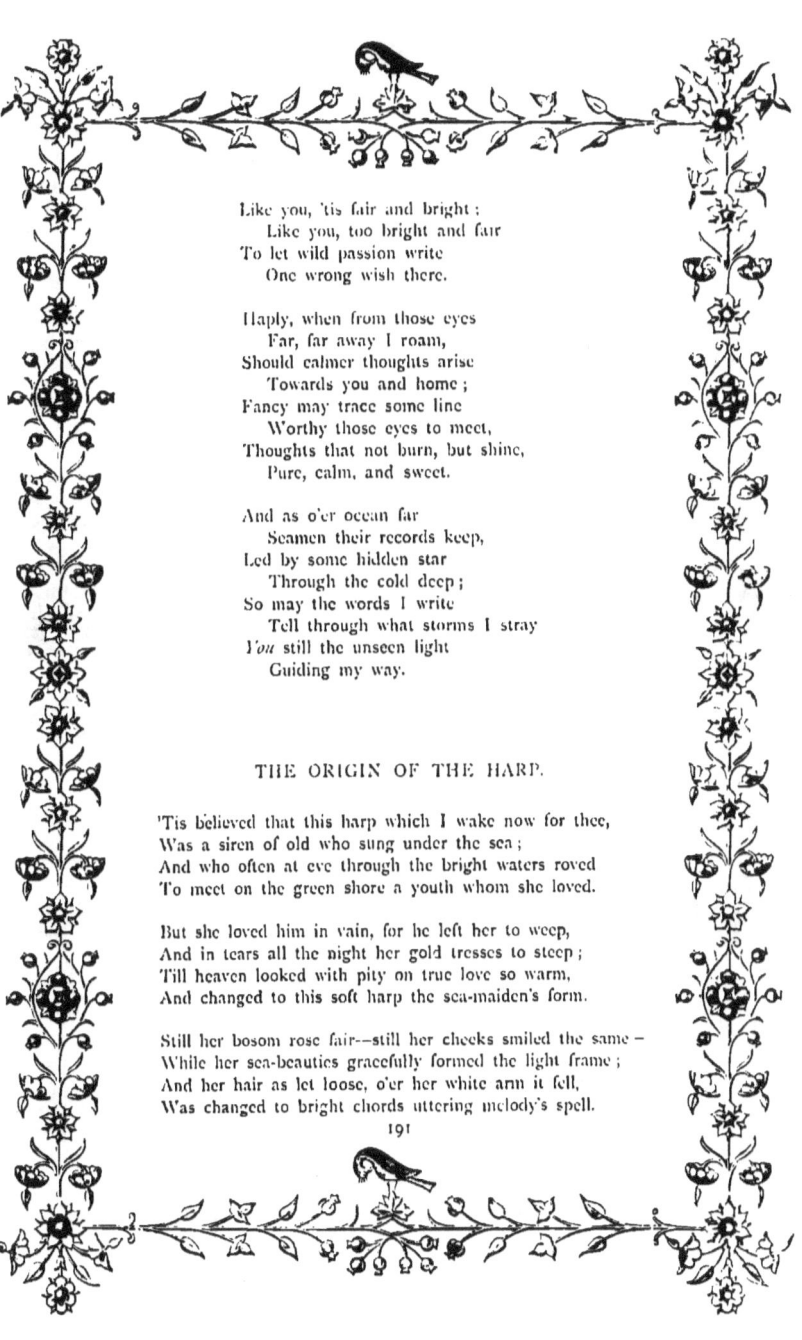

Like you, 'tis fair and bright;
Like you, too bright and fair
To let wild passion write
One wrong wish there.

Haply, when from those eyes
Far, far away I roam,
Should calmer thoughts arise
Towards you and home;
Fancy may trace some line
Worthy those eyes to meet,
Thoughts that not burn, but shine,
Pure, calm, and sweet.

And as o'er ocean far
Seamen their records keep,
Led by some hidden star
Through the cold deep;
So may the words I write
Tell through what storms I stray
You still the unseen light
Guiding my way.

THE ORIGIN OF THE HARP.

'Tis believed that this harp which I wake now for thee,
Was a siren of old who sung under the sea;
And who often at eve through the bright waters roved
To meet on the green shore a youth whom she loved.

But she loved him in vain, for he left her to weep,
And in tears all the night her gold tresses to steep;
Till heaven looked with pity on true love so warm,
And changed to this soft harp the sea-maiden's form.

Still her bosom rose fair—still her cheeks smiled the same—
While her sea-beauties gracefully formed the light frame;
And her hair as let loose, o'er her white arm it fell,
Was changed to bright chords uttering melody's spell.

Hence it came that this soft harp so long hath been known
To mingle love's language with sorrow's sad tone;
Till *thou* didst divide them, and teach the fond lay
To speak love when I'm near thee and grief when away.

THERE'S A BOWER OF ROSES BY BENDEMEER'S STREAM.

There's a bower of roses by Bendemeer's stream,
    And the nightingale sings round it all the day long;
In the time of my childhood 'twas like a sweet dream,
    To sit in the roses and hear the bird's song.

That bower and its music I never forget,
    But oft when alone, in the bloom of the year.
I think—Is the nightingale singing there yet?
    Are the roses still bright by the calm Bendemeer?

No, the roses soon withered that hung o'er the wave,
    But some blossoms were gathered while freshly they shone.
And a dew was distilled from their flowers that gave
    All the fragrance of summer when summer was gone.

Thus memory draws from delight ere it dies
    An essence that breathes of it many a year;
Thus bright to my soul, as 'twas then to my eyes,
    Is that bower on the banks of the calm Bendemeer!

SAMUEL ROGERS.

1763–1855.

It was a happy proof that, in our age, commerce and literature may sometimes join hands, when a great banker took to writing poems. The genius of Rogers was calm, equable, never soaring, and conscious of its own limitations. A purity and classical refinement, with something of the amateur or dilettante element, pervades them, but not unpleasantly.

TO —— .

Go — you may call it madness, folly ;
You shall not chase my gloom away.
There's such a charm in melancholy,
I would not, if I could, be gay.

Oh ! if you knew the pensive pleasure
That fills my bosom, when I sigh,
You would not rob me of a treasure
Monarchs are too poor to buy.

A WISH.

Mine be a cot beside the hill ;
A bee-hive's hum shall soothe my ear ;
A willowy brook that turns a mill
With many a fall shall linger near.

The swallow, oft, beneath my thatch,
Shall twitter from her clay-built nest ;
Oft shall the pilgrim lift the latch
And share my meal, a welcome guest.

Around my ivy'd porch shall spring
  Each fragrant flower that drinks the dew;
And Lucy at her wheel shall sing,
  In russet gown and apron blue.

The village-church among the trees,
  Where first our marriage-vows were given,
With merry peals shall swell the breeze,
  And point with taper spire to heaven.

ON —— ASLEEP.

Sleep on, and dream of heaven,
  Tho' shut so close thy laughing eyes,
Thy rosy lips still wear a smile,
  And move, and breathe delicious sighs!—

Ah! now soft blushes tinge her cheeks,
  And mantle o'er her neck of snow.
Ah! now she murmurs, now she speaks
  What most I wish—and fear to know.

She starts, she trembles, and she weeps!
  Her fair hands folded on her breast.
—And now, how like a saint she sleeps!
  A seraph in the realms of rest!

Sleep on secure! Above control,
  Thy thoughts belong to Heaven and thee!
And may the secret of thy soul
  Remain within its sanctuary!

AN ITALIAN SONG.

Dear is my little native vale,
  The ring-dove builds and murmurs there;
Close by my cot she tells her tale
  To every passing villager.
The squirrel leaps from tree to tree,
And shells his nuts at liberty.

In orange-groves and myrtle-bowers,
  That breathe a gale of fragrance round,
I charm the fairy-footed hours
  With my loved lute's romantic sound;
Or crowns of living laurel weave
For those that win the race at eve.

The shepherd's horn at break of day,
  The ballet danced in twilight glade,
The canzonet and roundelay
  Sung in the silent green-wood shade:
These simple joys, that never fail,
Shall bind me to my native vale.

LEIGH HUNT.

1784—1859.

THE days when this graceful and sensitive poet roused Tory indignation by deriding the portliness of the Prince Regent have long since passed away. We no longer glow with anger, to find Leigh Hunt in raptures at the simple beauty of Hampstead lanes. The grasshopper still "catches his heart up at the sound of June" in his verse, and will do so for centuries. His affectations and prettinesses we forget when we remember the honesty of his sympathies, and the cloudless sunshine of his happy gaiety.

RONDEAU.

Jenny kissed me when we met,
   Jumping from the chair she sat in;
Time, you thief, who love to get
   Sweets into your list, put that in:
Say I'm weary, say I'm sad,
   Say that health and wealth have missed me,
Say I'm growing old, but add,
   Jenny kissed me.

TO J. H., FOUR YEARS OLD.

A NURSERY SONG.

Ah! little ranting Johnny,
For ever blithe and bonny,
And singing nonny, nonny,
With hat just thrown upon ye;
Or whistling like the thrushes,
With voice in silver gushes;

Or twisting random posies
With daisies, weeds, and roses;
And strutting in and out so,
Or dancing all about so,
With cock-up nose so lightsome,
And sidelong eyes so brightsome,
And cheeks as ripe as apples,
And head as rough as Dapple's,
And arms as sunny shining
As if their veins they'd wine in;
And mouth that smiles so truly,
Heaven seems to have made it newly.
It breaks into such sweetness
With merry-lipped completeness;—
Ah Jack, ah Gianni mio,
As blithe as Laughing Trio,
— Sir Richard, too, you rattler,
So christened from the Tattler,—
My Bacchus in his glory,
My little Cor-di-fiori,
My tricksome Puck, my Robin,
Who in and out come bobbing,
As full of feints and frolic as
That fibbing rogue Autolycus,
And play the graceless robber on
Your grave-eyed brother Oberon,—
Ah Dick, ah Dolce-riso,
How can you, can you be so?

One cannot turn a minute,
But mischief,—there you're in it,
A getting at my books, John,
With mighty bustling looks, John;
Or poking at the roses,
In midst of which your nose is;
Or climbing on a table,
No matter how unstable,
And turning up your quaint eye
And half-shut teeth, with "Mayn't I?"
Or else you're off at play, John,
Just as you'd be all day, John,
With hat or not, as happens,
And there you dance and clap hands,

Or on the grass go rolling
Or plucking flowers, or bowling,
And getting me expenses
With losing balls o'er fences;
Or, as the constant trade is,
Are fondled by the ladies,
With "What a young rogue this is!"
Reforming him with kisses;
Till suddenly you cry out,
As if you had an eye out.
So desperately tearful,
The sound is really fearful;
When lo! directly after
It bubbles into laughter.

   Ah rogue! and do you know, John,
Why 'tis we love you so, John?
And how it is they let ye
Do what you like and pet ye,
Though all who look upon ye,
Exclaim, "Ah Johnny, Johnny!"
It is because you please 'em
Still more, John, than you tease 'em;
Because, too, when not present
The thought of you is pleasant;
Because, though such an elf, John,
They think that if yourself, John,
Had something to condemn too,
You'd be as kind to them too;
In short, because you're very
Good-tempered, Jack, and merry;
And are as quick at giving
As easy at receiving;
And in the midst of pleasure
Are certain to find leisure
To think, my boy, of ours,
And bring us lumps of flowers.

   But see, the sun shines brightly;
Come, put your hat on rightly,
And we'll among the bushes,
And hear your friends the thrushes;
And see what flowers the weather
Has rendered fit to gather;

And when we home must jog you
Shall ride my back, you rogue you,
Your hat adorned with fine leaves,
Horse-chestnut, oak, and vine-leaves ;
And so, with green o'erhead, John,
Shall whistle home to bed, John.

AN ANGEL IN THE HOUSE.

How sweet it were, if, without feeble fright,
Or dying of the dreadful beauteous sight,
An angel came to us, and we could bear
To see him issue from the silent air
At evening in our room, and bend on ours
His divine eyes, and bring us from his bowers
News of dear friends, and children who have never
Been dead indeed,—as we shall know for ever.
Alas! we think not what we daily see
About our hearths,—angels, that *are* to be,
Or may be, if they will, and we prepare
Their souls and ours to meet in happy air :—
A child, a friend, a wife, whose soft heart sings
In unison with ours, breeding its future wings.

LORD MACAULAY.

1800—1859.

WHO would ever have expected to find our great partisan historian and Indian statesman writing a valentine? It is Hercules spinning for Omphale. The Roman ballads are robust and glorious, but then they are not occasional poems, and would not suit our purpose.

SONG.

O STAY, MADONNA! STAY.

O stay, Madonna! stay;
'Tis not the dawn of day
That marks the skies with yonder opal streak:
The stars in silence shine;
Then press thy lips to mine,
And rest upon my neck thy fervid cheek.

O sleep, Madonna! sleep;
Leave me to watch and weep
O'er the sad memory of departed joys,
O'er hope's extinguished beam,
O'er fancy's vanished dream,
O'er all that nature gives and man destroys.

O wake, Madonna! wake;
  Even now the purple lake
Is dappled o'er with amber flakes of light;
  A glow is on the hill;
  And every trickling rill
In golden threads leaps down from yonder height.

  O fly, Madonna! fly,
  Lest day and envy spy
What only love and night may safely know;
  Fly, and tread softly, dear!
  Lest those who hate us hear
The sounds of thy light footsteps as they go.

VALENTINE

TO THE HON. MARY C. STANHOPE.

Hail! day of Music, day of Love,
On earth below, in air above.
In air the turtle fondly moans,
The linnet pipes in joyous tones;
On earth the postman toils along,
Bent double by huge bales of song,
Where, rich with many a gorgeous dye,
Blazes all Cupid's heraldry—
Myrtles and roses, doves and sparrows,
Love-knots and altars, lamps and arrows.
What nymph without wild hopes and fears
The double rap this morning hears?
Unnumbered lasses, young and fair,
From Bethnal Green to Belgrave Square,
With cheeks high flushed and hearts loud beating,
Await the tender annual greeting.
The loveliest lass of all is mine—
Good morrow to my Valentine!
  Good morrow, gentle child! and then
Again good morrow, and again,
Good morrow following still good morrow,
Without one cloud of strife or sorrow,

And when the god to whom we pay
In jest our homages to-day
Shall come to claim, no more in jest,
His rightful empire o'er thy breast,
Benignant may his aspect be,
His yoke the truest liberty:
And if a tear his power confess,
Be it a tear of happiness.
It shall be so. The Muse displays
The future to her votary's gaze;
Prophetic rage my bosom swells—
I taste the cake—I hear the bells!
From Conduit Street the close array
Of chariots barricades the way
To where I see, with outstretched hand,
Majestic, thy great kinsman stand,*
And half unbend his brow of pride,
As welcoming so fair a bride.
Gay favours, thick as flakes of snow,
Brighten S. George's portico:
Within I see the chancel's pale,
The orange flowers, the Brussels veil,
The page on which those fingers white,
Still trembling from the awful rite,
For the last time shall faintly trace
The name of Stanhope's noble race.
I see kind faces round thee pressing,
I hear kind voices whisper blessing;
And with those voices mingles mine—
All good attend my Valentine!

St. Valentine's Day, 1851.

* The statue of Pitt in Hanover Square.

ROBERT B. BROUGH.

1828—1860.

THIS young poet, whose life had no summer in it, but was all spring (a cold and bitter spring), was of a Liverpool family, and came to London to seek his fortunes. Glowing with genius and seething with irrestrainable radicalism, he produced no long and continuous work worthy of his fine powers. His *chef d'œuvre* was this following exquisite paraphrase from a writer whose pathos and genial drollery he could so deeply appreciate.

A STORY FROM BOCCACCIO.

I have got a certain habit that approacheth to a merit,
   Yet is something of a weakness, and a trifle of a bore ;
'Tis that, when I meet a pleasure, I must call a friend to share it,
   Or I miss of its enjoyment half the luxury or more.

Thus, — when some good-natured crony sends a partridge or a pheasant,
   Or a trout, or river-salmon, that is not enough for two,
For my life I can't sit down to dine alone, howe'er unpleasant
   Comes the mutton anti-climax that must eke the dinner through.

Or, again,— I've got a garden, rather famous for its roses,
   But still more so for its artichokes, its beans, and early peas ;
Well, when any of these favourites begin to show their noses,
   I approach the garden-wall and cry, "Step here, sir, if you please."

'Tis to Mr. Jones, my neighbour, to partake my exultation ;
   But, if Mr. Jones be absent from his rake and pruning-hook,
I must press the nearest biped in the cause of admiration,
   If it's only Tom the stable boy, or Margery the cook.

So, in Literature's garden, when I've met a song or story
   That has raised a pleasant smile, or caused a pleasant tear
       descend;
Should you chance to call upon me, be admonished I should bore ye
   With the whole of the transaction from beginning to the end.

I've been reading in Boccaccio, where I've stumbled o'er a treasure
   That I'd somehow overlooked, although I've loved the book for
       years;
It's a quarter after midnight, and I can't expect the pleasure
   Of a visitor to favour me with sympathy and ears.

So I'll put the tale on paper, just as well as I can do it
   (For I can't wait till the morning for a call from Mr. Jones)
And I fancy, e'en in my hands, you'll be able to get through it,
   As, in any clumsy setting, we can value precious stones.

—

It was in the land of gardens (by the way, I've never been there;
   So the charms of "local colour" you had better not expect)—
In a garden, among gardens, Nature's blue, and gold, and green,
       there
   Were concentred—as in Eden, Eve a bower might have deck'd.

By the way, pray understand me—misconception's always hum-
       bling—
   ('Tis of Italy I speak); a Roman villa there had stood;
And with moss and vines half hidden, broken columns lay a-
       crumbling,
   Which I won't attempt to paint, as only Mr. Ruskin could.

And, were I to try the beauties of the sky and sea and ocean
   To depict, our travelled critics would be quickly down on me;
All I want is to convey a golden, dreamy kind of notion
   Of a garden, in the sunset, by the Adriatic sea.

Well—there sat two lovers, loving, neither gossipping nor moving,
   Ne'er a sigh or kiss exchanging, not a word did either say;
They were simply, I repeat it, sitting quietly and loving;
   Which is quite an occupation, I can tell you, in its way.

They were young and good and happy—more description, where's
    the need of?
Is it necessary, even, to inform you they were fair?
Since that goodness, youth, and happiness, from all I see and
    read of,
Are to Beauty, just as Oxygen and Nitrogen to Air.

So I give you a *carte blanche* of their external forms and dresses,
    All the details to fill in; you may indulge your tastes at ease
In the choice of ladies' fashion, and in hue of eyes and tresses,
    And the gentleman may clothe in any coloured stuffs you please.

Well, they sat there, never moving, only sitting still and loving,
    With their hands and souls united, and their faces looking calm;
Drinking bliss at each heart's pore—no thought of questioning or
    proving!
    Do the lilies think of analyzing zephyr's pleasant balm?

But, alas!—(I'm but a Cockney; you must pardon me some
    triteness
In my images from Nature)—in its pride of dewy gem,
Little recks the happy Lily, with its snowy, saucy whiteness,
    Of the brewing gust from northward, that will snap it from
        its stem!

So, alas! with my two lovers, at their lazy, happy loving,
    With their hearts from doubt and trouble, as their sky from
        cloudlets, free;
With the hundred thousand influences round them sweetly moving,
    Of the garden, and the sunset, and the Adriatic Sea!

To the story!—it's a short one: 'faith, a line or two would tell it.
    Yet a folio not exhaust it (there's a verse in Holy Writ
That contains but two short words: in half a second you may
    spell it,
    Yet the mighty Volume's purport is concentred all in it).

In the grass, among the flowers, plucking crocus cup and daisy,
    (Plants that probably in Italy were never known to smile:
I repeat that I'm a Cockney)—there he lounged, serenely lazy,
    Picking, throwing, nibbling, dreaming, dozing—loving all the
        while.

Well; one leant upon his elbow, and his hand went idly roving
    Through the tresses of the other—not in rapture or amaze
At their beauty; for the lovers who were sitting there and loving,
    Were *as one*—and none but coxcombs will their own adorning
        praise.

No! he twirled the tresses hither, and he tossed the tresses thither,
    As he would his own moustaches, and the maiden never moved;
Ne'er a freedom could she dream of, for the hand that trifled with her
    Was her own, for they were one—and so they trifled, sat, and
        loved;

And his other hand strayed idly o'er the herbage of the garden
    (By the way, 'twas once a wizard's, of the noxious herbal school;
I'm a greenhorn at narration, so I trust that you will pardon
    Any trifling deviation from severe constructive rule).

Scarce within his reach of arm, he spied a plant of curious prickle;
    It was tempting from its distance (still one hand about her
        head)—
Could he reach it? lo, a triumph! it is plucked, its fibres tickle;
    He must chew it—he has done so—in a moment he is DEAD!

'Twas a poison! . . . (I admit it's unartistic, ill-worked up to;
    It's abrupt, it's coarse, it's cruel, harsh—entitles me to groans;
But, I've told you, ne'er a neighbour would look in to chat and
        sup too;
So, if any one's to blame, I think you'll own it's Mr. Jones!)

He was dead, and she was living! Earth and sea, and sky, and
        ocean,
    All were changed—the light of life was gone, rekindled ne'er
        to be;
In the dark she stood alone; the sun had sunk with plummet
        motion;
Not a star shone o'er the blackness of the Adriatic Sea!

It was black, and cold, and sudden—she was hopeless, calm, and
        frigid;
Ne'er a moan escaped her bosom, on her brow was ne'er a frown;
She was broken, she was frozen, she was pulseless, she was rigid;
    Can the Lily wave its petals when the north has blown it down?

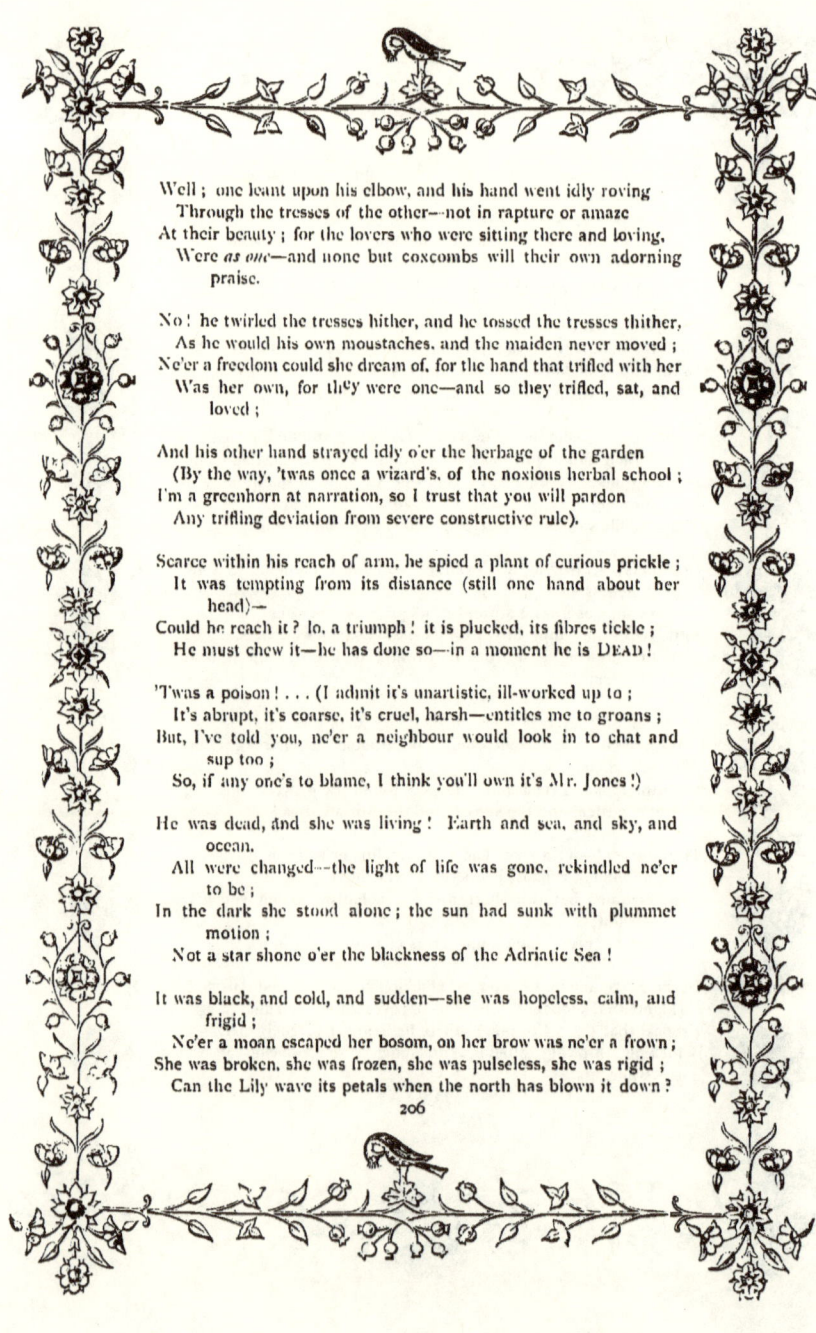

There she stood beside the body—not a kiss and not a murmur
　They were one, and he was dead beyond all human hopes and pains—
He was dead! the better part of her—the vital one, the firmer,
　And the mortifying virus worked through heart, and soul, and veins.

She was dying, and she waited. There, the neighbours came and found her,
　And they charged her with his murder; how, with magic art and wile,
She had poisoned her true lover; as the worldlings clamoured round her,
　She but met them with the spectre of a dead but lovely smile.

"Dearest friends," she said, "I love you, for you loved him and are wrathsome
　At his death, and thirst for many, in return for such a life;
And I love ye that ye'd slay me, with a death that's foul and loathsome;
　As you think 'tis I have slain him—I! who should have been his wife!

"Best of friends—do not hate me bitterly, and tear me into pieces;
　For you deem 'tis I have done it—nor give prayers up for my soul.
How you loved him! he was worth it. What! your honest fury ceases?
　Such true hearts must not be tortured, I'll confess to you the whole."

And she led them to the garden, whence they ruthlessly had torn her;
　And the people, still unsatisfied, were murmuring with ire;
ut the spirit flame within yet burnt, that upward still had borne her,
　And the vulgar, 'neath it, cowered, as the Heathen worship fire.

And she took them to the spot, where late with him she sat a-loving;
　And she told them of that happy time (years back it seemed to be!)
How they sat and loved, and idled, never thinking, never moving,
　In the garden, in the sunset, by the Adriatic Sea!

And she showed them how her lover had sat toying with her tresses,
  And with one hand plucked a poisoned leaf (the other at her head).
"Here's the plant!" she said, and picked it; "thus, its poison he
    expresses,
  Just as I do;" and she chewed it. In a moment she was dead!

There's my story—do you like it? from Boccaccio I've departed
  In the features; but I've given you, at all events, the bones.
It's a first attempt: if bullied, or but met with praise faint-hearted,
  . Why, in future, I shall go to bed, or knock up Mr. Jones.

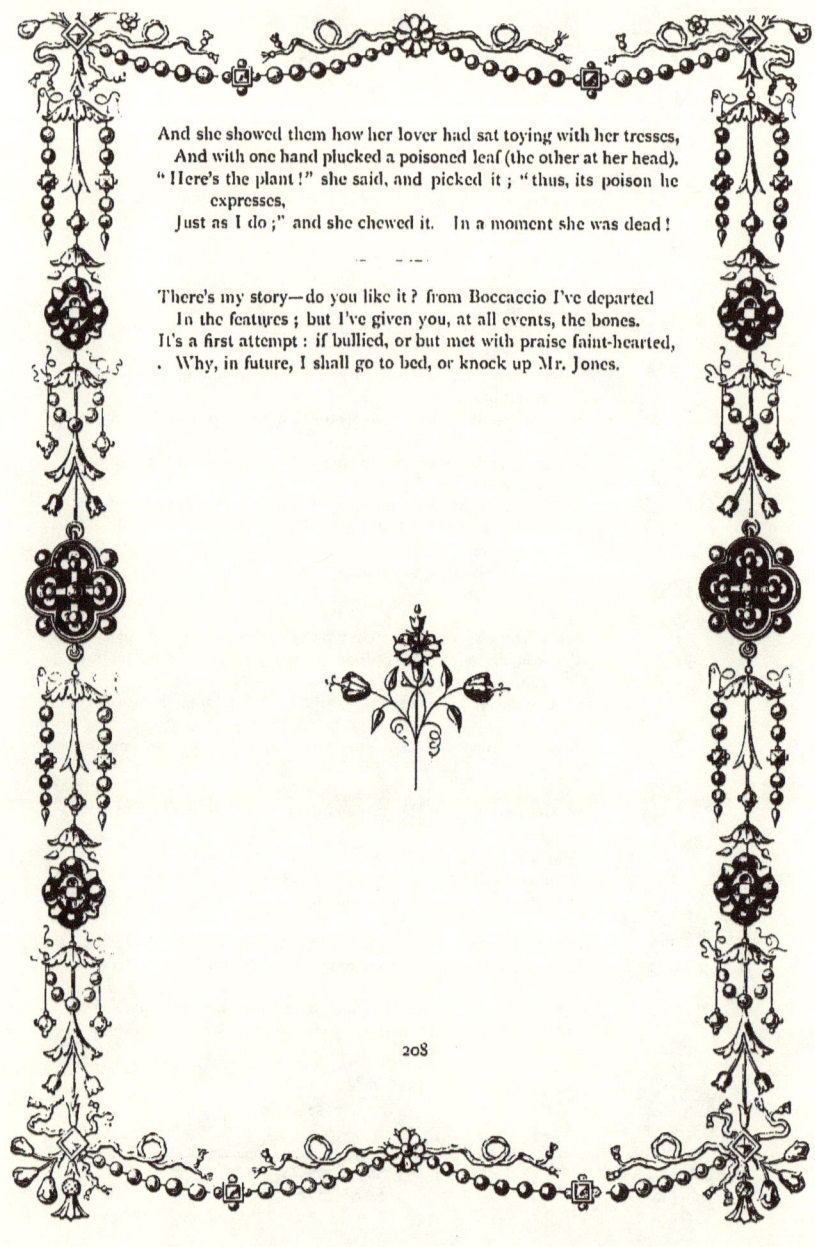

STEWART LOCKYER.

1833 1860.

THIS accomplished young poet was the son of a London architect. He attained considerable success as an artist of the pre-Raphaelite school. Impatient for quicker success (an impatience which is the peculiar curse of our age), he started for Pernambuco, where he entered an engineer's office, and in a few years fell a victim to the climate. His verses are peculiarly sweet and musical; and have an inner fervour and glow like a good Burgundy.

THE TOAST.

She who hath the gentle soul,
She who hath the winning way,
She who dare not favour grant
Lest a thousand hearts she slay—
Tender, fair, and wise, and good,
Choicest pearl of maidenhood;

She whose soft and lustrous hair,
Bright as golden vapoured sky,
Ever shines more richly fair
With the crown of modesty;
She who hath the form of grace,
She who hath the angel face;

She who hath a crowd of slaves,
Deeming servitude a bliss—
If her bondage be so sweet,
Heaven! what must be her kiss!
Well ye know her whom I mean,
Drink to her, our love, our queen!

Drink! 'tis all that we may do,
Chivalry is gone and dead,
Else in homage to her eyes
Gladly we'd have fought and bled ;
Days are gone for hearts to drain
For lady's love on battle plain.

But, behold! the vine hath shed
Purple drops to honour her,
Best and choicest that he hath,
As their perfume doth aver—
He hath done far more than we,
'Tis his heart's blood that ye see.

What! and will ye let her know
How ye have been put to shame?
Shall she think your ardour slow,
Your devotion dull and tame,
And your boasted love outdone
By this nursling of the sun?

He who is a lover staunch,
Quickly from his lady's eyes
Let him with a jealous fear
Hide the crimson sacrifice,
Lest the grape shall seem to be
Far more generous than he ;
Hide it, let no ruby stain
In the tell-tale glass remain ;
Drink, until no drop be seen,
Unto her, our love, our queen!

MRS. E. B. BROWNING.

1809–1861.

MRS. BROWNING ranks as the Queen of our female poets. She alone of them has thrown vigorous thought on national events into passionate verse; she alone has written a novel (almost a minor epic) in verse. Occasionally mannered, and daring in her mannerisms almost to affectation (coining phrases for her own intellectual coterie), her poetry is always true to nature, generous, and impassioned.

WINE OF CYPRUS.

Given to me by H. S. BOYD, Author of "Select Passages from the Greek Fathers," &c to whom these stanzas are addressed.

If old Bacchus were the speaker,
  He would tell you with a sigh
Of the Cyprus in this beaker
  I am sipping like a fly,—
Like a fly or gnat on Ida
  At the hour of goblet-pledge,
By Queen Juno brushed aside, a
  Full white arm-sweep, from the edge.

Sooth, the drinking should be ampler
  When the drink is so divine,
And some deep-mouthed Greek exemplar
  Would become your Cyprus wine:
Cyclops' mouth might plunge aright in,
  With his one eye over-leered,
Nor too large were mouth of Titan
  Drinking rivers down his beard.

Pan might dip his head so deep in
　　That his ears alone pricked out,
Fauns around him pressing, leaping,
　　Each one pointing to his throat:
While the Naiads, like Bacchantes,
　　Wild, with urns thrown out to waste,
Cry "O earth, that thou wouldst grant us
　　Springs to keep, of such a taste!"

But for me, I am not worthy
　　After gods and Greeks to drink,
And my lips are pale and earthy
　　To go bathing from this brink:
Since you heard them speak the last time
　　They have faded from their blooms,
And the laughter of my pastime
　　Has learnt silence at the tombs.

Ah, my friend! the antique drinkers
　　Crowned the cup and crowned the brow.
Can I answer the old thinkers
　　In the forms they thought of, now?
Who will fetch from garden-closes
　　Some new garlands while I speak,
That the forehead crowned with roses
　　May strike scarlet down the cheek?

Do not mock me! with my mortal
　　Suits no wreath again, indeed;
I am sad-voiced as the turtle
　　Which Anacreon used to feed:
Yet as that same bird demurely
　　Wet her beak in cup of his,
So without a garland surely
　　I may touch the brim of this.

Go,—let others praise the Chian!
　　This is soft as Muses' string,
This is tawny as Rhea's lion,
　　This is rapid as his spring,

Bright as Paphia's eyes ere met us,
   Light as ever trod her feet;
And the brown bees of Hymettus
   Make their honey not so sweet.

Very copious are my praises,
   Though I sip it like a fly!
Ah—but, sipping,—times and places
   Change before me suddenly:
As Ulysses' old libation
   Drew the ghosts from every part,
So your Cyprus wine, dear Grecian,
   Stirs the Hades of my heart.

And I think of those long mornings
   Which my thought goes far to seek,
When betwixt the folio's turnings
   Solemn flowed the rhythmic Greek:
Past the pane the mountain spreading,
   Swept the sheep's-bells tinkling noise,
While a girlish voice was reading,
   Somewhat low for *ais* and *ois*.

Then, what golden hours were for us!
   While we sat together there,
How the white vests of the chorus
   Seemed to wave up a live air!
How the cothurns trod majestic
   Down the deep iambic lines,
And the rolling anapæstic
   Curled like vapour over shrines!

Oh! our Æschylus, the thunderous,
   How he drove the bolted breath
Through the cloud, to wedge it ponderous
   In the gnarlèd oak beneath!
Oh! our Sophocles, the royal,
   Who was born to monarch's place,
And who made the whole world loyal,
   Less by kingly power than grace!

Our Euripides, the human,
    With his droppings of warm tears,
And his touches of things common
    Till they rose to touch the spheres!
Our Theocritus, our Bion,
    And our Pindar's shining goals!—
These were cup-bearers undying
    Of the wine that's meant for souls.

And my Plato, the divine one,
    If men know the gods aright,
By their motions as they shine on
    With a glorious trail of light!
And your noble Christian bishops
    Who mouthed grandly the last Greek!
Though the sponges on their hyssops
    Were distent with wine—too weak.

Yet, your Chrysostom, you praised him
    As a liberal mouth of gold;
And your Basil, you upraised him
    To the height of speakers old:
And we both praised Heliodorus
    For his secret of pure lies,—
Who forged first his linkèd stories
    In the heat of ladies' eyes.

And we both praised your Synesius
    For the fire shot up in his odes,
Though the Church was scarce propitious
    As he whistled dogs and gods.
And we both praised Nazianzen
    For the fervid heart and speech:
Only I eschewed his glancing
    At the lyre hung out of reach.

Do you mind that deed of Atè
    Which you bound me to so fast,—
Reading 'De Virginitate'
    From the first line to the last?

How I said at ending, solemn
 As I turned and looked at you,
That Saint Simeon on the column
 Had had somewhat less to do?

For we sometimes gently wrangled,
 Very gently, be it said,
Since our thoughts were disentangled
 By no breaking of the thread!
And I charged you with extortions
 On the nobler fames of old—
Ay, and sometimes thought your Porsons
 Stained the purple they would fold.

For the rest a mystic moaning
 Kept Cassandra at the gate,
With wild eyes the vision shone in,
 And wide nostrils scenting Fate.
And Prometheus, bound in passion
 By brute Force to the blind stone,
Showed us looks of invocation
 Turned to ocean and the sun.

And Medea we saw burning
 At her nature's planted stake:
And proud Œdipus fate-scorning
 While the cloud came on to break—
While the cloud came on slow, slower,
 Till he stood discrowned, resigned!—
But the reader's voice dropped lower
 When the poet called him BLIND.

Ah, my gossip! you were older,
 And more learned, and a man!
Yet that shadow, the enfolder
 Of your quiet eyelids, ran
Both our spirits to one level;
 And I turned from hill and lea
And the summer sun's green revel,
 To your eyes that could not see.

Now Christ bless you with the one light
    Which goes shining night and day!
May the flowers which grow in sunlight
    Shed their fragrance in your way!
Is it not right to remember
    All your kindness, friend of mine,
When we two sat in the chamber,
    And the poets poured us wine?

So, to come back to the drinking
    Of this Cyprus,—it is well,
But those memories, to my thinking,
    Make a better œnomel;
And whoever be the speaker,
    None can murmur with a sigh
That, in drinking from *that* beaker,
    I am sipping like a fly.

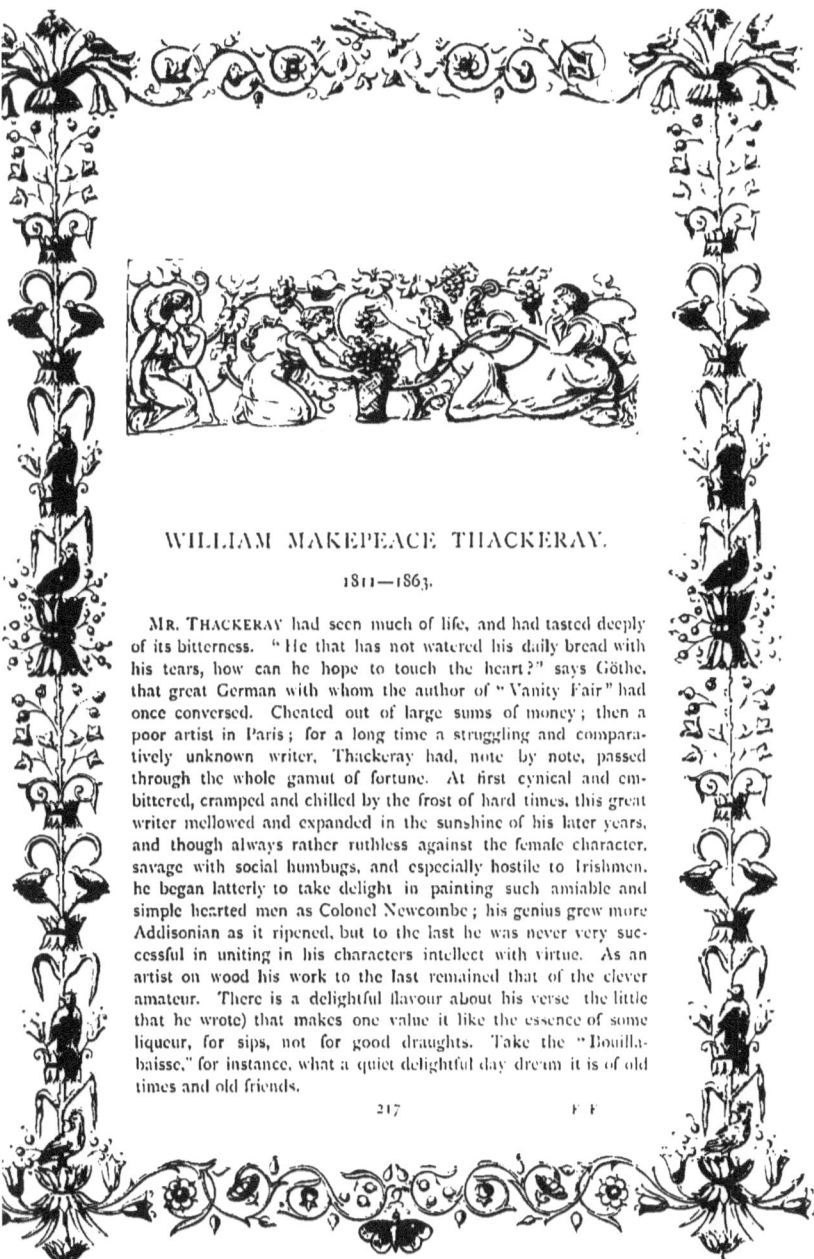

WILLIAM MAKEPEACE THACKERAY.
1811—1863.

MR. THACKERAY had seen much of life, and had tasted deeply of its bitterness. "He that has not watered his daily bread with his tears, how can he hope to touch the heart?" says Göthe, that great German with whom the author of "Vanity Fair" had once conversed. Cheated out of large sums of money; then a poor artist in Paris; for a long time a struggling and comparatively unknown writer, Thackeray had, note by note, passed through the whole gamut of fortune. At first cynical and embittered, cramped and chilled by the frost of hard times, this great writer mellowed and expanded in the sunshine of his later years, and though always rather ruthless against the female character, savage with social humbugs, and especially hostile to Irishmen, he began latterly to take delight in painting such amiable and simple hearted men as Colonel Newcombe; his genius grew more Addisonian as it ripened, but to the last he was never very successful in uniting in his characters intellect with virtue. As an artist on wood his work to the last remained that of the clever amateur. There is a delightful flavour about his verse (the little that he wrote) that makes one value it like the essence of some liqueur, for sips, not for good draughts. Take the "Bouillabaisse," for instance, what a quiet delightful day dream it is of old times and old friends.

THE BALLAD OF BOUILLABAISSE.

A street there is in Paris famous
    For which no rhyme our language yields,
Rue Neuve des Petits Champs its name is—
    The New Street of the Little Fields;
And here's an inn, not rich and splendid,
    But still in comfortable case,
The which in youth I oft attended,
    To eat a bowl of Bouillabaisse.

This Bouillabaisse a noble dish is—
    A sort of soup, or broth, or brew,
Or hotchpotch of all sorts of fishes,
    That Greenwich never could outdo;
Green herbs, red peppers, mussels, saffern,
    Soles, onions, garlic, roach, and dace;
All these you eat at Terré's tavern
    In that one dish of Bouillabaisse.

    *   *   *   *   *

I wonder if the house still there is?
    Yes, here the lamp is, as before;
The smiling red-cheeked écaillère is
    Still opening oysters at the door.
Is Terré still alive and able?
    I recollect his droll grimace;
He'd come and smile before your table,
    And hoped you liked your Bouillabaisse.

We enter—nothing's changed or older.
    "How's Monsieur Terré, Waiter, pray?"
The waiter stares and shrugs his shoulder—
    "Monsieur is dead this many a day."
"It is the lot of saint and sinner,
    So honest Terré's run his race."
"What will Monsieur require for dinner?"
    "Say, do you still cook Bouillabaisse?"

"Oh, oui, Monsieur,"'s the waiter's answer;
    "Quel vin Monsieur desire-t-il?"
"Tell me a good one"—"That I can, Sir,
    The Chambertin with yellow seal."

"So Terré's gone," I say, and sink in
    My old accustomed corner-place ;
"He's done with feasting and with drinking,
    With Burgundy and Bouillabaisse."

My old accustomed corner here is,
    The table still is in the nook ;
Ah ! vanished many a busy year is
    This well-known chair since last I took.
When first I saw ye, *Cari luoghi*,
    I'd scarce a beard upon my face,
And now a grizzled grim old fogy
    I sit and wait for Bouillabaisse.

Where are you, old companions trusty
    Of early days, here met to dine ?
Come, Waiter, quick, a flagon crusty —
    I'll pledge them in the good old wine.
The kind old voices and old faces
    My memory can quick retrace ;
Around the board they take their places
    And share the wine and Bouillabaisse.

There's Jack has made a wondrous marriage ;
    There's laughing Tom is laughing yet ;
There's brave Augustus drives his carriage ;
    There's poor old Fred in the Gazette ;
On James's head the grass is growing :
    Good Lord ! the world has wagged apace
Since here we set the claret flowing,
    And drank, and ate the Bouillabaisse.

Ah me ! how quick the days are flitting !
    I mind me of a time that's gone
When here I'd sit, as now I'm sitting,
    In this same place — but not alone.
A fair young form was nestled near me,
    A dear, dear face looked fondly up,
And sweetly spoke and smiled to cheer me
    There's no one now to share my cup.

I drink it as the Fates ordain it.
  Come, fill it, and have done with rhymes:
Fill up the lonely glass, and drain it
  In memory of dear old times.
Welcome the wine, whate'er the seal is;
  And sit you down and say your grace
With thankful heart, whate'er the meal is
  — Here comes the smoking Bouillabaisse!

In the "Age of Wisdom," the poet gives youth one of his cynical lessons with a profound experience of the vanity of human pleasures.

THE AGE OF WISDOM.

Ho, pretty page, with the dimpled chin
  That never has known the barber's shear,
All your wish is woman to win,
This is the way that boys begin,—
  Wait till you come to Forty Year!

Curly gold locks cover foolish brains,
  Billing and cooing is all your cheer,
Sighing and singing of midnight strains
Under Bonnybell's window panes,—
  Wait till you come to Forty Year.

Forty times over let Michaelmas pass,
  Grizzling hair the brain doth clear—
Then you know a boy is an ass,
Then you know the worth of a lass,
  Once you have come to Forty Year!
      * * * * *

The reddest lips that ever have kissed,
  The brightest eyes that ever have shone,
May pray and whisper, and we not list,
Or look away, and never be missed,
  Ere yet even a month is gone.

Gillian's dead, God rest her bier,
 How I loved her twenty years syne!
Marian's married, but I sit here
Alone and merry at Forty Year,
 Dipping my nose in the Gascon wine.

The "Mahogany Tree" is a wild Christmas song, full of good fellowship, and yet the mirth is thoughtful. The present Christmas reminds the poet of past Christmases; beyond the bright lights there is a gloom.

THE MAHOGANY TREE.

Christmas is here;
 Winds whistle shrill,
 Icy and chill,
  Little care we:
Little we fear
 Weather without,
 Sheltered about
  The Mahogany Tree.

Once on the boughs,
 Birds of rare plume
 Sang, in its bloom;
  Night-birds are we:
Here we carouse,
 Singing, like them,
 Perched round the stem
  Of the jolly old tree.

Here let us sport,
 Boys, as we sit;
 Laughter and wit
  Flashing so free.
Life is but short—
 When we are gone,
 Let them sing on
  Round the old tree.

Evenings we knew,
　Happy as this;
　Faces we miss,
　　Pleasant to see.
Kind hearts and true,
　Gentle and just,
　Peace to your dust!
　　We sing round the tree.

Care, like a dun,
　Lurks at the gate:
　Let the dog wait:
　　Happy we'll be!
Drink every one;
　Pile up the coals,
　Fill the red bowls,
　　Round the old tree!

In the "Cane Bottomed Chair," Thackeray sketches with tender regret the old bitter-sweet Bohemian life.

THE CANE-BOTTOMED CHAIR.

In tattered old slippers that toast at the bars,
And a ragged old jacket perfumed with cigars,
Away from the world and its toils and its cares,
I've a snug little kingdom up four pair of stairs.

　　*　　　*　　　*　　　*

This snug little chamber is crammed in all nooks
With worthless old knicknacks and silly old books,
And foolish old odds, and foolish old ends,
Cracked bargains from brokers, cheap keepsakes from friends.

Old armour, prints, pictures, pipes, china (all cracked);
Old rickety tables, and chairs broken-backed;
A twopenny treasury, worthless to see;
What matter? 'tis pleasant to you, friend, and me.

　　*　　　*　　　*　　　*

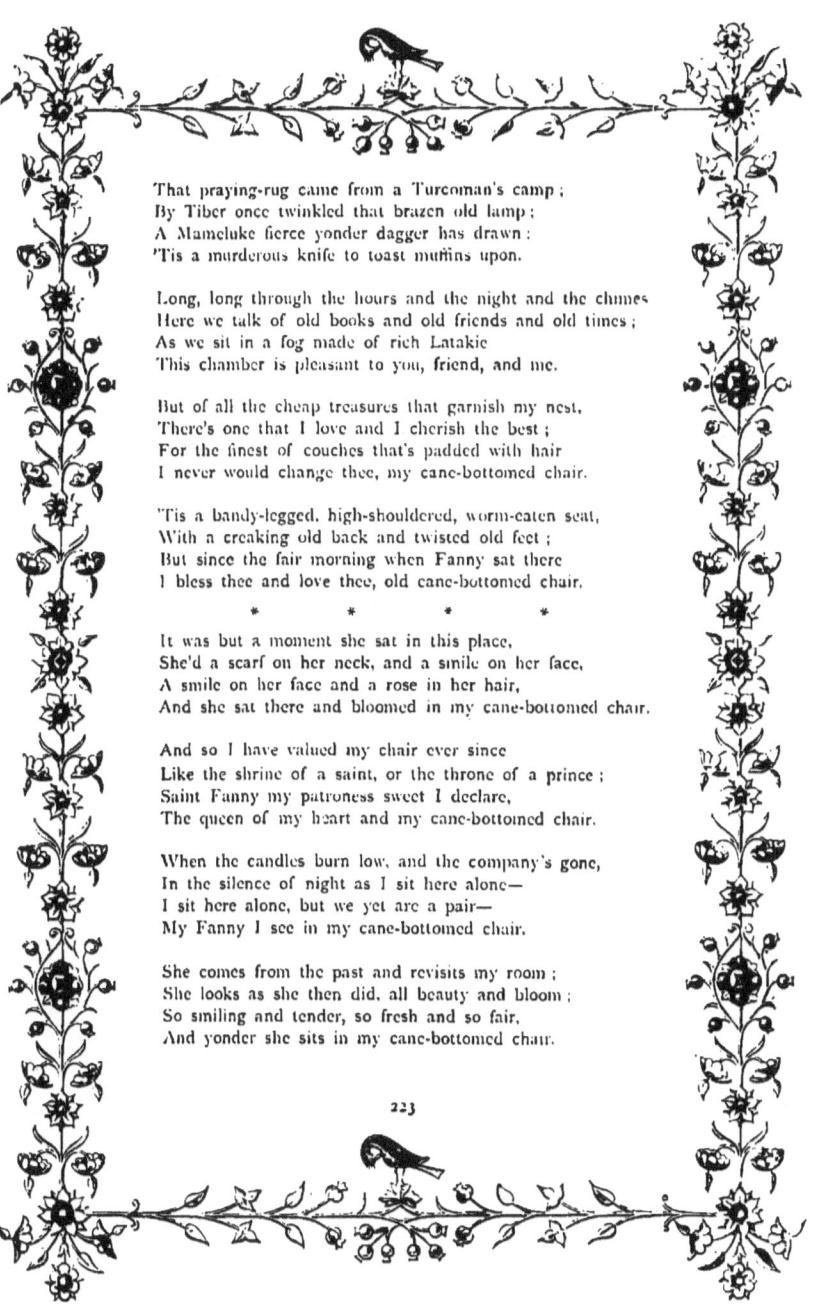

That praying-rug came from a Turcoman's camp;
By Tiber once twinkled that brazen old lamp;
A Mameluke fierce yonder dagger has drawn:
'Tis a murderous knife to toast muffins upon.

Long, long through the hours and the night and the chimes
Here we talk of old books and old friends and old times;
As we sit in a fog made of rich Latakie
This chamber is pleasant to you, friend, and me.

But of all the cheap treasures that garnish my nest,
There's one that I love and I cherish the best;
For the finest of couches that's padded with hair
I never would change thee, my cane-bottomed chair.

'Tis a bandy-legged, high-shouldered, worm-eaten seat,
With a creaking old back and twisted old feet;
But since the fair morning when Fanny sat there
I bless thee and love thee, old cane-bottomed chair.

   * * * *

It was but a moment she sat in this place,
She'd a scarf on her neck, and a smile on her face,
A smile on her face and a rose in her hair,
And she sat there and bloomed in my cane-bottomed chair.

And so I have valued my chair ever since
Like the shrine of a saint, or the throne of a prince;
Saint Fanny my patroness sweet I declare,
The queen of my heart and my cane-bottomed chair.

When the candles burn low, and the company's gone,
In the silence of night as I sit here alone—
I sit here alone, but we yet are a pair—
My Fanny I see in my cane-bottomed chair.

She comes from the past and revisits my room;
She looks as she then did, all beauty and bloom;
So smiling and tender, so fresh and so fair,
And yonder she sits in my cane-bottomed chair.

ALARIC ALEXANDER WATTS.
1799—1864.

AMONG the sentimental poets, Mr. Watts stands high, but the school is by no means a perfect one. Assumed melancholy and feigned Byronic emotions are as bad as the strained metaphors and hysterical fury of our spasmodic poets of a few years ago. In the "Keepsakes," which Mr. Watts originated, much of his graceful and always musical verse appears.

TEN YEARS AGO.

Ten years ago, ten years ago,
   Life was to us a fairy scene,
And the keen blasts of worldly woe
   Had seared not then its pathway green.
Youth and its thousand dreams were ours,
   Feelings we ne'er can know again;
Unwithered hopes, unwasted powers,
   And frames unworn by mortal pain:
Such was the bright and genial flow
Of life with us—ten years ago!

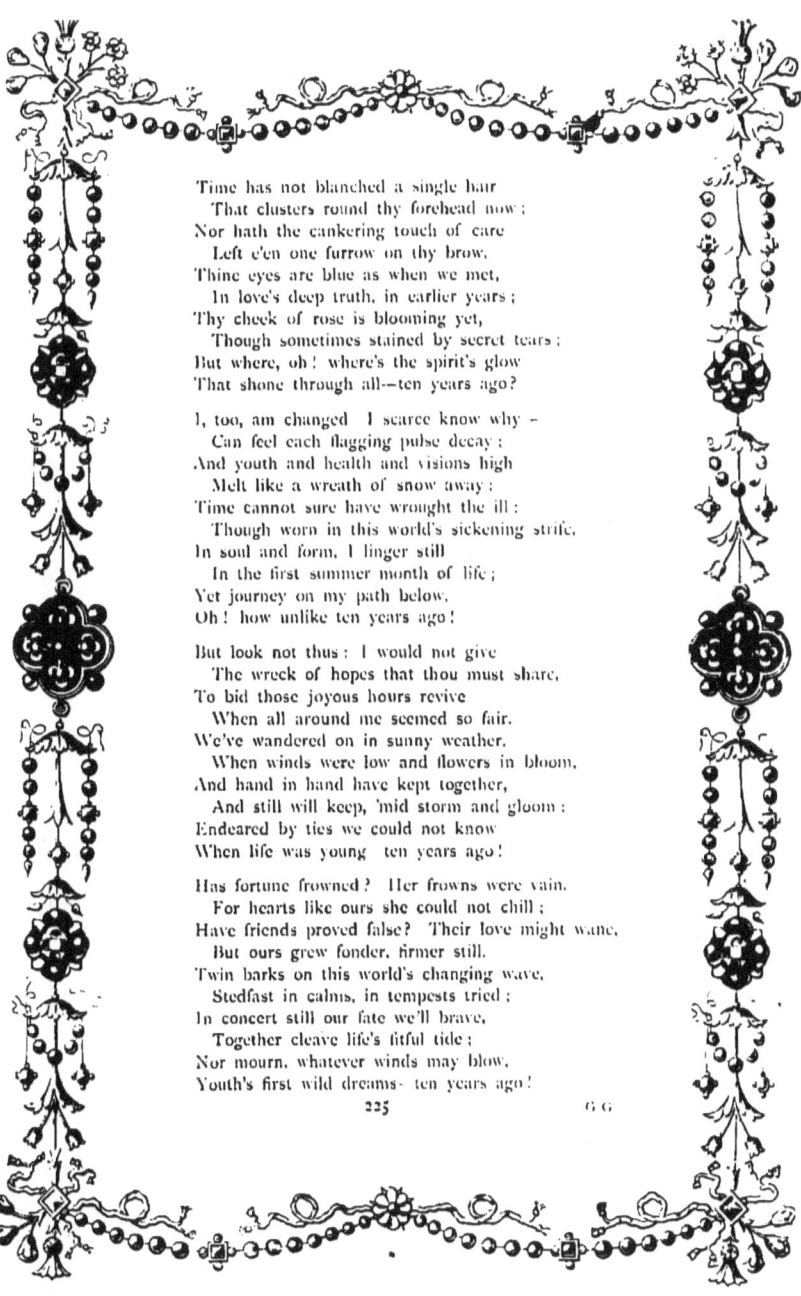

Time has not blanched a single hair
　That clusters round thy forehead now;
Nor hath the cankering touch of care
　Left e'en one furrow on thy brow.
Thine eyes are blue as when we met,
　In love's deep truth, in earlier years;
Thy cheek of rose is blooming yet,
　Though sometimes stained by secret tears;
But where, oh! where's the spirit's glow
That shone through all—ten years ago?

I, too, am changed—I scarce know why—
　Can feel each flagging pulse decay;
And youth and health and visions high
　Melt like a wreath of snow away;
Time cannot sure have wrought the ill;
　Though worn in this world's sickening strife,
In soul and form, I linger still
　In the first summer month of life;
Yet journey on my path below,
Oh! how unlike ten years ago!

But look not thus; I would not give
　The wreck of hopes that thou must share,
To bid those joyous hours revive
　When all around me seemed so fair.
We've wandered on in sunny weather,
　When winds were low and flowers in bloom,
And hand in hand have kept together,
　And still will keep, 'mid storm and gloom;
Endeared by ties we could not know
When life was young—ten years ago!

Has fortune frowned? Her frowns were vain,
　For hearts like ours she could not chill;
Have friends proved false? Their love might wane,
　But ours grew fonder, firmer still.
Twin barks on this world's changing wave,
　Stedfast in calms, in tempests tried;
In concert still our fate we'll brave,
　Together cleave life's fitful tide;
Nor mourn, whatever winds may blow,
Youth's first wild dreams—ten years ago!

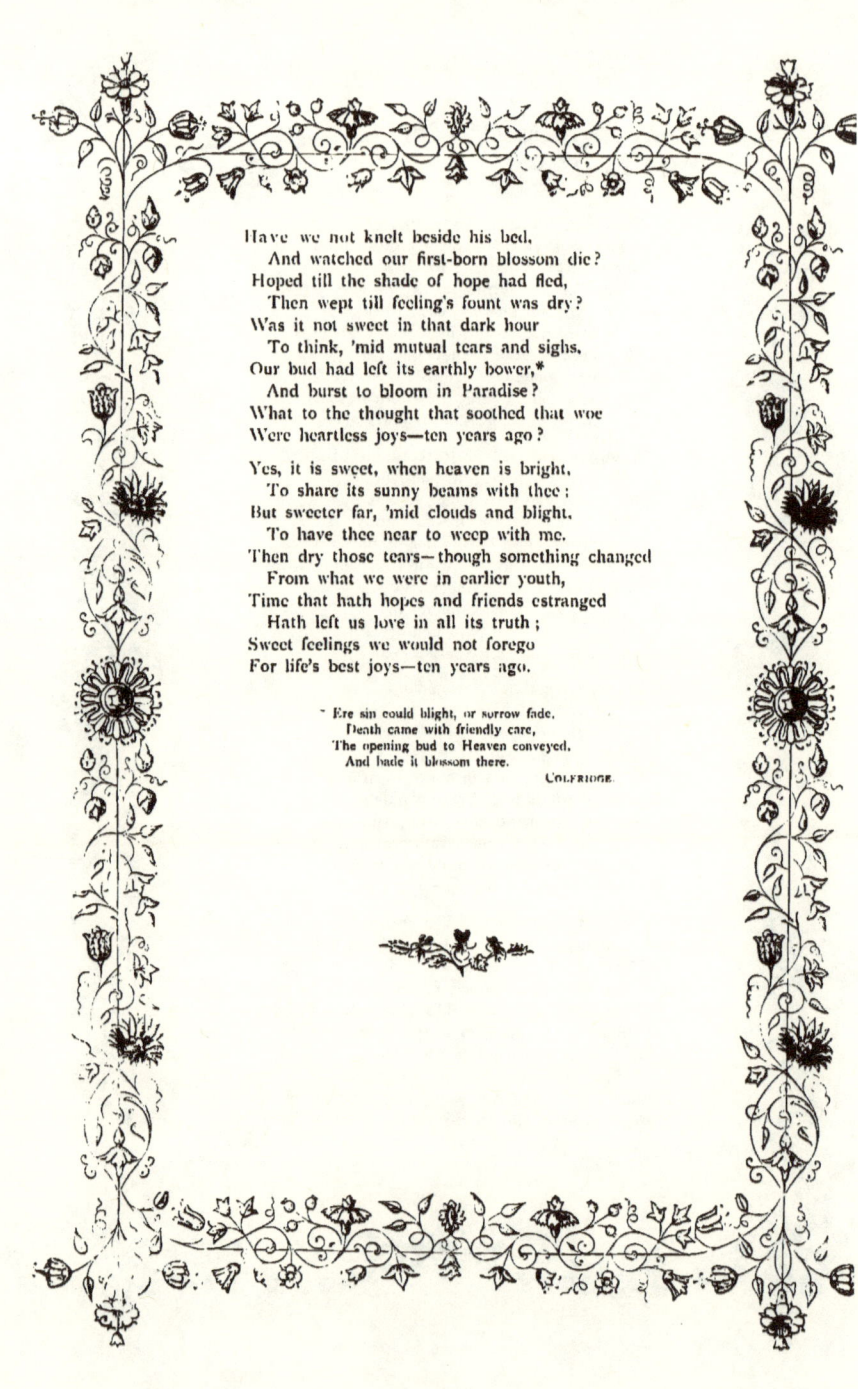

Have we not knelt beside his bed,
    And watched our first-born blossom die?
Hoped till the shade of hope had fled,
    Then wept till feeling's fount was dry?
Was it not sweet in that dark hour
    To think, 'mid mutual tears and sighs,
Our bud had left its earthly bower,*
    And burst to bloom in Paradise?
What to the thought that soothed that woe
Were heartless joys—ten years ago?

Yes, it is sweet, when heaven is bright,
    To share its sunny beams with thee;
But sweeter far, 'mid clouds and blight,
    To have thee near to weep with me.
Then dry those tears—though something changed
    From what we were in earlier youth,
Time that hath hopes and friends estranged
    Hath left us love in all its truth;
Sweet feelings we would not forego
For life's best joys—ten years ago.

    * Ere sin could blight, or sorrow fade,
      Death came with friendly care,
    The opening bud to Heaven conveyed,
      And bade it blossom there.
                  COLERIDGE.

ADELAIDE A. PROCTER.

1835—1864.

THIS accomplished young lady, the daughter of the poet Barry Cornwall, died of consumption in the very May time of her genius. A presentiment of early death pervades all her verse; her songs are as tender and as sad as those of the nightingale, and, like them, they seem fittest for the meditative twilight.

MY PICTURE GALLERY.

You write and think of me, my friend, with pity,
    While you are basking in the light of Rome,
Shut up within the heart of this great city,
    Too busy and too poor to leave my home.

You think my life debarred all rest or pleasure,
    Chained all day to my ledger and my pen;
Too sickly e'en to use my little leisure
    To bear me from the strife and din of men.

Well, it is true; yet, now the days are longer,
    At sunset I can lay my writing down,
And slowly crawl (summer has made me stronger)
    Just to the nearest outskirt of the town.

There a wide common, blackened though and dreary
    With factory smoke, spreads outward to the west;
I lie down on the parched-up grass, if weary,
    Or lean against a broken wall to rest.

So might a king, turning to Art's rich treasure,
    At evening when the cares of state were done,
Enter his royal gallery, drinking pleasure
    Slowly from each great picture, one by one.

Towards the west I turn my weary spirit,
  And watch my pictures: one each night is mine.
Earth and my soul, sick of day's toil, inherit
  A portion of that luminous peace divine.

There I have seen a sunset's crimson glory
  Burn as if earth were one great altar's blaze;
Or, like the closing of a piteous story,
  Light up the misty world with dying rays.

There I have seen the clouds in pomp and splendour
  Their gold and purple banners all unfurl;
There I have watched colours far more faint and tender
  Than pure and delicate tints upon a pearl.

Skies strewn with roses fading, fading slowly,
  While one star trembling watched the daylight die;
Or deep in gloom a sunset, hidden wholly
  Save through gold rents torn in a violet sky.

Or parted clouds, as if asunder riven
  By some great angel—and beyond a space
Of far-off tranquil light; the gates of Heaven
  Will lead as grandly to as calm a place.

Or stern dark walls of cloudy mountain ranges
  Hid all the wonders that we knew must be;
While far on high some little white clouds' changes
  Revealed the glory they alone could see.

Or in wild wrath th' affrighted clouds lay shattered,
  Like treasures of the lost Hesperides,
All in a wealth of ruined splendour scattered,
  Save one strange light on distant silver seas.

What land or time can claim the master painter
  Whose art could teach him half such gorgeous dyes?
Or skill so rare, but purer hues and fainter
  Melt every evening in my western skies?

So there I wait until the shade has lengthened,
  And night's blue misty curtain floated down;
Then, with my heart calmed and my spirits strengthened,
  I crawl once more back to the sultry town.

What monarch, then, has nobler recreations
  Than mine? Or where the great and classic land
Whose wealth of Art delights the gathered nations,
  That owns a Picture Gallery half as grand?

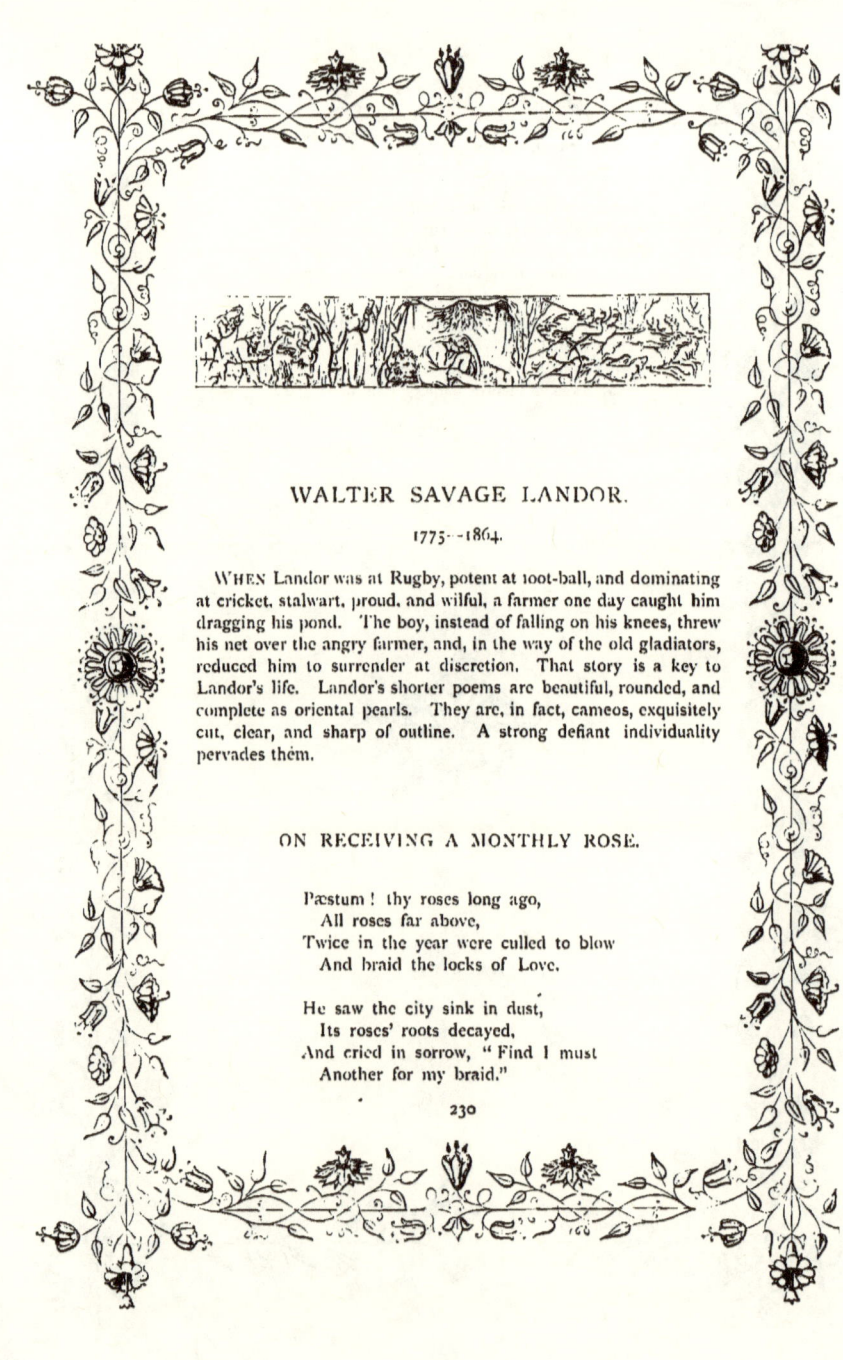

WALTER SAVAGE LANDOR.

1775--1864.

WHEN Landor was at Rugby, potent at foot-ball, and dominating at cricket, stalwart, proud, and wilful, a farmer one day caught him dragging his pond. The boy, instead of falling on his knees, threw his net over the angry farmer, and, in the way of the old gladiators, reduced him to surrender at discretion. That story is a key to Landor's life. Landor's shorter poems are beautiful, rounded, and complete as oriental pearls. They are, in fact, cameos, exquisitely cut, clear, and sharp of outline. A strong defiant individuality pervades them.

ON RECEIVING A MONTHLY ROSE.

Pæstum! thy roses long ago,
  All roses far above,
Twice in the year were culled to blow
  And braid the locks of Love.

He saw the city sink in dust,
  Its roses' roots decayed,
And cried in sorrow, "Find I must
  Another for my braid."

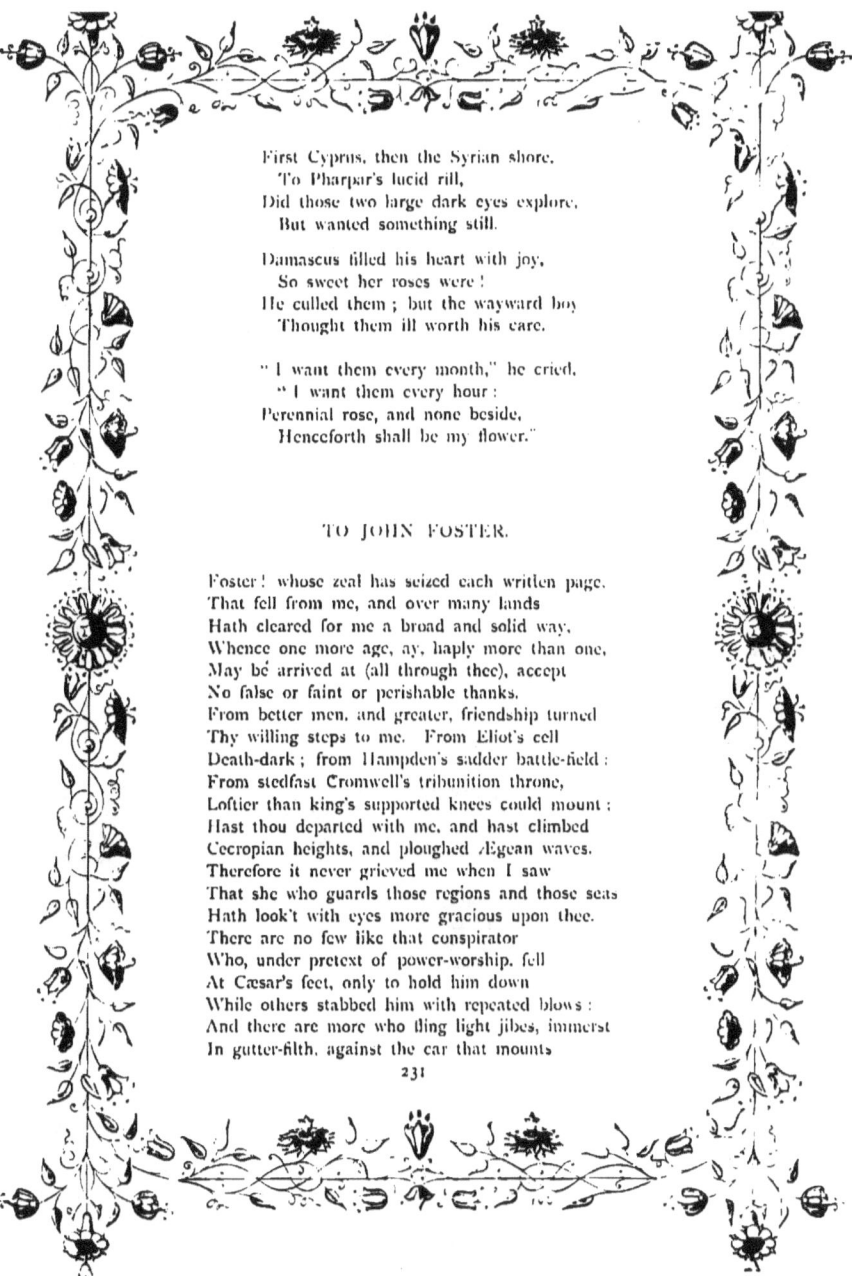

First Cyprus, then the Syrian shore,
  To Pharpar's lucid rill,
Did those two large dark eyes explore,
  But wanted something still.

Damascus filled his heart with joy,
  So sweet her roses were!
He culled them; but the wayward boy
  Thought them ill worth his care.

" I want them every month," he cried,
" I want them every hour:
Perennial rose, and none beside,
  Henceforth shall be my flower."

TO JOHN FOSTER.

Foster! whose zeal has seized each written page,
That fell from me, and over many lands
Hath cleared for me a broad and solid way,
Whence one more age, ay, haply more than one,
May be arrived at (all through thee), accept
No false or faint or perishable thanks.
From better men, and greater, friendship turned
Thy willing steps to me. From Eliot's cell
Death-dark; from Hampden's sadder battle-field;
From stedfast Cromwell's tribunition throne,
Loftier than king's supported knees could mount;
Hast thou departed with me, and hast climbed
Cecropian heights, and ploughed Ægean waves.
Therefore it never grieved me when I saw
That she who guards those regions and those seas
Hath look't with eyes more gracious upon thee.
There are no few like that conspirator
Who, under pretext of power-worship, fell
At Cæsar's feet, only to hold him down
While others stabbed him with repeated blows:
And there are more who fling light jibes, immerst
In gutter-filth, against the car that mounts

Weighty with triumph up the Sacred Way.
Protect in every place my stranger guests,
Born in the lucid land of free pure song,
Now first appearing on repulsive shores,
Bleak, and where safely none but natives move,
Red-polled, red-handed, siller-grasping men.
Ah! lead them far away, for they are used
To genial climes and gentle speech; but most
Cymodameia; warn the Tritons off
While she ascends, while through the opening plain
Of the green sea (brightened by bearing it)
Gushes redundantly her golden hair.

SIXTEEN.

In Clementina's artless mien
  Lucilla asks me what I see,
And are the roses of sixteen
      Enough for me

Lucilla asks if that be all,
  Have I not culled as sweet before?
Ah yes, Lucilla! and their fall
      I still deplore.

I now behold another scene,
  Where pleasure beams with heaven's own light,
More pure, more constant, more serene,
      And not less bright.

Faith, on whose breast the Loves repose,
  Whose chain of flowers no force can sever,
And Modesty, who, when she goes,
      Is gone for ever.

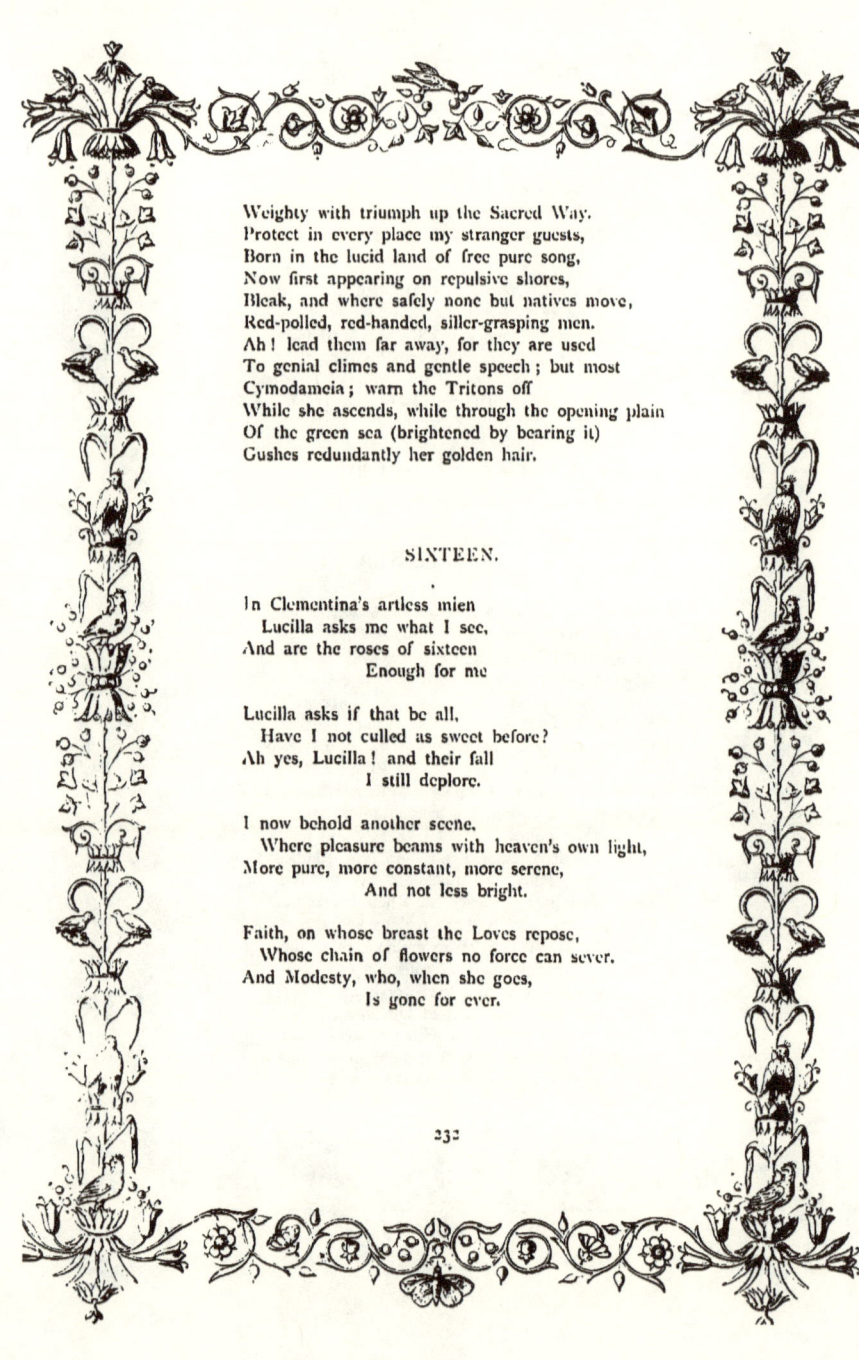

FRANCIS MAHONY, ESQ

FATHER PROUT. 1805—1866.

WHAT a singular transformation—a Jesuit priest turning newspaper correspondent and magazine writer! No one has paraphrased Horace more exquisitely than Father Prout, and of all his paraphrases, there is not one more exquisite and more close to the original (a merit sometimes overlooked in clever translations) than the following :—

ODE IX.

See how the winter blanches
   Soracte's giant brow!
Hear how the forest branches
   Groan for the weight of snow!
While the fix'd ice impanels
Rivers within their channels.

Out with the frost! expel her!
   Pile up the fuel block,
And from thy hoary cellar
   Produce a Sabine crock;
O Thaliarck! remember
It counts a fourth December.

Give to the gods the guidance
   Of earth's arrangements.—List!
The blasts at their high biddance
   From the vex'd deep desist,
Nor 'mid the cypress riot;
And the old elms are quiet.

The *chef d'œuvre* of Father Prout, however, is that reminiscence of his native city which he entitled

"THE BELLS OF SHANDON."

Of all the poems on bells ever written we prefer this. Even Edgar Poe's wonderful poem (though about that there is the subtlety and passion of insanity) is not so thoughtful nor so true.

THE SHANDON BELLS.

With deep affection
And recollection
I often think of
  Those Shandon bells,
Whose sounds so wild would
In the days of childhood
Fling round my cradle
  Their magic spells.
On this I ponder
Where'er I wander,
And thus grow fonder
  Sweet Cork, of thee.
With thy bells of Shandon,
That sound so grand on,
The pleasant waters
  Of the river Lee.

I've heard bells chiming,
Full many a clime in,
Tolling sublime in
  Cathedral shrine,
While at a glib rate
Brass tongues would vibrate,
But all their music
  Spoke nought like thine.
For memory dwelling
On each proud swelling,
  Its bold notes free,
Made the bells of Shandon,
Sound far more grand on
The pleasant waters
  Of the river Lee.

I've heard bells toll in
Old "Adrian's Mole" in
Their thunder rolling
 From the Vatican,
And cymbals glorious
Swinging uproarious
In the gorgeous turrets
 Of Nôtre Dame.
But thy sounds were sweeter,
Than the dome of Peter
Flings o'er the Tiber
 Pealing solemnly;
O! the bells of Shandon.
Sound far more grand on,
The pleasant waters
 Of the river Lee.

With his deep scholarship, wonderful versatility as a linguis and profound knowledge of ecclesiastical learning in its least known branches, Father Prout combined all the ardour and sparkle of an Irish genius. His rhymes are as audacious as they are ingenious—he tried "each mode of the lyre and was master of all." How admirable is this eccentric jingle on a hamlet near Cork.

The town of Passage
Is both large and spacious.
And situated
 Upon the say.
'Tis nate and dacent,
And quite adjacent
To come from Cork
 On a summer's day;
There you may slip in
To take a dipping,
Fornent the shipping
 That at anchor ride;
Or in a wherry,
Cross o'er the ferry,
To Carrigaloe
 On the other side.

Mud cabins swarm in
This place so charming.
With sailors' garments,
  Hung out to dry.
And each abode is
Snug and commodious
With pigs melodious
  In their straw-built sty.
'Tis there the turf is,
And lots of murphies,
Dead sprats and herrings
  And oyster shells;
Nor any lack O
Of good tobacco,
Though what is smuggled
  By far excels.

There are ships from Cadiz
And from Barbadoes,
But the leading trade is
  In whisky-punch.
    *   *   *
Of ships—there's one fixt
For lodging convicts
A floating "stone-jug"
  Of amazing bulk;
The hake and salmon
Playing at backgammon
Swim for diversion
  All round this "hulk;"
There Saxon jailors
Keep brave Repailers
Who soon with sailors
  Must anchor weigh
From th' Emerald Island,
Ne'er to see dry land
Until they spy land
  In sweet Bot'ny Bay.

LIVING AUTHORS.

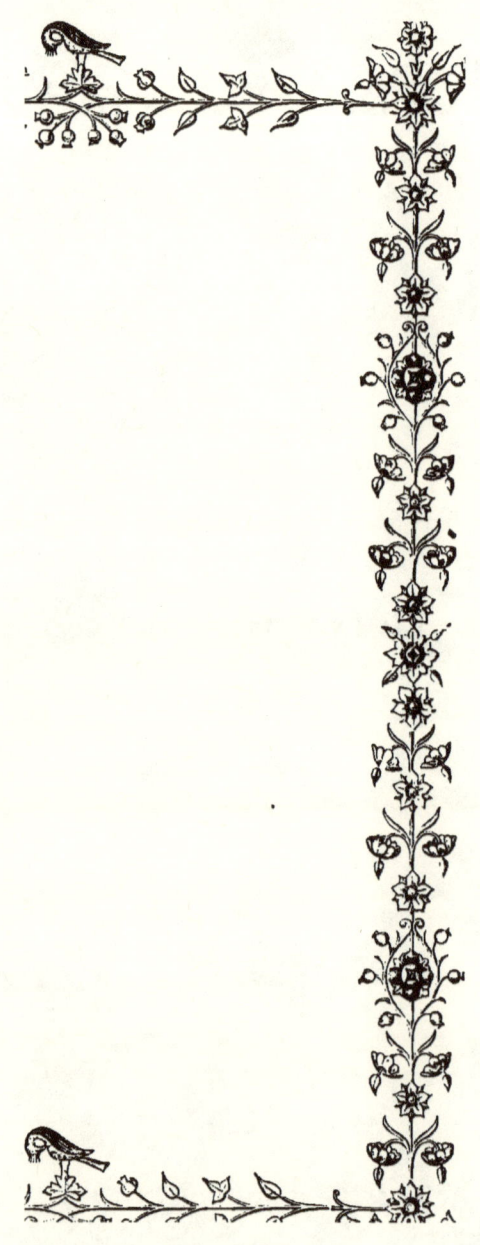

WILLIAM ALLINGHAM.

THE LOVER AND BIRDS.

Within a budding grove,
In April's ear sang every bird his best,
But not a song to pleasure my unrest,
Or touch the tears unwept of bitter love.
Some spake, methought, with pity, some as if in jest.
To every word
Of every bird
I listened, and replied as it behove.

Screamed Chaffinch, "Sweet, sweet, sweet!
O bring my pretty love to meet me here!"
"Chaffinch," quoth I, "be dumb awhile, in fear
Thy darling prove no better than a cheat,
And never come, or fly when wintry days appear."
Yet from a twig
With voice so big
The little fowl his utterance did repeat.

Then I, "The man forlorn
Hears Earth send up a foolish noise aloft."
"And what'll *he* do? what'll *he* do!" scoffed
The Blackbird, standing in an ancient thorn;
Then spread his sooty wings, and flitted to the croft
  With cackling laugh:
  Whom I, being half
Enraged, called after, giving back his scorn.

 Worse mocked the Thrush, "Die! die!
O could he do it! could he do it? Nay!
Be quick! be quick! Here, here, here!" (went his lay)
"Take heed! take heed!" then, "Why? why? why? why? why?
See-ee now! see-ee now! (he drawled) Back! back! back!
 R-r-r-run away!"
  "O Thrush, be still!
  Or, at thy will,
Seek some less sad interpreter than I!"

 "Air, air! blue air and white!
Whither I flee, whither, O whither, O whither I flee!"
('Thus the Lark hurried, mounting from the lea)
" Hills, countries, many waters glittering bright,
Whither I see, whither I see! deeper, deeper, deeper, whither I
 see, see, see!"
  "Gay Lark," I said,
  "The song that's bred
In happy nest may well to heaven make flight."

 "There's something, something sad,
I half remember"—piped a broken strain.
Well sung, sweet Robin! Robin sung again,
"Spring's opening cheerily, cheerily! be we glad!"
Which moved, I wist not why, me melancholy mad,
  Till now, grown meek,
  With wetted cheek,
Most comforting and gentle thoughts I had.

PHILIP JAMES BAILEY.

SONG, FROM "FESTUS."

Oh! the wee green neuk, the sly green neuk,
    The wee sly neuk for me!
Whare the wheat is wavin' bright and brown,
    And the wind is fresh and free.
Whare I weave wild weeds, and out o' reeds
    Kerve whissles as I lay;
And a douce low voice is murmurin' by
    Through the lee-lang simmer day.
        Oh! the wee green neuk, &c.

And whare a' things luik as though they lo'ed
    To languish in the sun;
And that, if they feed the fire they dree,
    They wadna ae pang were gone.
Whare the lift aboon is still as death,
    And bright as life can be;
While the douce low voice says, Na, na, na!
    But ye mauna luik sae at me.
        Oh! the wee green neuk, &c.

Whare the lang rank bent is saft and cule,
    And freshenin' till the feet;
And the spot is sly, and the spinnie high,
    Whare my luve and I mak' seat:
And I tease her till she rins, and then
    I catch her roun' the tree;
While the poppies shak' their heids and blush:
    Let 'em blush till they drap for me!
        Oh! the wee green neuk, &c.

HENRY S. LEIGH.

THE SEE-SAW.

Sickness and health have been having a game with me,
    Tossing me, just like a ball, to and fro.
Pleasure and pain have been doing the same with me,
    Treating me simply like something to throw.
Joy took me up to the clouds for a holiday,
    In a balloon that she happens to keep;
Then, as a damp upon rather a jolly day,
    Grief in her diving-bell took me down deep.

Poverty came pretty early—bad luck to her!—
    Truly she makes an affectionate wife.
I, like a fool, have been faithful, and stuck to her;
    She'll stick to *me* for the rest of my life.
As for our children (I wish we had drowned them all)—
    Those I regard as the worst of my ills.
How can you wonder to hear me *confound* them all,
    Seeing that most of those children are *Bills?*

Hope, who was once an occasional visitor,
    Never looks in on us now for a chat.
Memory comes, though—the cruel inquisitor!
    (Not that I feel much the better for *that!*)
Hope was a liar, there's no use denying it:
    Memory's tales are decidedly true;
Yet I confess that I like, after trying it,
    Hope's conversation the best of the two.

MARY HOWITT.

THE BARLEY-MOWERS' SONG.

Barley-mowers here we stand,
One, two, three, a steady band;
True of heart and strong of limb,
Ready in our harvest-trim;
All a-row, with spirits blithe,
Now we whet the bended scythe.
　　Rink-a-tink, rink-a-tink, rink-a-tink-a-tink!

Side by side now, bending low,
Down the swaths of barley go;
Stroke by stroke, as true as chime
Of the bells we keep in time:
Then we whet the ringing scythe,
Standing 'mid the barley lithe.
　　Rink-a-tink, rink-a-tink, rink-a-tink-a-tink!

After labour cometh ease;
Sitting now beneath the trees,
Round we send the barley-wine,
Life-infusing, clear and fine;
Then refreshed, alert and blithe,
Rise we all, and whet the scythe.
　　Rink-a-tink, rink-a-tink, rink-a-tink-a-tink!

Barley-mowers must be true,
Keeping still the end in view;
One with all, and all with one,
Working on till set of sun;
Bending all with spirits blithe,
Whetting all at once the scythe.
　　Rink-a-tink, rink-a-tink, rink-a-tink-a-tink!

Day and night, and night and day,
Time, the mower, will not stay:
We may hear him in our path
By the falling barley-swath;
While we sing with spirits blithe,
We may hear his ringing scythe—
    Rink-a-tink, rink-a-tink, rink-a-tink-a-tink!

Time, the mower, cuts down all,
High and low, and great and small:
Fear him not, for we will grow
Ready like the field we mow;
Like the bending barley lithe,
Ready for Time's whetted scythe.
    Rink-a-tink, rink-a-tink, rink-a-tink-a-tink!

RICHARD CHENEVIX TRENCH.

ATLANTIS.

I could loose my boat,
And could bid it float
Where the idlest wind should pilot,
So its glad course lay
From this earth away,
Toward any untrodden islet.

For this earth is old,
And its heart is cold,
And the palsy of age has bound it;
And my spirit frets
For the viewless nets
Which are hourly clinging round it.

And with joyful glee
We have heard of thee,
Thou Isle in mid-ocean sleeping;
And thy records old,
Which the Sage has told
How the Memphian tombs are keeping.

But we know not where,
'Neath the desert air,
To look for the pleasant places
Of the youth of Time,
Whose austerer prime
The haunts of his childhood effaces.

Like the golden flowers
Of the western bowers,
Have waned their immortal shadows;
And no harp may tell
Where the asphodel
Clad in light those Elysian meadows.

And thou, fairest Isle
In the daylight's smile,
Hast thou sunk in the boiling ocean,
While beyond thy strand
Rose a mightier land
From the wave in alternate motion?

Are the isles that stud
The Atlantic flood
But the peaks of thy tallest mountains,
While repose below
The great waters' flow
Thy towns and thy towers and fountains?

EDMUND F. BLANCHARD.

WHAT WILL YOU DO, LOVE?

If all that you adore,—
  You confess—
Fairest hair, little lips,
  Finger-tips,
Nose, chin, and large slow eyes
  That surprise
Quick dimples when Love seeks
  Them in cheeks.
All—all—from neck to feet,
  All complete:
If all that you adore,
  You confess,—
Fade! would you love me more?
  Love me less?

Or—say—your heart retains
  All the pains—
The proud pains of Love's faith.
  Would the death
Of beauty only be
  Felt for me?
For me alone. For you
  What keeps true
Contenting. Still draw bliss
  From my kiss?
Or must I not retain
  Too much faith,
Less Love you'd but regain
  After Death?

ELIZA COOK.

OUR NATIVE SONG.

Our native song,—our native song!
    Oh! where is he who loves it not?
The spell it holds is deep and strong,
    Where'er we go, whate'er our lot.
Let other music greet our ear
    With thrilling fire or dulcet tone;
We speak to praise, we pause to hear,
    But yet—oh, yet—'tis not our own!
The anthem chant, the ballad wild,
    The notes that we remember long—
The theme we sung with lisping tongue—
    'Tis *this* we love—our native song!

The one who bears the felon's brand
    With moody brow and darkened name,
Thrust meanly from his father-land,
    To languish out a life of shame;
Oh! let him hear some simple strain—
    Some lay his mother taught her boy—
He'll feel the charm, and dream again
    Of home, of innocence, and joy!
The sigh will burst, the drops will start,
    And all of virtue buried long—
The best, the purest in his heart,—
    Is wakened by his native song.

Self-exiled from our place of birth,
    To climes more fragrant, bright, and gay,
The memory of our own fair earth
    May chance awhile to fade away:

HOME SWEET HOME

But should some minstrel-echo fall
   Of chords that breathe Old England's fame,
Our souls will burn, our spirits yearn,
   True to the land we love and claim.
The high—the low—in weal or woe,
   Be sure there's something coldly wrong
About the heart that does not glow
   To hear its own, its native song.

ALGERNON CHARLES SWINBURNE.

CHORUS IN "ATALANTA IN CALYDON."

Before the beginning of years
    There came to the making of man
Time, with a gift of tears;
    Grief, with a glass that ran;
Pleasure, with pain for leaven;
    Summer, with flowers that fell;
Remembrance fallen from heaven,
    And madness risen from hell;
Strength without hands to smite;
    Love that endures for a breath;
Night, the shadow of light,
    And life, the shadow of death.

And the high gods took in hand
    Fire, and the falling of tears,
And a measure of sliding sand
    From under the feet of the years;
And froth and drift of the sea;
    And dust of the labouring earth;
And bodies of things to be
    In the houses of death and of birth;
And wrought with weeping and laughter,
    And fashioned with loathing and love,
With life before and after,
    And death beneath and above;

For a day and a night and a morrow,
    That his strength might endure for a span
With tranquil and heavy sorrow,
    The holy spirit of man.

From the winds of the north and the south
    They gathered as unto strife;
They breathed upon his mouth,
    They filled his body with life;
Eyesight and speech they wrought
    For the veils of the soul therein,
A time for labour and thought,
    A time to serve and to sin;
They gave him light in his ways,
    And love, and a space for delight,
And beauty, and length of days,
    And night, and sleep in the night.
His speech is a burning fire;
    With his lips he travaileth;
In his heart is a blind desire,
    In his eyes foreknowledge of death:
He weaves, and is clothed with derision;
    Sows, and he shall not reap;
His life is a watch or a vision
    Between a sleep and a sleep.

H. CHOLMONDELEY-PENNELL.

DERBY DAY.

"Oh! who will over the Downs with me?"
　　Over Epsom Downs, and away—
The sun has got a tear in his eye,
And the morning mists are light and high;—
　　We shall have a splendid day.

　　　　　*　　*　　*

And splendid it is, by all that's hot!—
　　A regular blaze on the hill;
And the turf rebounds from the light-shod heel
And the tapering spokes of the delicate wheel
With a springy-velvety sort of a feel
　　That fairly invites "a spill."

Splendid it is, but we musn't stop,
　　The folks are beginning to run,—
Is yonder a cloud that covers the course?
No, it's fifty thousand—man and horse—
　　Come out to see the fun.

　　　*　　*　　*　　*　　*

So—just in time for the trial spurt;
　　The jocks are cantering in,—
We shall have the leaders round in a crack,
And a hundred voices are shouting "back,"
　　But nobody stirs a pin!
　　There isn't a soul will budge
　　So much as an inch from his place,
Tho' the hue of the master's scarlet coat
　　Is a joke compared to his face.

"To the ropes! to the ropes!" Now stick to your hold;
A breezy flutter of crimson and gold,
And the crowd are swept aside,
You can see the caps as they fall and rise
　　Like a swarm of variegated flies
　　Coming glittering up the ride;

"To the ropes, for your life! Here they come—there they go"—
　　The exquisite graceful things!
In the very sport of their strength and pride;
Ha! that's the Favourite,—look at his *stride*,
　　It suggests the idea of wings:
And the glossy neck is arched and firm
　　In spite of the flying pace;
The jockey sticks to his back like glue,
And his hand is quick and his eye is true,
And whatever skill and pluck can do
　　They will do to win the race.
The colt with the bright broad chest,
　　Will run to win the day;
There's fame and fortune in every bound,
And a hundred and fifty thousand pound
　　Staked on the gallant Bay!

　　　*　　　*　　　*　　　*

　　　"*They're off!*" . . . .
　　And away at the very first start,
　　　"Hats down! hats down in front!
Hats down, you sir in the wide-awake!"
The tightened barriers quiver and shake,
　　But they bravely bear the brunt.

A hush like death is over the crowd;
　　D'you hear that distant cry?
Then hark how it gathers, far and near,
One rolling, ringing, rattling cheer,
　　As the race goes dashing by,
And away with the hats and the caps in the air,
　　And the horses seem to FLY . . . .
Forward! forward! at railway speed,
There's one that has fairly taken the lead
In a style that can scarce miscarry;

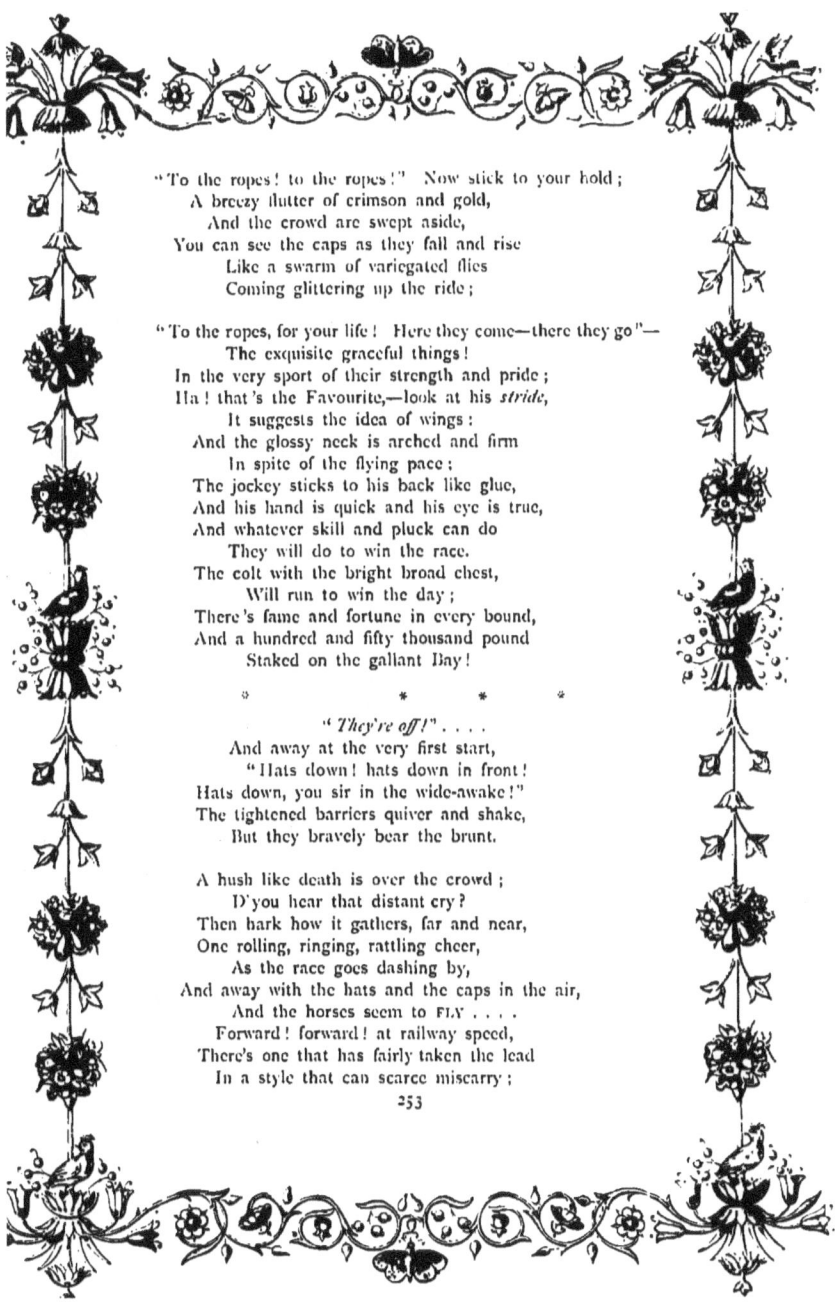

Over and on, like a flash of light,
And now his colours are coming in sight.
Favourite! Favourite!—scarlet and white—
    He'll win, by the Lord Harry!!

If he can but clear the corner, I say,
    The Derby is lost and won:
It's an awful shave, but he'll do the trick,
Now! Now or never—he's passing it quick.—
He's round! . . . .
    No, he isn't; he's broken his neck,
    And the jockey his collar bone;
And the whirlwind race is over his head,
Without stopping to ask if he's living or dead.—
    Was there ever such rudeness known?
He fell like a trump in the foremost place—
He died with the rushing wind on his face—
At the wildest bound of his glorious pace—
    In the mad exulting revel;
He left his shoes to his son and heir,
His hocks to a champagne dealer at Ware,
    A lock of his hair
    To the Lady-Mare,
And his hoofs and his tail—to the * * * *

LORD HOUGHTON.

MONCKTON MILNES.

I WANDERED BY THE BROOK-SIDE.

I wandered by the brook-side,
  I wandered by the mill,
I could not hear the brook flow,
  The noisy wheel was still;
There was no burr of grasshopper,
  No chirp of any bird,
But the beating of my own heart
  Was all the sound I heard.

I sat beneath the elm-tree,
  I watched the long, long shade.
And as it grew still longer,
  I did not feel afraid;
For I listened for a footfall,
  I listened for a word,
But the beating of my own heart
  Was all the sound I heard.

He came not,—no, he came not,—
  The night came on alone,—
The little stars sat, one by one,
  Each on his golden throne;
The evening air passed by my cheek,
  The leaves above were stirred,—
But the beating of my own heart
  Was all the sound I heard.

Fast silent tears were flowing,
  When something stood behind,
A hand was on my shoulder,
  I knew its touch was kind;
It drew me nearer—nearer,
  We did not speak one word,
For the beating of our own hearts
  Was all the sound we heard.

ALEXANDER SMITH.

A BALLAD FROM THE "LIFE DRAMA."

In winter, when the dismal rain
  Came down in slanting lines,
And wind, that grand old harper, smote
  His thunder harp of pines,

A Poet sat in his antique room,
  His lamp the valley kinged,
'Neath dry crusts of dead tongues he found
  Truth, fresh and golden-winged.

When violets came, and woods were green,
  And larks did skyward dart,
A Love alit, and white did sit
  Like an angel on his heart.

From his heart he unclasped his love
  Amid the trembling trees,
And sent it to the Lady Blanche
  On wingèd poesies.

The Lady Blanche was saintly fair,
  Nor proud, but meek her look;
In her hazel eyes her thoughts lay clear
  As pebbles in a brook.

Her father's veins ran noble blood,
  Her hall rose 'mid the trees;
Like a sunbeam she came and went
  'Mong the white cottages.

The peasants thanked her with their tears,
  When food and clothes were given, —
"This is a joy," the Lady said,
  "Saints cannot taste in Heaven!"

They met, — the Poet told his love,
  His hopes, despairs, his pains,—
The Lady with her calm eyes marked
  The tumult in his veins.

He passed away—a fierce song leapt
  From cloud of his despair,
As lightning, like a bright wild beast,
  Leaps from its thunder lair.

He poured his frenzy forth in song,
  Bright heir of tears and praises!
Now resteth that unquiet heart
  Beneath the quiet daisies.

The world is old,—oh, very old,—
  The wild winds weep and rave;
The world is old, and grey, and cold,
  Let it drop into its grave!

CHRISTINA ROSSETTI.

WHEN I AM DEAD, MY DEAREST.

When I am dead, my dearest,
  Sing no sad song for me;
Plant thou no roses at my head,
  Nor shady cypress tree:
Be the green grass above me
  With showers and dewdrops wet;
And if thou wilt, remember,
  And if thou wilt, forget.

I shall not see the shadows,
  I shall not feel the rain;
I shall not hear the nightingale
  Sing on, as if in pain:
And dreaming through the twilight
  That doth not rise nor set,
Haply I may remember,
  And haply may forget.

LORD LYTTON.

MEMORIES, THE FOOD OF LOVE.

When shall we come to that delightful day,
   When each can say to each, "Dost thou remember?"
Let us fill urns with rose leaves in our May,
   And hive the thrifty sweetness for December!

For who may deem the throne of love secure,
   Till o'er the *Past* the conqueror spreads his reign?
That only land where human joys endure,
   That dim elysium where they live again!

Swelled by a thousand streams, the deeps that float
   The bark on which we risk our all, should be.
A rill suffices for the idler's boat:
   It needs an ocean for the argosy.

The heart's religion keeps, apart from time
   The sacred burial-ground of happy hours:
The past is holy with the haunting chime
   Of dreamy Sabbath bells from distant towers.

Oft dost thou ask me, with that bashful eye,
  "If I shall love thee evermore as now!"
Feasting as fondly on the sure reply,
  As if my lips were virgin of the vow.

Sweet does that question, "Wilt thou love me?" fall
  Upon the heart that has forsworn its will:
But when the words hereafter we recall,
  "Dost thou remember?" shall be sweeter still.

THE HOLLOW OAK.

Hollow is the oak beside the sunny waters drooping;
Thither came, when I was young, happy children trooping;
Dream I now, or hear I now—far, their mellow whooping?

Gay below the cowslip bank see the billow dances,
There I lay, beguiling time, when I lived romances;
Dropping pebbles in the wave, fancies into fancies;—

Farther, where the river glides by the wooded cover,
Where the merlin singeth low, with the hawk above her,
Came a foot and shone a smile—woe is me, the Lover!

Leaflets on the hollow oak still as greenly quiver,
Musical amid the reeds murmurs on the river;
But the footstep and the smile?—woe is me for ever!

TOM TAYLOR.

"TEN, CROWN OFFICE ROW."

A TEMPLAR'S TRIBUTE TO HIS OLD CHAMBERS AND HIS OLD CHUM.

" There is another block of old houses in the Temple now condemned, which are said to be upwards of 200 years old. They form what is called Crown Office Row. Their destruction will commence forthwith." DAILY PAPER.

They were fusty, they were musty, they were grimy, dull, and dim,
The paint scaled off the panelling, the stairs were all untrim;
The flooring creaked, the windows gaped, the door-posts stood awry;
The wind whipt round the corner with a wild and wailing cry.
In a dingier set of chambers no man need wish to stow,
Than those, old friend, wherein we denned, at Ten, Crown Office Row.

But *we* were young, if *they* were old; we never cared a pin,
So the windows kept the rain out and let the sunshine in;
Our stout hearts mocked the crazy roofs, our hopes bedecked the wall;
We were happy, we were hearty, strong to meet what might befall;
Will sunnier hours be ever ours, than those which used to go,
Gay to their end, my dear old friend, at Ten, Crown Office Row?

We were two sucking barristers; briefs few and far between,
Upon our reading-tables, in their red-tape bands, were seen;
But we had friends, and we had books, a pewter, pipes, and weeds,
And tin enough to pay our way, or credit for our needs;
And so we doffed the world aside—gave Father Care to know,
Go where he might, he must not light at Ten, Crown Office Row.

Narrow and dark the Clerk's room; our kitchen 'twas, as well:
Whence a pleasant sound of frizzling at breakfast time befell:

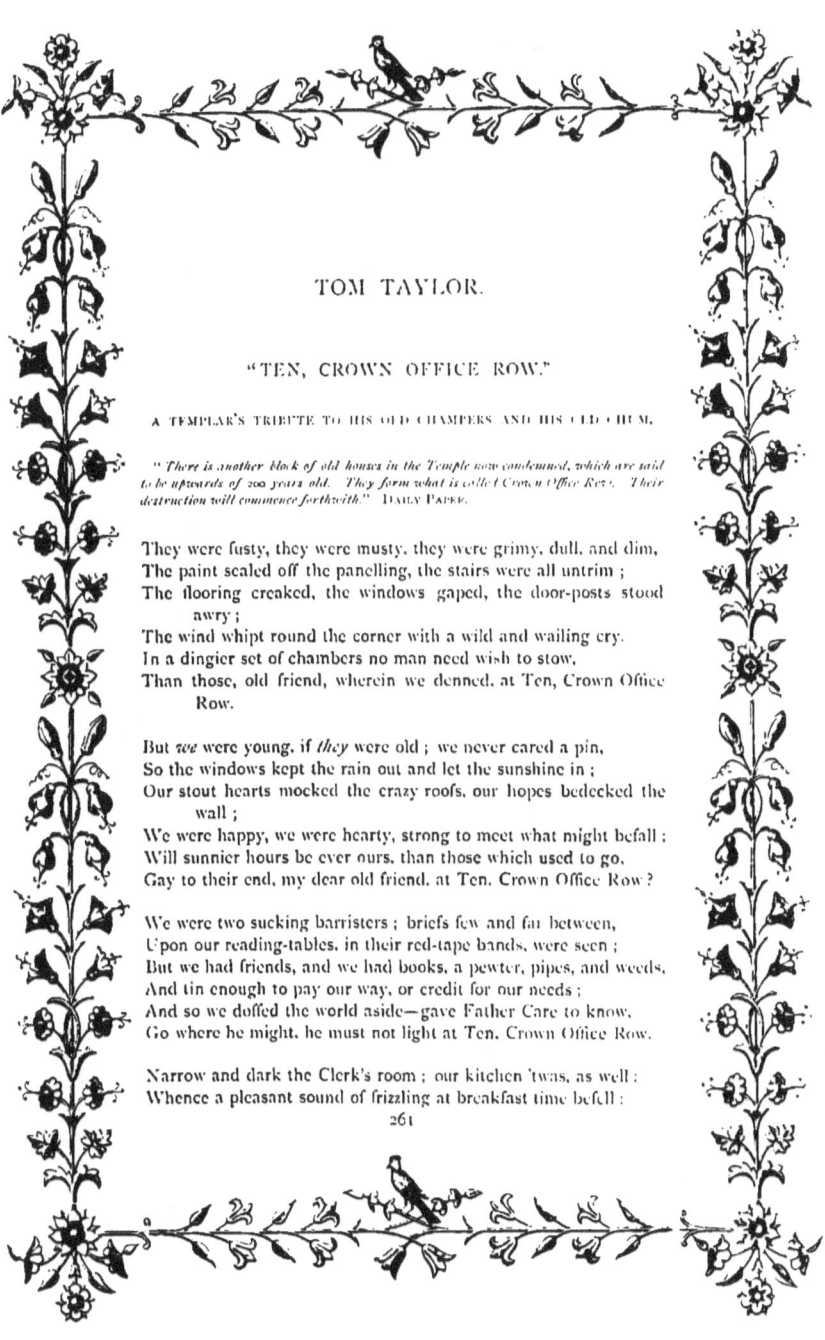

Narrow and dark the bed-rooms, where we snored and splashed
    and sung
Each in his tub, and took the rub of life with sinews strung,
Where we parted, in the small hours, friends, with a glad "good
    night,"
When the struggling sunshine found us, still friends, at morning
    light :
Glad morning times, glad midnight chimes, come back from long
    ago,
To light the glooms of those old rooms at Ten, Crown Office Row!

Those merry Sunday breakfasts—they never could be wrong—
When you made such famous toast, and I brewed the tea so
    strong,—
Were ever sausages like those from TUCKER's famous shop?
Where could the sheep have grazed whose loins produced our
    special chop ?
And then the lounge and weed, with the Garden green below,
And the Thames all smile and sparkle, past Ten, Crown Office Row.

You remember those queer dinners—from the Rainbow and from
    Dicks ?
That great day of Kabòbs—with fair hands to cut the sticks?
How deftly those white fingers on the skewers disposed the meat—
Till for pleasure in the cooking we scarcely cared to eat—
I've often since dined *à la Russe*, with G. H. M.—but, oh,
What are his dinners to those meals at Ten, Crown Office Row?

Those scrambling, screaming dinners, where all was frolic-fun,
From the eager clerks, who rushed about like bullet out of gun,
To the sore-bewildered laundress, with Soyer's shilling book,
Thrust, of a sudden, in her hand, and straightway bade to cook.
What silver laughs, what silver songs, from these old walls might
    flow,
Could they give out all they drank in at Ten, Crown Office Row!

Some of those tuneful voices will never sound again,
And some of them will read these lines, far o'er the Indian main ;
And smiles will come to some wan lips, tears to some sunken eyes,
To think of all these lines recall of Temple memories ;
And they will sigh as we have sighed, to learn the bringing low
Of those old chambers, dear old friend, at Ten, Crown Office Row

And one whose voice awaked the song, whose hand aroused the strings,
One of our guests, in those old rooms, even now beside me sings;
To eat our bach'lor dinner one time she deigned to come,
And now she smiles my wife, by the hearthstone of our home.
You too have found a loving mate—ah—well—'twas time to go—
No wives we had—'twas the one thing bad, at Ten, Crown Office Row.

Good-bye, old rooms, where we chummed years, without a single fight,
Far statelier sets of chambers will arise upon your site;
More airy bed-rooms, wider panes, our followers will see;
And wealthier, wiser tenants, the Inn may find than we;—
But lighter hearts or truer I'll defy the Bench to show,
Than yours, old friend, and his who penned this "Ten, Crown Office Row."

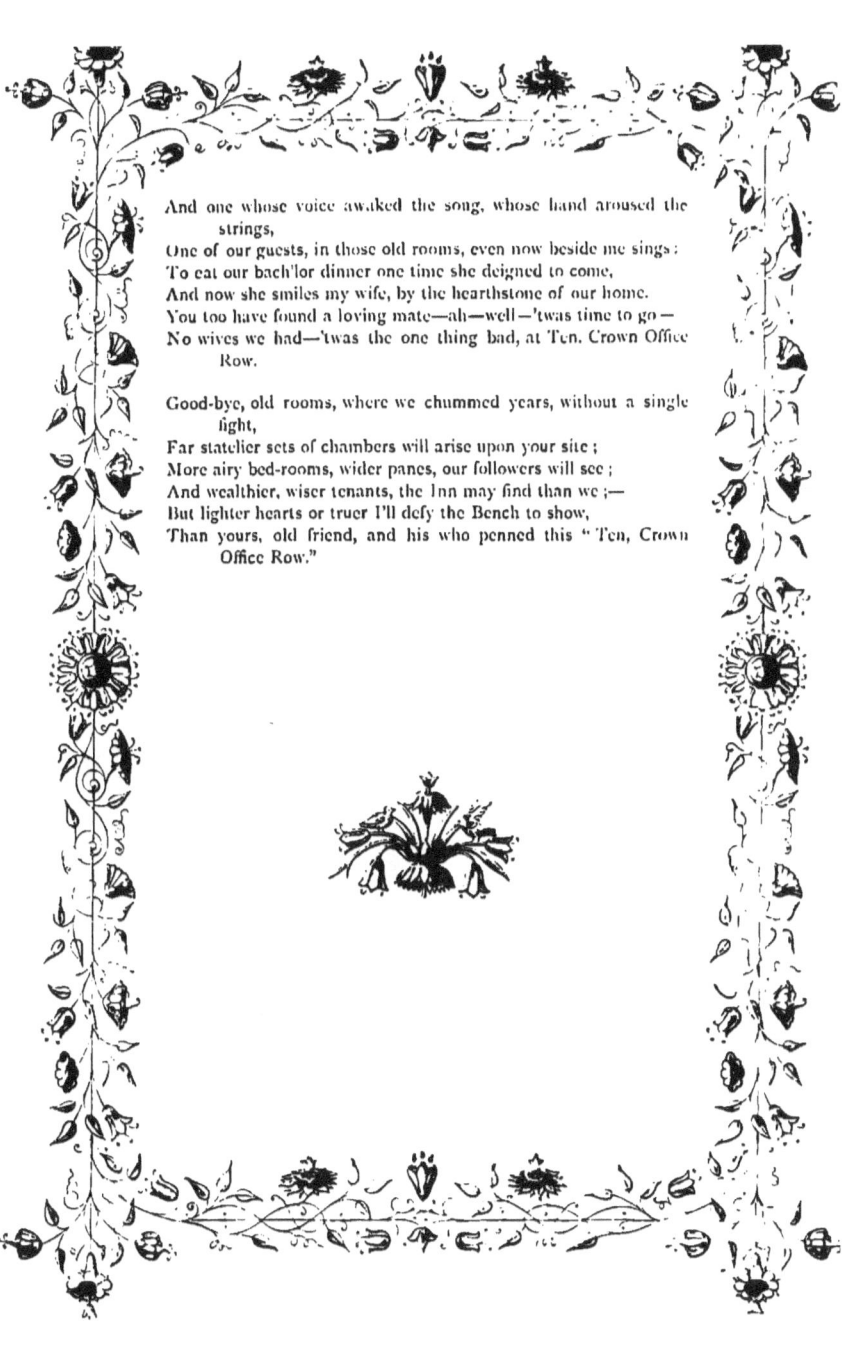

CHARLES MACKAY.

STREET COMPANIONS.

Whene'er through Gray's Inn porch I stray
I meet a spirit by the way;
He wanders with me all alone,
And talks with me in under-tone.

The crowd is busy seeking gold,
It cannot see what I behold;
I and the spirit pass along
Unknown, unnoticed, in the throng.

While on the grass the children run,
And maids go loitering in the sun,
I roam beneath the ancient trees,
And talk with him of mysteries.

The dull brick houses of the square,
The bustle of the thoroughfare,
The sounds, the sights, the crush of men,
Are present, but forgotten then.

I see them, but I heed them not,
I hear, but silence clothes the spot;
All voices die upon my brain,
Except that spirit's in the lane.

He breathes to me his burning thought,
He utters words with wisdom fraught,
He tells me truly what I am—
I walk with mighty Verulam.

He goes with me through crowded ways,
A friend and mentor in the maze,
Through Chancery Lane to Lincoln's Inn,
To Fleet Street, through the moil and din.

I meet another spirit there,
A blind old man with forehead fair,
Who ever walks the right-hand side
Toward the fountain of Saint Bride.

He hath no need of common eyes,
He sees the fields of Paradise;
He sees, and pictures unto mine,
A gorgeous vision most divine.

He tells the story of the Fall,
He names the fiends in battle-call,
And shows my soul, in wonder dumb,
Heaven, Earth, and Pandemonium.

He tells of Lycidas the good,
And the sweet Lady in the wood,
And teaches wisdom high and holy
In Mirth and heavenly Melancholy.

With such companions at my side
I float on London's human tide;
An atom on its billows thrown,
But lonely never, nor alone.

TOM HOOD, Junior.

SPRING.

Here, where the tall plantation firs
   Slope to the river down the hill,
Strange impulses—like vernal stirs,—
   Have made me wander at their will.

I see with half-attentive eyes
   The buds and flowers that mark the Spring,
And Nature's myriad prophecies
   Of what the Summer suns will bring.

For every sense I find delight—
   The new-wed cushat's murmured tones,
Young blossoms bursting into sight,
   And the rich odour of the cones.

The larch, with tassels purple-pink,
   Whispers like distant falling brooks;
And sun-forgotten dew-drops wink
   Amid the grass in shady nooks.

CAREY SPRING.

The breeze that hangs round every bush
   Steals sweetness from the tender shoots,
With here and there a perfumed gush
   From violets among the roots.

See—where behind the ivied rock
   Grow drifts of white anemones,
As if the Spring, in Winter's mock,
   Were mimicking his snows with these.

The single bloom those furzes bear
   Gleams like the fiery planet Mars;—
The creamy primroses appear
   In galaxies of vernal stars;

And grouped in Pleiad clusters round,
   Lent-lilies blow—some six or seven:—
With blossom-constellations crowned
   This quiet nook resembles Heaven.

JAMES PAYN.

"THE BACKS," (CAMBRIDGE.)

Dropping down the river,
Down the glancing river,
Through the fleet of shallops,
Through the fairy fleet,
Underneath the bridges,
Carvèd stone and oaken,
Crowned with sphere and pillar,
Linking lawn with lawn,
Sloping swards of garden,
Flowering bank to bank;
'Midst the golden noon-tide,
'Neath the stately trees,
Reaching out their laden
Arms to overshade us;
'Midst the summer evens,
Whilst the winds were heavy
With the blossom-odours,
Whilst the birds were singing
From their sleepless nests :
  Dropping down the river,
Down the branchèd river,
Through the hidden outlet
Of some happy stream,
Lifting up the leafy
Curtain that o'erhung it,
Fold on fold of foliage
Not proof against the stars.

Drinking ruby claret
From the silvered "Pewter,"
Spoil of ancient battle
On the "*ready*" Cam,
Ne'er to be forgotten
Pleasant friendly faces
Mistily discerning
Through the glass below ;
Ah ! the balmy fragrance
Of the mild Havannah !
Down amidst the purple
Of our railway wrappers,
Solemn-thoughted, glorious
On the verge of June.
  Musical the rippling
Of the tardy current,
Musical the murmur
Of the wind-swept trees,
Musical the cadence
Of the friendly voices
Laden with the sweetness
Of the songs of old.

MORTIMER COLLINS.

THE WAYSIDE WELL.

Full of beauty is the wayside well,
    Overcanopied with leafage pleasant,
Where the spirits of coolness love to dwell
    'Mid the heat incessant.

Here you see the weary wayfarer
    Cool himself beneath the leafy shadow,
While the long grass scarcely seems to stir
    In the unshaven meadow.*

Here full often rest the smoking team,
    Toiling movers of the broad-wheeled wagon:
Here the vagrant artist stays to dream
    O'er his pocket-flagon.

Hither also trips the rustic maiden
    Singing blithely through the wind-swept barley,
With her dark red earthen pitcher laden,
    In the morning early.

Talk of palm-tree shade and Arab lymph
    In the bosom of a green oasis:
Talk of water which the Naiad nymph
    'Mid dark Tempe places:

Talk of icy wine Italian quaffed
    In a cave of Pulciano's mountain:
There is nothing like a joyous draught
    From the wayside fountain.

---

* See Spenser's Faerie Queene, Book ii. canto v. stanza 30:—
    And fast beside there trickled softly down
    A gentle stream   .   .   .   .   .
    The weary traveller, wandering that way,
    Therein did often quench his thirsty heat,
    And then by it his weary limbs display.

THE WAYSIDE WELL.

A CAMEO.

He sat the quiet stream beside—
His white feet laving in the tide—
And watched the pleasant waters glide
   Beneath the skies of summer.
She singing came from mound to mound,
Her footfall on the thymy ground
Unheard; his tranquil haunt she found—
   That beautiful new comer.

He said,—" My own Glycerium!
The pulses of the woods are dumb,
How well I knew that thou wouldst come
   Beneath the branches gliding."
The dreamer fancied he had heard
Her footstep, whensoever stirred
The summer wind, or languid bird
   Amid the boughs abiding.

She dipped her fingers in the brook,
And gazed awhile with happy look
Upon the windings of a book
   Of Cyprian hymnings tender.
The ripples to the ocean raced—
The flying minutes passed in haste:
His arm was round the maiden's waist—
   That waist so very slender.

O cruel Time! O tyrant Time!
Whose winter all the streams of rhyme,
The flowing waves of love sublime,
   In bitter passage freezes.
I only see the scrambling goat,
The lotos on the waters float,
While an old shepherd with an oat
   Pipes to the autumn breezes.

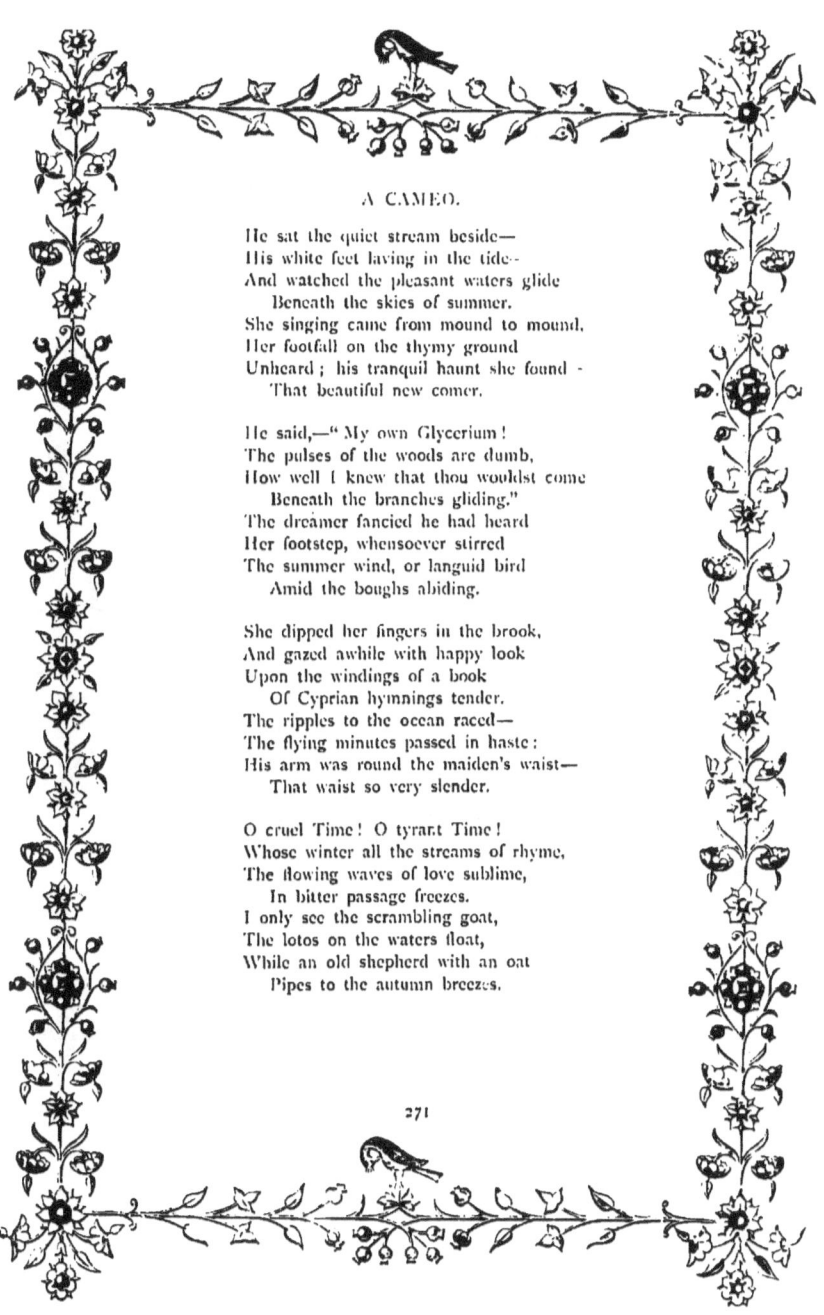

GODFREY TURNER.

THE TEMPLE FOUNTAIN.

Salutation to you now, you learned Temple Benchers:
Falling-off was there, I trow, in your account of trenchers;
Falling-off was there of rent, as well as fees and feeding—
Chancellors *in gemmâ* went elsewhere for legal breeding!
Falling-off, my countrymen, was there in chamber-letting,
Coupled with a falling-off that causes more regretting.
Empty sets in Temple courts had raised some consternation;
Emptiness in Templars calls for louder reprobation,
But these signs degenerate with satisfaction leave I,
Seeing now *auspicium melioris ævi*;
Seeing now a state of things that promises improvement—
Manifest machinery for going in a groove meant;
Going in a groove exact—smooth—level—rectilinean;
Going in the safety groove—Popular Opinion.

You have got a little nook—every Cockney knows it;
Every Cockney picture-book has a print that shows it.
Gossip-lore (green-spectacled, amiably dozy)
Pokes and potters oftentimes about that corner cosy,
Little Cockney girls and boys, with, oh! such pretty "nusses,"
Play there out of harm's way of the cabs and omnibuses.
Puzzle-browed, pale, stooping men pace the sunny gravel,—
Pace, and pace, and, now and then, some hard knot unravel.

Oh! but I have loved the spot, any time you'll mention,
Since, indeed, I started in the trade of Good Intention.
When that business hung on hand, then I've left my duty—
Left "the fever and the fret," and dreamed awhile of Beauty.
And—when others fled from town to lake and moor and mountain—
I have laid my trouble down beside the Temple Fountain.

Benchers, you are men, as we. You, as we, have haply
Read the book of Gamp—the book of Pecksniff, and of Tapley;
Conned the book of Chuzzlewit, and gathered from its pages
That for which in vain you'd search a library of sages.
Knowledge of the kindred life that flows along the highways,
Throbs with equal pulse, in poor and great and wealthy byways.
There's a passage in the book to which I have alluded—
Passage rare!—which overlook I don't imagine you did.
Is it not cap. 45, so pleasant, wise and witty?—
Don't you know the cap. as well as any cap. in Chitty?
Is it not, I say, the cap, that fits the "general reader,"
Just as Love to all must hap—clown, lord, and special pleader?
Is it not the cap., in short, which one might fairly count an
Epic upon Friendship, Love, Law, Beauty, and the Fountain?

Benchers, guard the spot in which the Fountain flashes brightly :—
Mr. Abraham, C.E. go find a site less sightly.
(Mind, no spoiling King's Bench Walk, quadrangle quaint, where trees are ;
No pert "elevation" there, in style as dead as Cæsar !)
Be your praise, O Benchers, sung by city-dwelling mortals,
Long as wingèd horse and lamb shall decorate your portals !
Company in Upper Hall, ye miscellaneous diners,
Reading men, and rowing men, Queen's Counsel, swells, and liners,—
Pledge me straight the Benchers all, and pledge them in a brimmer :—
May their lives be gladdened by the Fountain's pleasant shimmer ;
May their shadows not be less while hereabout they linger,
Holding friendly button with communicative finger ;
May the Fountain, ages hence, keep babbling still their praises ;
Babbling, too, of pastures green, lambs, lovers' walks, and daisies.

ALFRED TENNYSON.

THE BROOK.

I come from haunts of coot and hern,
  I make a sudden sally,
And sparkle out among the fern
  To bicker down a valley.

By thirty hills I hurry down,
  Or slip between the ridges,
By twenty thorps, a little town,
  And half a hundred bridges.

Till last by Philip's farm I flow
  To join the brimming river:
For men may come, and men may go,
  But I go on for ever.

I chatter over stony ways
  In little sharps and trebles,
I babble into eddying bays,
  I bubble on the pebbles.

With many a curve my banks I fret
  By many a field and fallow,
And many a fairy foreland set
  With willow-weed and mallow.

I chatter, chatter, as I flow
  To join the brimming river:
For men may come, and men may go,
  But I go on for ever.

I wind about, and in and out,
  With here a blossom sailing,
And here and there a lusty trout,
  And here and there a grayling;

PHILIP'S FARM.

And here and there a foamy flake
Upon me, as I travel,
With many a silvery waterbreak
Above the golden gravel;

And draw them all along, and flow
To join the brimming river:
For men may come, and men may go,
But I go on for ever.

I steal by lawns and grassy plots,
I slide by hazel covers;
I move the sweet forget-me-nots
That grow for happy lovers.

I slip, I slide, I gloom, I glance
Among my skimming swallows,
I make the netted sunbeam dance
Against my sandy shallows.

I murmur under moon and stars
In brambly wildernesses;
I linger by my shingly bars,
I loiter round my cresses.

And out again I curve, and flow
To join the brimming river;
For men may come, and men may go,
But I go on for ever.

TO THE REV. F. D. MAURICE.

Come, when no graver cares employ,
Godfather, come and see your boy:
  Your presence will be sun in winter,
Making the little one leap for joy.

For, being of that honest few
Who give the Fiend himself his due,
  Should eighty thousand College Councils
Thunder "Anathema," friend, at you;

Should all our Churchmen foam in spite
At you, so careful of the right,
    Yet one lay-hearth would give you welcome
(Take it and come) to the Isle of Wight;

Where, far from noise and smoke of town,
I watch the twilight falling brown
    All round a careless-ordered garden,
Close to the ridge of a noble down.

You'll have no scandal while you dine,
But honest talk and wholesome wine,
    And only hear the magpie gossip
Garrulous under a roof of pine:

For groves of pine on either hand
To break the blast of winter stand;
    And further on, the hoary Channel
Tumbles a breaker on chalk and sand;

Where, if below the milky steep
Some ship of battle slowly creep,
    And on through zones of light and shadow
Glimmer away to the lonely deep,

We might discuss the northern sin
Which made a selfish war begin;
    Dispute the claims, arrange the chances,
Emperor, Ottoman, which shall win:

Or whether war's avenging rod
Shall lash all Europe into blood;
    Till you should turn to dearer matters,
Dear to the man that is dear to God;

How best to help the slender store,
How mend the dwellings of the poor;
    How gain in life, as life advances,
Valour and charity more and more.

Come, Maurice, come; the lawn as yet
Is hoar with rime, or spongy-wet;
   But when the wreath of March has blossomed,
Crocus, anemone, violet,

Or later, pay one visit here,
For those are few we hold as dear;
   Nor pay but one, but come for many,
Many and many a happy year.

FREDERICK LOCKER.

AN INVITATION TO ROME.

O, come to Rome, it is a pleasant place,
  Your London sun is here seen shining brightly:
The Briton too puts on a cheery face,
  And Mrs. Bull is *suave* and even sprightly.
The Romans are a kind and cordial race,
  The women charming, if one takes them rightly;
I see them at their doors, as day is closing,
More proud than duchesses—and more imposing.

A *far niente* life promotes the graces;—
  They pass from dreamy bliss to wakeful glee,
And in their bearing and their speech one traces
  A breadth of grace and depth of courtesy
That are not found in more inclement places;
  Their clime and tongue seem much in harmony;
The Cockney met in Middlesex or Surrey
Is often cold—and always in a hurry.

Though *far niente* is their passion, they
  Seem here most eloquent in things most slight:
No matter what it is they have to say,
  The manner always sets the matter right.

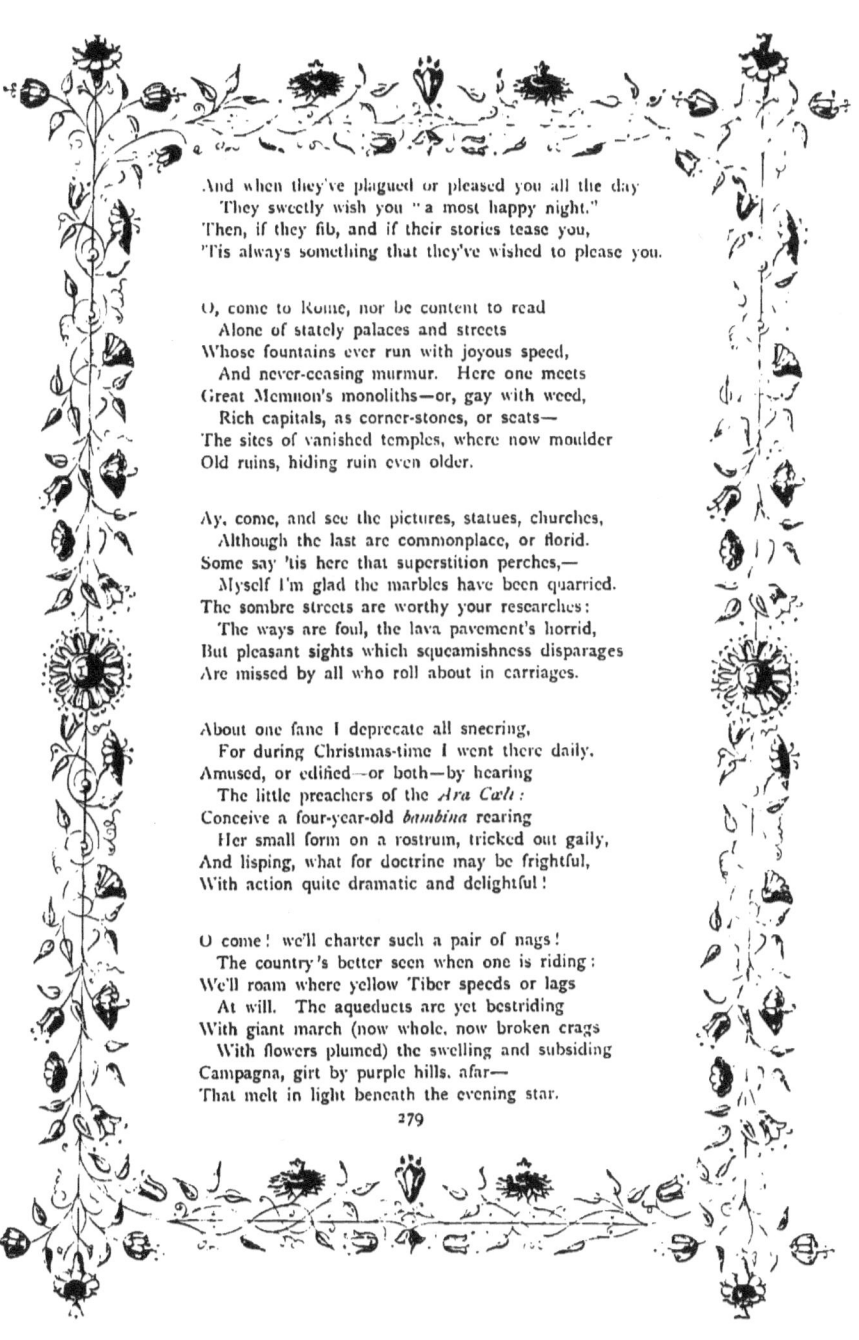

And when they've plagued or pleased you all the day
They sweetly wish you "a most happy night."
Then, if they fib, and if their stories tease you,
'Tis always something that they've wished to please you.

O, come to Rome, nor be content to read
  Alone of stately palaces and streets
Whose fountains ever run with joyous speed,
  And never-ceasing murmur. Here one meets
Great Memnon's monoliths—or, gay with weed,
  Rich capitals, as corner-stones, or seats—
The sites of vanished temples, where now moulder
Old ruins, hiding ruin even older.

Ay, come, and see the pictures, statues, churches,
  Although the last are commonplace, or florid.
Some say 'tis here that superstition perches,—
  Myself I'm glad the marbles have been quarried.
The sombre streets are worthy your researches:
  The ways are foul, the lava pavement's horrid,
But pleasant sights which squeamishness disparages
Are missed by all who roll about in carriages.

About one fane I deprecate all sneering,
  For during Christmas-time I went there daily,
Amused, or edified—or both—by hearing
  The little preachers of the *Ara Cœli*:
Conceive a four-year-old *bambina* rearing
  Her small form on a rostrum, tricked out gaily,
And lisping, what for doctrine may be frightful,
With action quite dramatic and delightful!

O come! we'll charter such a pair of nags!
  The country's better seen when one is riding;
We'll roam where yellow Tiber speeds or lags
  At will. The aqueducts are yet bestriding
With giant march (now whole, now broken crags
  With flowers plumed) the swelling and subsiding
Campagna, girt by purple hills, afar—
That melt in light beneath the evening star.

A drive to Palestrino will be pleasant—
   The wild fig grows where erst her turrets stood;
There oft, in goatskins clad, a sun-burnt peasant
   Like Pan comes frisking from his ilex wood,
And seems to wake the past time in the present.
   Fair *contadina*, mark his mirthful mood,
No antique satyr he. The nimble fellow
Can join with jollity your *Salterello*.

Old sylvan peace and liberty! The breath
   Of life to unsophisticated man.
Here Mirth may pipe, here Love may weave his wreath,
   "*Per dar' al mio bene.*" When you can,
Come share their leafy solitudes. Grim Death
   And Time are grudging of Life's little span:
Wan Time speeds swiftly o'er the waving corn,
Death grins from yonder cynical old thorn.

I dare not speak of Michael Angelo—
   Such theme were all too splendid for my pen.
And if I breathe the name of Sanzio
   (The brightest of Italian gentlemen),
It is that love casts out my fear—and so
   I claim with him a kindredship. Ah! when
We love, thy name is on our hearts engraven,
As is thy name, my own dear Bard of Avon!

Nor is the Colosseum theme of mine,
   'Twas built for poet of a larger daring;
The world goes there with torches—I decline
   Thus to affront the moonbeams with their flaring.
Some time in May our forces we'll combine
   (Just you and I), and try a midnight airing,
And then I'll quote this rhyme to you—and then
You'll muse upon the vanity of men.

O come! I send a leaf of tender fern,—
   'T was plucked where Beauty lingers round decay:
The ashes buried in a sculptured urn
   Are not more dead than Rome—so dead to-day!

That better time, for which the patriots yearn,
　Enchants the gaze, again to fade away.
They wait and pine for what is long denied,
And thus I wait till thou art by my side.

Thou'rt far away! Yet, while I write, I still
　Seem gently, Sweet, to press thy hand in mine;
I cannot bring myself to drop the quill,
　I cannot yet thy little hand resign!
The plain is fading into darkness chill,
　The Sabine peaks are flushed with light divine,
I watch alone, my fond thought wings to thee,
O come to Rome—O come, O come to me!

PICCADILLY.

Piccadilly! shops, palaces, bustle, and breeze,
The whirring of wheels, and the murmur of trees,
By daylight, or nightlight,—or noisy, or stilly,—
Whatever my mood is—I love Piccadilly!

Wet nights, when the gas on the pavement is streaming,
And young Love is watching, and old Love is dreaming,
And Beauty is whirled off to conquest, where shrilly
Cremona makes nimble thy toes, Piccadilly!

Bright days, when we leisurely pace to and fro,
And meet all the people we do or don't know,—
Here is jolly old Brown and his fair daughter Lillie;
—No wonder, young pilgrim, you like Piccadilly!

See yonder pair riding, how fondly they saunter!
She smiles on her poet, whose heart's in a canter:
Some envy her spouse, and some covet her filly,
He envies them both,—he's an ass, Piccadilly!

Now were I that gay bride, with a slave at my feet,
I would choose me a house in my favourite street:

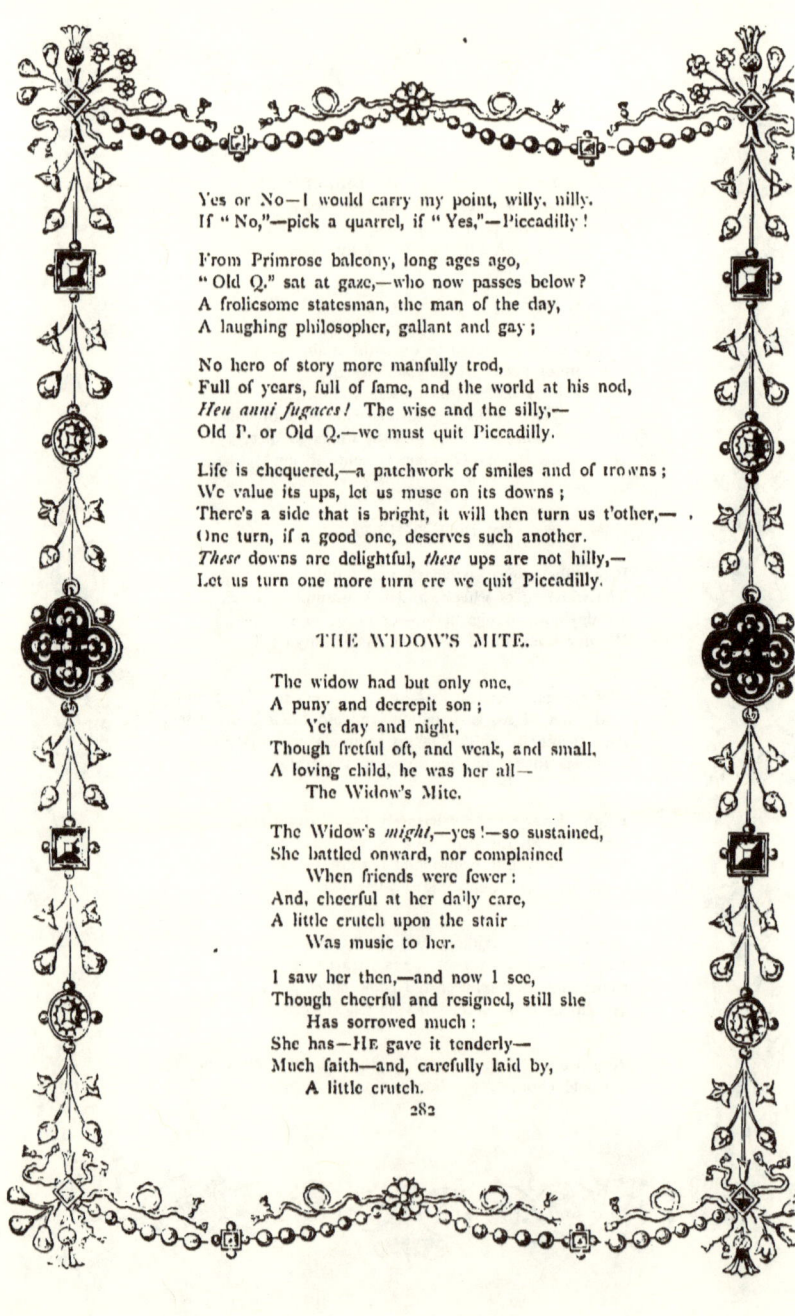

Yes or No—I would carry my point, willy, nilly,
If " No,"—pick a quarrel, if " Yes,"—Piccadilly!

From Primrose balcony, long ages ago,
" Old Q." sat at gaze,—who now passes below?
A frolicsome statesman, the man of the day,
A laughing philosopher, gallant and gay;

No hero of story more manfully trod,
Full of years, full of fame, and the world at his nod,
Heu anni fugaces! The wise and the silly,—
Old P. or Old Q.—we must quit Piccadilly.

Life is chequered,—a patchwork of smiles and of frowns;
We value its ups, let us muse on its downs;
There's a side that is bright, it will then turn us t'other,—
One turn, if a good one, deserves such another.
These downs are delightful, *these* ups are not hilly,—
Let us turn one more turn ere we quit Piccadilly.

THE WIDOW'S MITE.

The widow had but only one,
A puny and decrepit son;
   Yet day and night,
Though fretful oft, and weak, and small,
A loving child, he was her all—
   The Widow's Mite.

The Widow's *might*,—yes!—so sustained,
She battled onward, nor complained
   When friends were fewer:
And, cheerful at her daily care,
A little crutch upon the stair
   Was music to her.

I saw her then,—and now I see,
Though cheerful and resigned, still she
   Has sorrowed much:
She has—HE gave it tenderly—
Much faith—and, carefully laid by,
   A little crutch.

BAFFLED!

BROWNING.

A SONG FROM "PARACELSUS."

FESTUS. Softly the Mayne river glideth
Close by where my love abideth;
Sleep's no softer: it proceeds
On through lawns, on through meads,
On and on, whate'er befall,
Meandering and musical,
Though the niggard pasture's edge
Bears not on its shaven ledge
Aught but weeds and waving grasses
To view the river as it passes,
Save here and there a scanty patch
Of primroses, too faint to catch
A weary bee . . .
  The river pushes
Its gentle way through strangling rushes,
Where the glossy king-fisher
Flutters when noon-heats are near,
Glad the shelving banks to shun,
Red and steaming in the sun,
Where the shrew-mouse with pale throat
Burrows, and the speckled stoat;
Where the quick sand-pipers flit
In and out the marl and grit
That seems to breed them, brown as they.
Nought disturbs the river's way,
Save some lazy stork that springs,
Trailing it with legs and wings,
Whom the shy fox from the hill
Rouses, creep he ne'er so still.

HOME THOUGHTS, FROM THE SEA.

Nobly, nobly Cape Saint Vincent to the north-west died away;
Sunset ran, one glorious blood-red, reeking into Cadiz Bay;
Bluish mid the burning water, full in face Trafalgar lay;
In the dimmest north-east distance, dawned Gibraltar grand
 and gray;
"Here and here did England help me,—how can I help
 England?—say,"
Whoso turns as I, this evening, turn to God to praise and pray,
While Jove's planet rises yonder, silent over Africa.

MEETING AT NIGHT.

The grey sea and the long black land;
And the yellow half-moon large and low;
And the startled little waves that leap
In fiery ringlets from their sleep,
As I gain the cove with pushing prow,
And quench its speed in the slushy sand.
Then a mile of warm sea-scented beach;
Three fields to cross till a farm appears;
A tap at the pane, the quick sharp scratch
And blue spurt of a lighted match,
And a voice less loud, thro' its joys and fears,
Than the two hearts beating each to each!

SONG FROM "PIPPA PASSES."

PIPPA. The year's at the spring,
    And day's at the morn;
    Morning's at seven;
    The hill-side's dew-pearled:
    The lark's on the wing;
    The snail's on the thorn;
    God's in his heaven—
    All's right with the world!

IN A YEAR.

Never any more
  While I live,
Need I hope to see his face
  As before.
Once his love grown chill,
  Mine may strive—
Bitterly we re-embrace,
  Single still.

Was it something said,*
  Something done,
Vexed him? was it touch of hand,
  Turn of head?
Strange! that very way
  Love begun.
I as little understand
  Love's decay.

When I sewed or drew,
  I recall
How he looked as if I sang,
  —Sweetly too.
If I spoke a word,
  First of all
Up his cheek the colour sprang,
  Then he heard.

Sitting by my side,
  At my feet,
So he breathed the air I breathed,
  Satisfied!
I, too, at love's brim
  Touched the sweet:
I would die if death bequeathed
  Sweet to him.

---

* A something, light as air—a look,
  A word unkind or wrongly taken—
Oh! love, that tempests never shook,
  A breath, a touch like this hath shaken.
      MOORE, "*Light of the Haram.*"

" Speak, I love thee best!
　He exclaimed.
" Let thy love my own foretell,"
　I confessed :
" Clasp my heart on thine
　Now unblamed,
Since upon thy soul as well
　Hangeth mine!"

Would he loved me yet,
　On and on,
While I found some way undreamed
　Paid my debt!
Gave more life and more,
　Till, all gone,
He should smile " She never seemed
　Mine before.

" What—she felt the while,
　Must I think?
Love's so different with us men,"
　He should smile.
" Dying for my sake—
　White and pink!
Can't we touch these bubbles then
　But they break?"

Dear, the pang is brief.
　Do thy part,
Have thy pleasure. How perplext
　Grows belief!
Well, this cold clay clod
　Was man's heart,
Crumble it—and what comes next?
　Is it God?

CHARLES F. KENT.

TWENTY-ONE.

To-day a Man! I enter Life,
   And note on either hand
How the white chapels of young sects
   By grey cathedrals stand;
And senate-houses built in stone
   By palaces in sand.

Brothers! I ask my right to pass
   Through every open door,
To span the girth of this thin shaft,
   And test that creaking floor,
Search out yon dark recess, and lift
   The veil that hangs before.

I ask, when image-vendors come,
   And press some hero's claim,
My right to know if he hath won
   And how deserved his fame:
Then 'mong my Lares, if I will,
   Refuse to class his name.

From childhood's long-lost innocence
　To God's far-distant shrine,
Some journey by the banks of Nile,
　Between the unbroken line
Of Sphinxes linking fane to fane :
　That life-path may be mine.

If with stunned sense and blistered feet
　I fall where I should stand ;
If in vain rage and fool's despair
　I strike my clenchèd hand
Into the dumbest blankest face
　Among that solemn band,

And madly strive to rend apart
　Its calm unpitying lips ;—
Must not tumultuous auguries
　Of Nature's last eclipse
Herald from each man's Sinai
　His Law's apocalypse?

Yet if it might be I would choose
　That in my listening brain
The thunder-voicèd mysteries
　Should breathe a peaceful strain,
And vibrate my attunèd heart
　To echo the refrain.

God knoweth.　May He grant that I
　Shall at the last attain,
If painfully o'er rugged rocks,
　Or gently through the plain,
The worthiest goal of every man,
　To be a child again !

OWEN MEREDITH.

ON MY TWENTY-FOURTH YEAR.

From "The Wanderer."

The night's in November : the winds are at strife :
  The snow's on the hill, and the ice on the mere :
The world to its winter is turned : and my life
    To its twenty-fourth year.

The swallows are flown to the south long ago :
  The roses are fallen : the woodland is sere.
Hope's flown with the swallows : Love's rose will not grow
    In my twenty-fourth year.

The snow on the threshold : the cold at the heart :
  But the fagot to warm, and the wine-cup to cheer :
God's help to look up to : and courage to start
    On my twenty-fourth year.

And 'tis well that the month of the roses is o'er!
  The last, which I plucked for Neræa to wear,
She gave her new lover. A man should do more
    With his twenty-fourth year

Than mourn for a woman because she's unkind,
  Or pine for a woman because she is fair.
Ah! I loved you, Neræa. But now . . . never mind,
    'Tis my twenty-fourth year!

What a thing! to have done with the follies of youth,
  Ere Age brings ITS follies ! . . . tho' many a tear
It should cost, to see Love fly away, and find Truth
    In one's twenty-fourth year.

The Past's golden vallies are drained. I must plant
　　On the Future's rough upland new harvests, I fear.
Ho, the plough and the team! . . . who would perish of want
　　　　In his twenty-fourth year?

Man's heart is a well which for ever renews
　　The void at the bottom, no sounding comes near:
And Love does not die, though its object I lose
　　　　In my twenty-fourth year.

The great and the little are only in name.
　　The smoke from my chimney casts shadows as drear
On the heart, as the smoke from Vesuvius in flame:
　　　　And my twenty-fourth year.

From the joys that have cheered it, the cares that have troubled,
　　What is wise to pursue, what is well to revere,
May judge all as fully as tho' life were doubled
　　　　To its forty-eighth year.

If the prospect grow dim 'tis because it grows wide.
　　Every loss hath its gain. So from sphere on to sphere
Man mounts up the ladder of Time: so I stride
　　　　Up my twenty-fourth year!

Exulting? . . . no . . . sorrowing? . . . no . . . with a mind
　　Whose regret chastens hope, whose faith triumphs o'er fear:
Not repining: not confident: no, but resigned
　　　　To my twenty-fourth year.

THE CHESS-BOARD.

My little love, do you remember,
　　Ere we were grown so sadly wise,
Those evenings in the bleak December,
Curtained warm from the snowy weather,
When you and I played chess together,
　　Checkmated by each other's eyes?

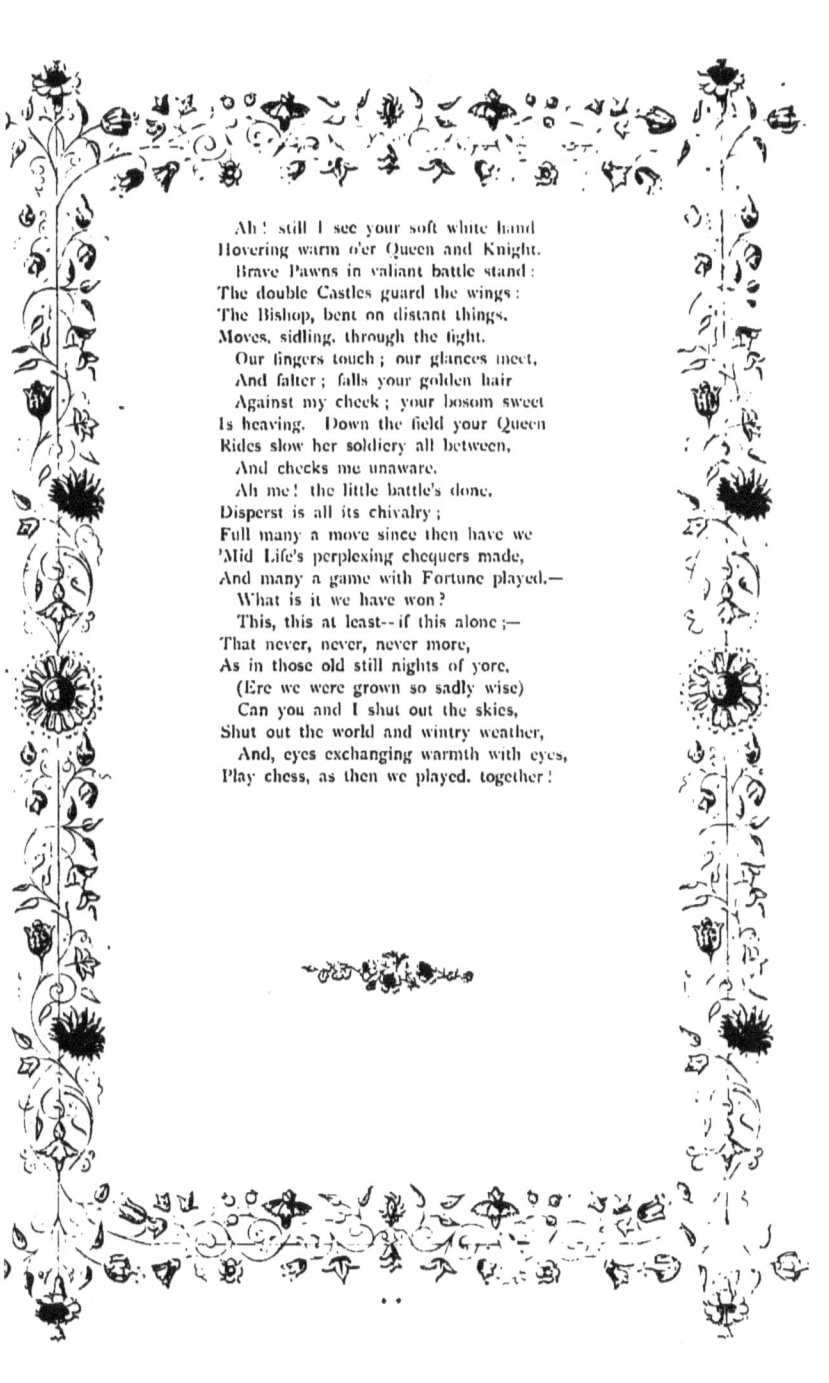

    Ah! still I see your soft white hand
Hovering warm o'er Queen and Knight.
Brave Pawns in valiant battle stand:
The double Castles guard the wings:
The Bishop, bent on distant things,
Moves, sidling, through the fight.
    Our fingers touch; our glances meet,
And falter; falls your golden hair
Against my cheek; your bosom sweet
Is heaving. Down the field your Queen
Rides slow her soldiery all between,
And checks me unaware.
    Ah me! the little battle's done,
Disperst is all its chivalry;
Full many a move since then have we
'Mid Life's perplexing chequers made,
And many a game with Fortune played.—
    What is it we have won?
    This, this at least—if this alone;—
That never, never, never more,
As in those old still nights of yore,
    (Ere we were grown so sadly wise)
    Can you and I shut out the skies,
Shut out the world and wintry weather,
    And, eyes exchanging warmth with eyes,
Play chess, as then we played, together!

MATTHEW ARNOLD.

TO MY FRIENDS,

WHO RIDICULED A TENDER LEAVE-TAKING.

Laugh, my friends, and without blame
Lightly quit what lightly came:
Rich to-morrow as to-day,
Spend as madly as you may.
I, with little land to stir,
Am the exacter labourer.
    Ere the parting kiss be dry,
    Quick, thy tablets, Memory!

But my youth reminds me—"Thou
Hast lived light as these live now:
As these are thou too wert such:
Much hast had, hast squandered much."
Fortune's now less frequent heir,
Ah! I husband what's grown rare.
    Ere the parting kiss be dry,
    Quick, thy tablets, Memory!

Young, I said, "A face is gone
If too hotly mused upon:
And our best impressions are
Those that do themselves repair."

Many a face I then let by,
Ah! is faded utterly.
    Ere the parting kiss be dry,
    Quick, thy tablets, Memory!

Paint that figure's pliant grace
As she towards me leaned her face,
Half-refused and half-resigned,
Murmuring, art thou still unkind?"
Many a broken promise then
Was new made - to break again.
    Ere the parting kiss be dry,
    Quick, thy tablets, Memory!

Paint those eyes, so blue, so kind,
Eager tell-tales of her mind:
Paint, with their impetuous stress
Of enquiring tenderness,
Those frank eyes where deep doth lie
An angelic gravity.
    Ere the parting kiss be dry,
    Quick, thy tablets, Memory!

What, my friends, these feeble lines
Show, you say, my love declines?
To paint ill as I have done
Proves forgetfulness begun?
Time's gay minions, pleased you see,
Time, your master, governs me.
    Pleased, you mock the fruitless cry,
    "Quick, thy tablets, Memory!"

Ah! too true. Time's current strong
Leaves us true to nothing long.
Yet if little stays with man,
Ah! retain we all we can!
If the clear impression dies,
Ah! the dim remembrance prize!
    Ere the parting kiss be dry,
    Quick, thy tablets, Memory!

BRYAN WALTER PROCTER.

(BARRY CORNWALL.)

A PHANTASY.

Feed her with the leaves of Love,
(Love, the rose, that blossoms here!)
Music, gently round her move!
Bind her to the cypress near!
Weave her round and round
With skeins of silken sound!
'Tis a little stricken deer
Who doth from the hunter fly,
And comes here to droop,—to die,
Ignorant of her wound!

Soothe her with sad stories,
O poet, till she sleep!
Dreams, come forth with all your glories!
Night, breathe soft and deep!
Music, round her creep!
If she steal away to weep
Seek her out,—and when you find her
Gentle, gentlest Music, wind her
Round and round,
Round and round,
With your bands of softest sound:
Such as we at nightfall hear
In the wizard forest near,
When the charmèd maiden sings
At the wizard springs!

SING, MAIDEN, SING!

Sing, maiden, sing!
  Mouths were made for singing;
Listen,—songs thou'lt hear
  Through the wide world ringing;
Songs from all the birds,
  Songs from winds and showers,
Songs from seas and streams,
  Even from sweet flowers.

Hear'st thou the rain,
  How it gently falleth?
Hearest thou the bird,
  Who from forest calleth?
Hearest thou the bee
  O'er the sunflower ringing?
Tell us, Maiden, *now*
  Should'st thou not be singing?

Hear'st thou the breeze
  Round the rose-bud sighing?
And the small sweet rose,
  Love to love replying?
So should'st *thou* reply
  To the prayer we're bringing;
So that bud, thy mouth,
  Should burst forth in singing!

CHARLES DICKENS.

THE IVY GREEN.

Oh, a dainty plant is the Ivy green
  That creepeth o'er ruins old!
Of right choice food are his meals, I ween,
  In his cell so lone and cold.
The wall must be crumbled, the stone decayed,
  To pleasure his dainty whim:
And the mouldering dust that years have made
  Is a merry meal for him.
    Creeping where no life is seen,
    A rare old plant is the Ivy green!

Fast he stealeth on, though he wears no wings,
  And a staunch old heart has he.
How closely he twineth, how tight he clings
  To his friend, the huge oak tree!
And slily he traileth along the ground,
  And his leaves he gently waves,
As he joyously hugs and crawleth round
  The rich mould of dead men's graves.
    Creeping where grim Death has been,
    A rare old plant is the Ivy green!

Whole ages have fled, and their works decayed,
  And nations have scattered been;
But the stout old Ivy shall never fade
  From its hale and hearty green.
The brave old plant in its lonely days
  Shall fatten upon the past,
For the stateliest building man can raise
  Is the Ivy's food at last.
    Creeping on, where Time has been,
    A rare old plant is the Ivy green.

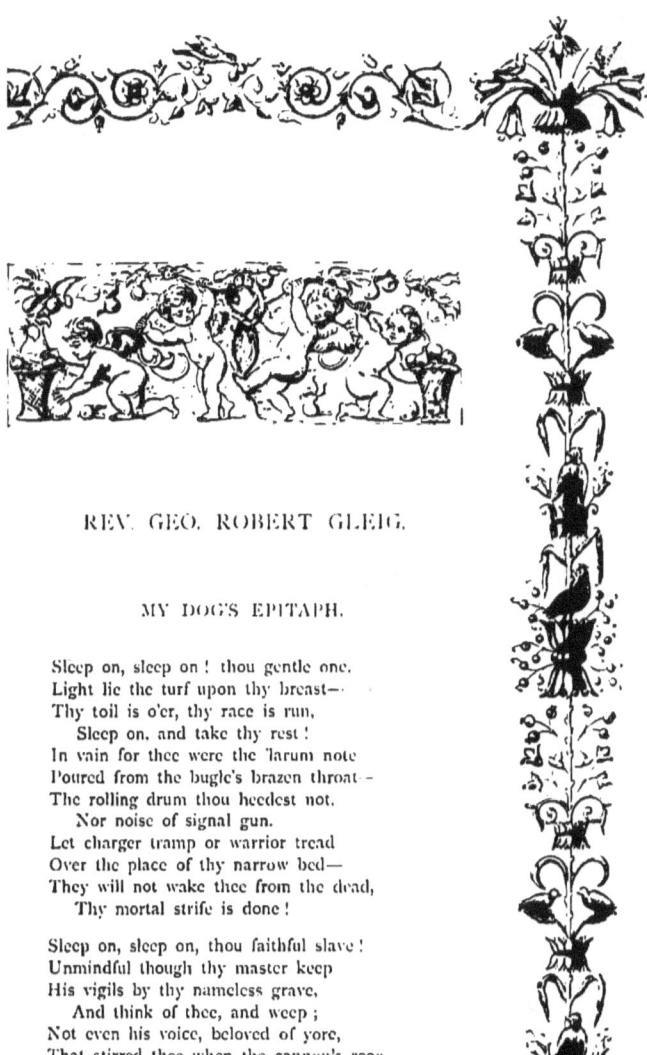

REV. GEO. ROBERT GLEIG.

MY DOG'S EPITAPH.

Sleep on, sleep on! thou gentle one,
Light lie the turf upon thy breast—
Thy toil is o'er, thy race is run,
   Sleep on, and take thy rest!
In vain for thee were the 'larum note
Poured from the bugle's brazen throat —
The rolling drum thou heedest not,
Nor noise of signal gun.
Let charger tramp or warrior tread
Over the place of thy narrow bed—
They will not wake thee from the dead,
   Thy mortal strife is done!

Sleep on, sleep on, thou faithful slave!
Unmindful though thy master keep
His vigils by thy nameless grave,
   And think of thee, and weep;
Not even his voice, beloved of yore,
That stirred thee when the cannon's roar
Hath failed to rouse, shall rouse thee more
   Out of thy slumbers deep!

No more for thee his whistle shrill
Shall sound through wood, o'er moor and hill—
Thy cry is mute, thy limbs are still
    In everlasting sleep!

Sleep on, sleep on! no morrow's sun
Shall light thee to the battle back—
Thy fight hath closed, thy laurel's won,
    And this thy bivouac.
On tented field, or bloody plain,
For thee the watchfire flares in vain—
Thou wilt not share its warmth again
    With him who loved thee well;
Nor when, with toil and danger spent,
He rests beneath the firmament,
Thine eye upon his form be bent,
    Thou trusty sentinel.

Sleep on, thou friend and comrade tried
In battle, broil, and peaceful bower:
Thou hast left for once thy master's side,
    But never in danger's hour.
Not thus inactive wert thou laid,
On that night of perilous ambuscade,
When levelled tube and brandished blade
    Were at thy master's throat:
Then fierce and forward was thy bound,
And proud thy footstep pressed the ground,
While the tangled greenwood echoed round
    With thy loud warning note.

Then sleep, though gladly would I give
Half of the life preserved by thee,
Could'st thou once more, my comrade, live
    Thy short space o'er with me.
Vain wish, and impotent as vain;
'Tis but a mockery of pain
To dream that aught may bring again
    The spirit that hath flown.
But years steal by, and they who mourn
Another's fate, each in his turn
Shall tread one path, and reach one bourne,—
    Then, faithful friend, sleep on!

WALTER THORNBURY.

EVERLASTING FLOWERS.

I send thee but a simple gift,
A little bunch of dry, crisp flowers
Still rainbow-coloured, though 'tis long
Since sunshine fed them or the showers.

Mere phantoms of those thoughts of love
Whose flying seeds from Eden blew,
God's hand in pity cast them forth,
If Talmud legends are but true.

Dear, promise me that when I'm dead
You'll press within my clay-cold hand
These same bright everlasting flowers,
—I'll bear them through the Silent Land.

I shall not need remembrances
Of thee, my own, but still I'll keep
These always with me through the dim
Sad shadow of Death's long, long sleep.

Dark waters, in thy blackest gulf,
Dark valley, in thy ghastliest cleft,
I'll guard these flowers, the types of love,
Though nothing but these flowers be left.

Come flame, come torture for my sins,
Or mercy ope the golden portal.
Still, still I'll grasp those changeless flowers,
To prove my boundless love immortal.

God's angels calling me, my soul
Shall climb to wiser, nobler powers,
Approving angels' greeting smiles,
Will hail those everlasting flowers.

FINIS.

Finis—the fittest word to end
   Life's book, so mystical and solemn;
The fiat of a Roman judge;
   The last stone of the finished column.

Finis—our thrilling, parting word,
   As standing by the grave we linger,
And hear the earth fall where the yew
   Points downward with its sable finger.

Finis—the saddest word of all,
   Irrevocable, changeless, certain;
The parting sigh beside the dead;
   The prompter's word to drop the curtain.

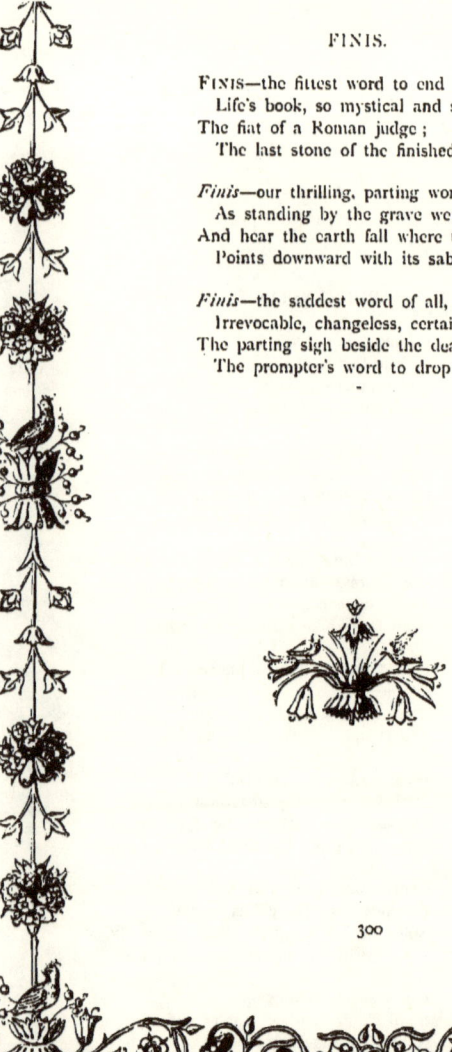

INDEX OF FIRST LINES.

About the sweet bag of a bee	7
A feeling sad came o'er me as I trod the sacred ground	175
Ah, Chloris! could I now but sit	39
Ah! County Guy, the hour is nigh	127
Ah! little ranting Johnny	196
All my past life is mine no more	25
All thoughts, all passions, all delights	131
Amaryllis I did woo	2
An hour with thee!—When earliest day	128
A rose-bud by my early walk	98
As after noon, one summer's day	51
As I laye a-thynkynge, a-thynkynge, a-thynkynge	176
As some fond virgin, whom her mother's care	64
A street there is in Paris famous	218
At the corner of Wood Street when daylight appears	183
Away! let nought to love displeasing	77
Barley-mowers here we stand	243
Before the beginning of years	250
Behind her neck her comely tresses tied	51
Bird of the wilderness	137
Born in yon blaze of orient sky	101
Bright Stella, formed for universal reign	90
Busy, curious, thirsty fly	70
Celia and I, the other day	52
Chloris! yourself you so excel	30
Christmas is here	221
Come all ye jolly shepherds	138
Come from my First, ay, come	149
Come, let us now resolve at last	33

Come, when no graver cares employ . . . . *Page*	275
Cyriac, whose grandsire on the royal bench	15
Dear Chloe, how blubbered is that pretty face	49
Dear is my little native vale.	194
Dear object of my late and early prayer	106
Deem not devoid of elegance the sage	93
Dropping down the river . . . . ; . . .	268
Ever let the Fancy roam	111
Fair Daffodils, we weep to see	11
Fairest isle, all isles excelling	34
Fair pledges of a fruitful tree	11
Farewell! Farewell! the voice you hear	127
Feed her with the leaves of Love	294
Finis—the fittest word to end	300
Foster! whose zeal has seized each written page . . . ; . .	231
From Stirling Castle we had seen	185
Full of beauty is the wayside well	270
Gather the rosebuds while ye may	10
Get up, get up, for shame, the blooming morn	13
Go, lovely Rose . . . ; . . . . ; . . .	29
Go—you may call it madness, folly	193
Had I a heart for falsehood framed . ; . . .	108
Hail! beauteous stranger of the grove	91
Hail! day of Music, day of Love . . . ;	201
Happy and free, securely blest	35
Happy the man, whose wish and care	66
Hears not my Phyllis, how the birds . . ;	38
Here, where the tall plantation firs	266
Her eyes the glow-worm lend thee	9
He sat the quiet stream beside	271
Hollow is the oak beside the sunny waters drooping	260
Ho, pretty page, with the dimpled chin	220
How brightly glistening in the sun	178
How is it that before mine eyes	140
How soon hath Time, the subtle thief of youth	16
How sweet it were, if, without feeble fright	199
How vainly men themselves amaze	18
I arise from dreams of thee	114
I come from haunts of coot and hern	274

I could loose my boat	245
I'd be a Butterfly, born in a bower	156
If all that you adore	247
If I live to be old, for I find I go down	44
If old Bacchus were the speaker	211
If wine and music have the power	54
I give my soldier-boy a blade	165
I have got a certain habit that approacheth to a merit	203
I have had playmates, I have had companions	135
I in these flowery meads would be	26
I met Louisa in the shade	182
In a drear-nighted December	113
In Clementina's artless mien	232
I ne'er could any lustre see	107
In female hearts did sense and merit rule	106
In London I never know what to be at	125
In some rude spot where vulgar herbage grows	107
In tattered old slippers that toast at the bars	222
In winter, when the dismal rain	256
I send thee but a simple gift	290
I thought 'twas a toy of the fancy — a dream	188
It was not in the winter	170
I've oft been asked by prosing souls	123
I wandered by the brook-side	255
I wandered lonely as a cloud	187
Jenny kissed me when we met	196
Just like Hope is yonder bow	103
Lately on yonder swelling bush	28
Laugh, my friends, and without blame	292
Lawrence, of virtuous father virtuous son	16
Life! I know not what thou art	120
Little bird, with bosom red	88
Love is by fancy led about	61
Love still has something of the sea	37
Maid of Athens, ere we part	118
Margarita first possest	4
May! queen of blossoms	121
Mild offspring of a dark and sullen sire	102
Mine be a cot beside the hill	193
My banks they are furnished with bees	74
My dear mistress has a heart	24
My little love, do you remember	290

My sheep I neglected, I broke my sheep-hook . . . . . *Page*	87
My time, O ye Muses, was happily spent	71
Never any more	285
Nobly, nobly Cape Saint Vincent to the north-west died away . .	284
Not, Celia, that I juster am	36
No ! those days are gone away	109
Now fruitful Autumn lifts his sun-burnt head	145
Now gentle sleep hath closèd up those eyes	3
Now the bright morning-star, day's harbinger	17
O, come to Rome, it is a pleasant place	278
Of all the girls that are so smart	62
Of a' the airts the wind can blaw	97
Of Time and Nature eldest born	94
Oft in danger, yet alive	89
Oh, a dainty plant is the Ivy green	296
Oh never another dream can be	144
Oh ! the wee green neuk, the sly green neuk	241
Oh ! what a weary race my feet have run	93
Oh ! who will over the Downs with me	252
Oh ye ! who so lately were blithesome and gay	159
O ! my love's like the stedfast sun	163
O Nancy, wilt thou go with me	104
One kind wish before we part	76
On Leven's banks while free to rove	81
O Reader ! hast thou ever stood to see	166
Orphan hours, the year is dead	115
O say ! what is that thing called Light	69
O stay, Madonna ! stay	200
Our native song,—our native song	248
Pæstum ! thy roses long ago	230
Parson, these things in thy possessing	66
Phyllis is my only joy	39
Phyllis ! why should we delay	30
Piccadilly ! shops, palaces, bustle, and breeze	281
Resolve me, Chloe, what is this . . .	53
Salutation to you now, you learned Temple Benchers	272
School, that in Burford's honoured time	146
See how the winter blanches	233
See, whilst thou weep'st, fair Chloe, see	51
Shall I, wasting in despair	1

She dwelt among the untrodden ways	*Page* 183
She walks in beauty, like the night	117
She was a phantom of delight	184
She who hath the gentle soul	209
Sickness and health have been having a game with me	242
Sleep on, and dream of heaven	194
Sleep on, sleep on ! thou gentle one	297
Softly the Mayne river glideth	283
Some years ago, ere Time and Taste	150
Sweet country life, to such unknown	7
Sweet is the vale where virtue dwells	161
Take back the Virgin Page	199
Take these flowers, which, purple waving	128
Ten years ago, ten years ago	221
Thanks, my Lord, for your venison, for finer or fatter	83
That which her slender waist confined	29
Thee, Mary, with this ring I wed	96
The fountains mingle with the river	115
The grey sea and the long black land	284
The merchant, to secure his treasure	48
The night's in November : the winds are at strife	289
The poplars are felled ; farewell to the shade	99
The pride of every grove I chose	56
The rose had been washed, just washed in a shower	100
The stricken deer that in his velvet side	107
The sun from the east tips the mountains with gold	82
The thirsty earth soaks up the rain	4
The town of Passage	235
The wanton troopers riding by	20
The widow had but only one	282
The year's at the spring	284
There be none of Beauty's daughters	119
There's a bower of roses by Bendemeer's stream	192
There sits a bird on yonder tree	174
They were fusty, they were musty, they were grimy, dull, and dim	261
This sycamore, oft musical with bees	134
Thus Kitty, beautiful and young	55
Timely blossom, infant fair	68
'Tis believed that this harp which I wake now for thee	191
'Tis like unto that dainty flower	172
To all you ladies now at land	41
To-day a Man ! I enter Life	287
Too late I stayed - forgive the crime	130

Twas on a lofty vase's side . .	Page 79
Twelve years ago I made a mock .	153
What ecstasies her bosom fire	58
What is she writing? watch her now .	179
Whene'er through Gray's Inn porch I stray	264
When I am dead, my dearest .	258
When I was a school-boy, aged ten .	157
When lovely woman stoops to folly .	83
When maidens such as Hester die .	136
When shall we come to that delightful day .	259
When the black-lettered list to the gods was presented .	129
Whilst I am scorched with hot desire .	50
Whilst in this cold and blustering clime .	31
Who has e'er been in London, that overgrown place .	142
Why do ye weep, sweet babes? Can tears .	12
With deep affection .	234
Within a budding grove .	239
Ye field flowers! the gardens eclipse you, 'tis true .	168
You write and think of me, my friend, with pity .	227

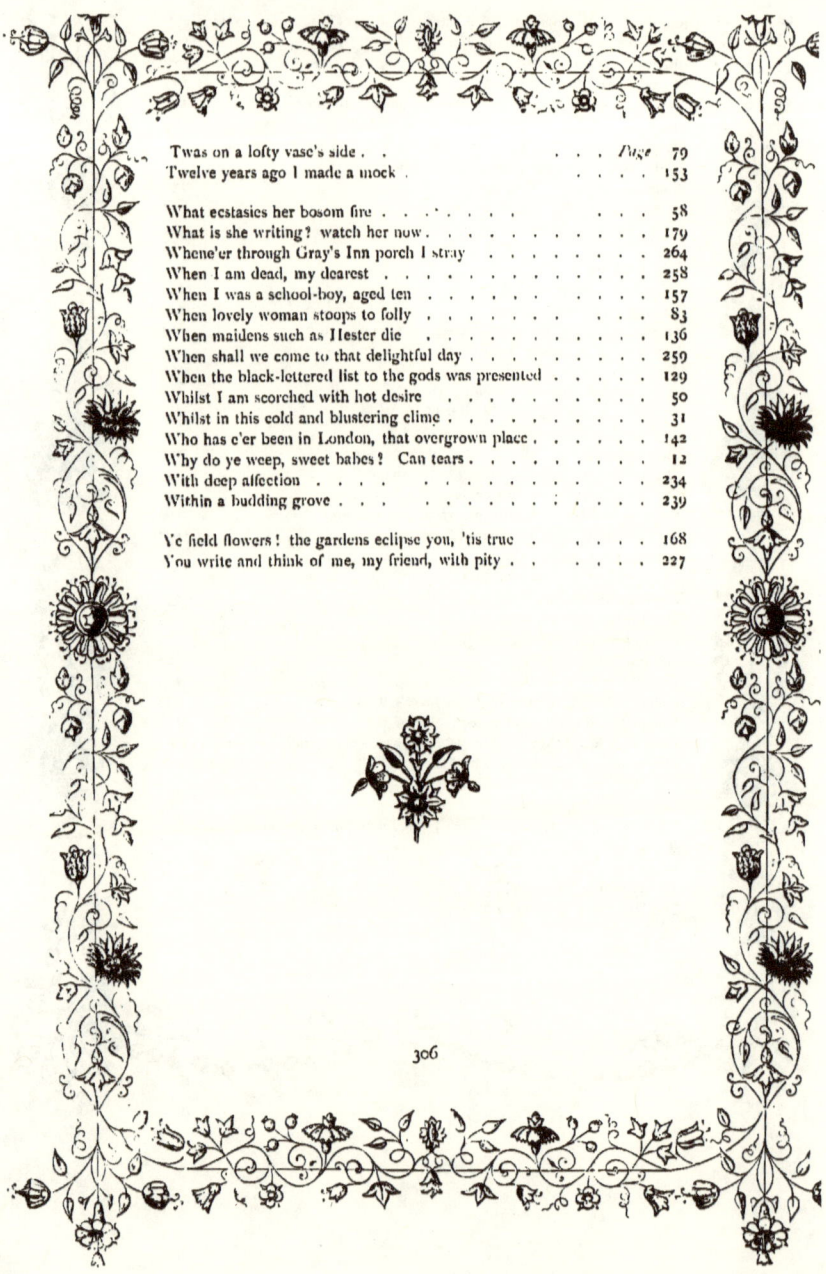

INDEX OF AUTHORS' NAMES.

Allingham, William . *Page* 239	Cooper, John Gilbert *Page* 77
Arnold, Matthew . . . 292	Cornwall, Barry . . . 294
Bailey, Philip James . . 241	Cotton, Charles 31
Barbauld, Mrs. . . . 120	Cowley, Abraham . . 4
Barham, Richard Harris . . 174	Cowper, William 99
Bayly, Thomas Haynes . 156	Cunningham, Allan 163
Bishop, Samuel . . . 96	Darwin, Erasmus . 101
Blacklock, Thomas . 94	Dickens, Charles . 296
Blanchard, Edmund F. . . 247	Dodsley, Robert 76
Blanchard, Laman . 172	Dorset, Earl of . 41
Bowles, William Lisle . 188	Dryden, John 34
Brontë, Anne . . . 178	
Brontë, Charlotte . . 179	Elliot, Sir Gilbert . 87
Brough, Robert B. . . . 203	Gay, John 58
Browning, Elizabeth Barrett 211	Gleig, George Robert . . 297
Browning, Robert . . 283	Goldsmith, Oliver . 83
Brummell, Beau . . . 159	Gray, Thomas . . 79
Buckingham, Duke of 33	
Burns, Robert . 97	Hemans, Felicia D. 140
Byrom, John . . 71	Herrick, Robert 7
Byron, Lord . . . 117	Hogg, James . . 137
	Hood, Thomas 170
Campbell, Thomas . . . 168	Hood, Thomas, the Younger. 266
Carey, Henry . . 62	Hook, Theodore E. . 161
Cibber, Colley 69	Houghton, Lord . . 255
Coleridge, Samuel Taylor . 131	Howitt, Mary . . 243
Collins, Mortimer . . . 270	Hunt, Leigh . . 196
Colman, George, Junior . . 112	
Cook, Eliza . 248	Johnson, Samuel 89

Keats, John	*Page* 109	
Kent, Charles F.	287	
Lamb, Charles	135	
Landon, Letitia Elizabeth	144	
Landor, Walter Savage	230	
Langhorne, John	88	
Lansdowne, Lord	61	
Leigh, Henry S.	242	
Locker, Frederick	278	
Lockyer, Stewart	209	
Logan, John	91	
Lytton, Lord	259	
Macaulay, Lord	200	
Mackay, Charles	264	
Maginn, William	165	
Mahony, Francis	233	
Marvell, Andrew	18	
Meredith, Owen	289	
Milton, John	15	
Moore, Thomas	190	
Morris, Captain	123	
Oldys, William	70	
Payn, James	268	
Pennell, Henry Cholmondeley	252	
Percy, Thomas	104	
Philips, Ambrose	68	
Pope, Alexander	64	
Pope, Walter	44	
Praed, Winthrop Mackworth	149	
Prior, Matthew	48	
Procter, Adelaide Anne	227	
Procter, Bryan Waller	*Page* 294	
Prout, Father	233	
Rochester, Earl of	24	
Rogers, Samuel	193	
Rossetti, Christina	258	
Scott, Sir Walter	127	
Sedley, Sir Charles	36	
Shelley, Percy Bysshe	114	
Shenstone, William	74	
Sheridan, Richard Brinsley	106	
Smith, Alexander	256	
Smith, Charlotte	103	
Smith, James	145	
Smollett, Tobias George	81	
Southey, Robert	166	
Spencer, William Robert	129	
Swinburne, Algernon Charles	250	
Taylor, Tom	261	
Tennyson, Alfred	274	
Thackeray, Wm. Makepeace	217	
Thornbury, Walter	299	
Thurlow, Lord	121	
Trench, Richard Chenevix	245	
Turner, Godfrey	272	
Waller, Edmund	28	
Walton, Izaak	26	
Warton, Thomas	93	
Watts, Alaric Alexander	224	
White, Henry Kirke	102	
Whitehead, Paul	82	
Wither, George	1	
Wordsworth, William	182	

www.ingramcontent.com/pod-product-compliance
Lightning Source LLC
Chambersburg PA
CBHW030254240426
43673CB00040B/968